LOVE
AS A
CHANGE
STRATEGY

LOVE AS A CHANGE STRATEGY

Innovation, Growth, and Transformation

MOHAMMAD F. ANWAR | FRANK E. DANNA
JEFFREY F. MA | CHRISTOPHER J. PITRE

WILEY

For general information on our other products and services or for technical support, please contact our Customer Care Department within the United States at (800) 762-2974, outside the United States at (317) 572-3993 or fax (317) 572-4002.

Wiley also publishes its books in a variety of electronic formats. Some content that appears in print may not be available in electronic formats. For more information about Wiley products, visit our web site at www.wiley.com.

Library of Congress Cataloging-in-Publication Data is Available:

ISBN: 9781394332182 (Cloth)
ISBN: 9781394332199 (ePub)
ISBN: 9781394332205 (ePDF)

Cover Design by Derek George
Author Photo by Dominique Carter

To the past, present, and future employees and customers of Softway.

Contents

Foreword

Dear Reader,

I first met "the guys"—Mohammad, Chris, Frank, and Jeff—when we invited them to speak at the American Leadership Forum (ALF). From the moment they stepped into the room, their energy was undeniable: bold, passionate, and utterly committed to their mission of bringing humanity back into the workplace. Their message of love as a business strategy wasn't just a refreshing idea—it was a call to action. One that resonated deeply with me as the leader of an organization rooted in heart-centered, ethical leadership.

Years later, as Mohammad and Chris have become ALF Senior Fellows and Frank and Jeff prepare to begin their own fellowships, I find myself reflecting not just on their journey but also mine.

Love as a Change Strategy invites you into the messy, courageous, and often uncomfortable reality of what it means to lead change. It challenges the notion that transformation is just a matter of process or persuasion. In truth, it's personal. It's human. And it rarely goes as planned.

I've lived that reality.

Early in my career, I was tasked with leading a respected organization through a period of transformation. Armed with stakeholder feedback, data, and a bold new vision, I was ready to guide the change we needed. What I wasn't ready for was the resistance from the very people I respected and depended on most.

I remember being told, "If it's not broken, why fix it?" Despite the data, despite the clarity of purpose, I was met with fear, hesitation, and even quiet rebellion. I thought I had done everything right. But I'd overlooked something essential: the emotional, human side of change. My efforts—no matter how well-intentioned—were being perceived as threats. Not solutions.

That's when I paused. Slowed down. And leaned into the lessons I'd learned from the *Art & Practice of Adaptive Leadership*: that real change happens at the rate people can absorb, and that what often looks like resistance is actually protection—of identity, legacy, and meaning.

So, we retreated—literally and figuratively. I invited the team into conversation, not confrontation. We named what was sacred. We grieved what we had to leave behind. And only then—when we centered our humanity—were we able to move forward together.

That's the heartbeat of this book.

Love as a Change Strategy doesn't promise shortcuts. It doesn't sugarcoat the struggle. What it offers is something far more powerful: a way to lead change that honors people as people—not just resources, roles, or resistance.

It reminds us that change is survival—but change with love is evolution.

May you find in these pages both the courage to lead and the compassion to listen.

With hope,

Nory Angel, MBA
President
American Leadership Forum - Houston/Gulf Coast
Houston, Texas

The Elephant in the Room

Mohammad sat back in his chair, sighed, and looked out the conference room window. It was another beautiful spring day in Houston—not much to complain about, other than the ever-present humidity. Instead of enjoying the weather outside, though, he was stuck in this room in another full-day reorganization meeting that was going absolutely nowhere.

He should have been used to it by now. After all, this is exactly how the previous reorg meeting went, and the one before that, and the one before that, and the one before that. He loved, trusted, and respected the people on his executive leadership team. They'd been through hell together and always emerged stronger on the other end, so why were they stuck in perpetual reorganization limbo?

Mohammad looked over at Lacee. She was trying to keep her cool, but he knew that look on her face too well. She was frustrated. Really, really frustrated. It was all she could do to read through the graveyard that was the leadership team's agenda and rattle off all the outstanding work. [Task 1], incomplete. [Task 2], incomplete. [Task 3], incomplete. None of these tasks were hard, and yet none of them were getting done either. So what was going on? Why was no one taking ownership of their work?

Because everyone was scared of what the work actually meant.

The reorganization they were planning was no joke. For a few years now, Mohammad had known that Softway, the company he'd founded and led for over twenty years, needed to change. Sure, they'd had some successful years and were still profitable, but they weren't growing. They were stagnating. To set the company up for an ambitious growth strategy over the next ten years, the company needed to evolve. To evolve, they needed to intentionally shift some people into different seats. This meant a change in positions, a change in roles, a change in responsibilities, a change in departments, a change in just about everything.

No one's current role was guaranteed in the new org structure. Company vets who'd served over ten years would be asked to shift into new positions. Experienced team leaders who'd successfully driven results would be asked to become individual contributors. Even some executive leadership team members would be transitioning into different parts of the company. Greg, for instance, would be shifting from account management to the head of tech services—and one of his first jobs would be to tell all the lead architects on his team that they would now be consultants. Totally different role, totally different responsibility, and totally what we needed of Greg and the tech team to make this reorg work.

Everyone on the leadership team knew these planned changes might affect them, but Mohammad could see that no one wanted to discuss them. If he were being honest, he didn't want to, either. Like everyone else, he was scared.

He was scared to tell Saif, who'd been with the company for nineteen years, that he would no longer be vice president of technology services. He was scared to tell Saquib, who had cofounded the company with him, that he would become a level-four consultant. He was scared to tell Taj, his own brother, that he was also going to move off his current position and that they weren't sure where to slot him after that.

None of these conversations would be easy, so Mohammad avoided them. He'd hoped to create an environment where these conversations would come naturally through dialogue, and he'd hoped the leadership team would be introspective and self-aware enough to recognize these issues independently. Unfortunately, no one appeared willing to admit their own shortcomings and explore what seat in the organization might suit them best. The team was defensive, deflective, or dismissive, doing whatever they could to shift negative attention away from themselves and focus on their strengths.

Mohammad sighed again and let the tension in the room wash over him. *Mohammad 1.0 would have told it like it is,* he thought to himself. Moh 1.0 would backflip onto the table, rip a phonebook in half, and give 'em all a piece of his mind. But he wasn't Mohammad 1.0 anymore, and phonebooks were hard to come by these days. That version of him got a much-needed upgrade when he pivoted the company—and himself—to embrace a culture of love. Mohammad 2.0 led with compassion and curiosity, but increasingly, he also struggled with being honest. Now, at version 2.1.3, when his team needed that honesty more than ever, Mohammad found himself lacking the courage to do what he knew was right.

Across the table sat Chris. Like Mohammad, Chris was detecting some master-level avoidance in the room. Sure, *some* issues were brought up, but their significance was being walked back, rationalized, or minimized. If only he'd brought his "weak excuses" bingo card with him. With all the "Well, I didn't mean it like that," or "I dunno, I'm just thinking out loud," or "We're good, just a minor hiccup, but we handled it," he'd have filled out the whole thing out by now.

"So, wait, are things good or not?" Chris asked after the most recent updates, genuinely unsure where things stood. He'd heard the summaries and all the upbeat spin, but he couldn't square those picture-perfect stories with the reality he saw. As we mentioned, nearly every single task was incomplete, and things weren't adding up. For several weeks, he'd watched that same leadership team struggle through some big client-facing projects and swept those struggles under the rug. If this leadership team couldn't be honest about its performance on these known, black-and-white issues, then what reason did Chris have to think that they were being honest about their work on the reorg project?

Chris saw this contradiction. *Everyone* saw this contradiction. And yet, no one wanted to talk about it. It was like an elephant had followed the team into the meeting, staked out a seat in the corner of the room, and sat there silently judging the group as everyone went on and on about their strengths and how well everything was going.

Chris thought about his own contributions to the conversation, which, well, hadn't been much. He had plenty to say—Chris *always* has plenty to say—but he felt like he was at a Greek organization meeting where it was impossible to get a word in edgewise. Besides, he was much more comfortable sharing with Mohammad during their one-on-ones than in large groups. But nearly half of Softway's US team was in this room, so his mouth stayed shut. Now well into his own personal transformation journey, Chris knew that his sharp wit cut deep, and he didn't want to embarrass anybody or let that be the first time they got real feedback inside a public setting.

Chris resolved to introspect more on why he hadn't been willing to speak up. In the meantime, he'd keep doing what he'd always done, quietly working by himself on his task list. On a team with no ownership, any supposed collaboration would just mean he'd end up doing all the work anyway. It was like suffering through group projects in high school all over again.

A few spots down the table to Chris's right, Frank was thinking the same thing. *Man, someone should really address the elephant in the room and say something about all this darn tension!* He'd do it, but it wasn't his problem. *He'd* been with the company for twelve years. *He* wasn't the one who had to change roles. *He* was fine. After feeling like an impostor his entire adult life, Frank finally felt like Softway had given him a place to belong. Why would he want to give that up now?

From his privileged position in the room, Frank felt detached and aloof. *I'm not the one who sucks,* he told himself. *It's everyone else. They can pry my title from my cold, dead hands.*

Frank looked down the table toward Jeff. Good old Jeff, master of the pickleball court. Frank had always admired Jeff for his attentiveness and insights. But now, Jeff didn't look like he was doing too good. He looked tired.

He was. He was *really* tired—tired of watching people do nothing but convert oxygen into carbon dioxide, tired of seeing people jockey for a better position in the org structure, tired of watching everyone duck responsibility for the fact that they weren't getting any meaningful work done. As far as he could see, the only person getting anything done was Lacee, and no one was making her job any easier.

And in that moment, it hit him. *Crap,* Jeff thought, *I'm part of the problem, too.*

His mind started to swirl. He used to bristle when others would complain that Softway had been dealing with the same problems for over a decade. He disagreed. Sure, some issues still lingered from before, but the naysayers were missing the bigger picture. Look how much they'd accomplished! In less than a decade, Softway had transformed from a toxic, failing culture to a team of connected, aligned, and *human* high performers. Why couldn't the naysayers see that?

Because, he realized, it wasn't enough. What good was a culture of love if Softway's leadership team still couldn't get out of its own way?

Jeff glanced over at the elephant. The elephant glanced back. Then, almost imperceptibly, it looked him dead in the eye and nodded.

Jeff knew what he had to do. Slowly, he readjusted his glasses, cleared his throat, and stood up to speak.

"This isn't working," he said. "What are we even doing here?"

Everyone froze.

"Every meeting, we commit to the same things. Then at the next meeting, we all get together to learn no one's done anything they committed to," Jeff continued. "We keep failing over and over again. Are we serious about this change or not?"

Then, Jeff proceeded to outline all the problems he'd seen with the reorg. First, he talked about himself and his position—or, should he say, his *three* positions. He hadn't been quite clear about his job since the last reorganization. All he knew was that one of his roles was project manager director, and he hadn't been that great at it. Next, Jeff took aim at Saif and discussed how he probably didn't belong in his position either. Hand in hand with the elephant, he went through the room one by one, highlighting the challenges each person faced in their current jobs and the challenges Softway faced if they remained in them.

"Look, I know I bring some value," Jeff said, "but like many of us, I was put in my role out of necessity, not because I deserved it. And I'm not the only person that has happened to over the years."

Harsh. But Jeff was right, and everybody knew it.

"We can't hold onto these positions so tightly when they might not be the best fit for us," he said. "If we want to do something different with the company, then we have to *be* something different in this company."

Yeah, you go, Jeff. Frank thought to himself. *That's just what everyone else who's not me needed to hear. What a brave thing to say.*

"If we're going to be in this, then we must all agree in this space that, after today, we're releasing our grip on any preconceived notions regarding our jobs or titles," Jeff said. "Do we agree that we're all willing to do whatever it takes to make this reorganization successful, even if that means losing our status?"

The room fell silent. It was deafening.

Then, from the corner, the elephant stood up and started to slow clap, followed by Mohammad, Chris, Frank, and the rest of the leadership team. Applause filled the air as the elephant hoisted Jeff onto its shoulders, paraded him around the room, and celebrated Jeff for single-handedly saving the company. Off in the distance, Chris swore he could hear a choir of Beyoncés singing the most heavenly of melodies.

Okay, so none of that last bit happened. But that's what it felt like to be in that room.

By addressing the elephant in the room, Jeff articulated the core problem preventing Softway from achieving meaningful change for the better part of a year: everyone. In all of their previous meetings, they had agreed to discuss the reorganization only in terms of structures, needs, and roles. They were *designing*, not *assigning*, and they were convinced that now wasn't the time to consider who would occupy which seat on the org chart.

Except it was. People are going to be people. That's what they do. Softway leadership were all in alignment on what the restructure should look like, but they were all concerned about how they would fit into the equation. Unable to divorce themselves and their stakes in the reorganization plan, they had been unwilling to take ownership and lead the change they wanted to create.

But then Jeff threw down the gauntlet. If Softway was going to change the organization, first they had to commit, in that room, to doing what it took to move the company forward. If that meant a "lesser" position for some of those within the company, then so be it.

So, one by one, each committed to the reorganization project once and for all. Then they nailed their change journey perfectly, and they all lived happily ever after.

Just kidding.

We still struggled with our reorg. *Every* organization will struggle with a change that big. As we embarked on this journey, some of the team weren't fully bought in, some of their objectives needed to be refined, and some of their timelines were overly ambitious.

That's okay. Change is a process, not a snap of the fingers. Eventually, we arrived at our destination with a fully aligned team, a realigned org chart, and a wide-open path to growth.

So, what was the secret sauce? Love.

Yes, really: L-O-V-E.

Love as a Change Strategy is not your grandfather's change management book. Actually, it's not a change management book at all, because we are not your typical change management consultants.

This is a change leadership book written *for* change leaders *by* change leaders. We know our stuff: we've read the research, led workshops and strategic initiatives, and walked the talk. In this book, we distill our broad experiences into a practical approach you can apply to your organization *today*.

At the center of this framework are people. Not processes, not systems, not technology, but *people*.

People make the change machine run. They are the beginning, middle, and end of the change journey. Fail to engage your people, and you will fail to create meaningful change. This truth holds no matter the scale or nature of your change. You can set your alarm and join a gym, but that alone won't get you shredded. You can enter your new role as the chair of the local parent-teacher association (PTA) with dreams and ambitions, but you still need to engage the other volunteers to realize your plans. You can map out the most amazing reorganization plan and lay out the steps meticulously, but your people still have to see themselves in that plan before committing. Get the people part right, or the rest won't matter.

Of course, change is still hard, even when you put people at the center. You won't find five surprising life hacks or seven daily habits to fake your way through change leadership here. Expect things to get messy at times—*really* messy.

Most books on change leave the messy part out. Like a real estate agent staging a house, they stuff all the unseemly bits into the guest room closet and pretend it isn't there. We lean into these moments—or, as one of our clients calls them, *rumbles*. Why? Because you don't lead change with warm fuzzies. That's not what we mean by leading with love. Leading change the right way is just as hard, if not harder, than leading change the wrong way. We want you to lead change the right way. So, we're going to throw the doors open to that crammed closet and show you what real, human-driven change looks like.

The following chapters are filled with stories, lessons, and examples like the one you just read. Some of these stories will be about us, and some will be about our clients. They won't always be sunshine and roses, but they will always be human. As you read through everything, give yourself permission to feel actual human emotions. You might laugh a little. You might cry a little. Both are okay. Actually, they're great. To get in the rumble and lead change with love, we must be direct, honest, and unburdened by ego. Only by working through our experiences and extracting our own lessons can we hope to move forward as humans trying to do right in the world.

Remember to bring yourself to this work, too. Whether you're an intentional change leader tasked with transforming a large company or an accidental change leader tasked with overhauling the local PTA, your experiences and perspective matter. We're glad to have you here and to share part of our journey with you.

With that said, and with apologies to famed boxing announcer Michael Buffer, let's get ready to rumble.

The Elephant in the Room

- ◆ Have you ever been in a situation where you knew, liked, and trusted the people around you, but for some reason, those people weren't producing results? If so, what did that feel like? What did the group finally do to get unstuck?
- ◆ For whatever change you're planning, what are you willing to sacrifice as a leader to get there? If nothing, why not?
- ◆ When you read the Introduction title, "The Elephant in the Room," what did you expect? How did the content match or differ from those expectations?
- ◆ Have you ever found yourself avoiding difficult conversations in the workplace? What held you back?
- ◆ How does the story of Mohammad and his team resonate with the challenges you've faced during an organizational change?
- ◆ Jeff's willingness to address the elephant shifted the entire room. Reflect on a time when you or someone else took a similar courageous step in your team. What happened?

◆ The authors emphasize that people, not processes, are at the center of change. Do you agree? Why or why not?

◆ How do you define *love* in the context of leadership and change? What examples from your own experience support that definition?

◆ Reflect on Jeff's realization that he was "part of the problem." How might you identify and address ways you could unintentionally be contributing to stagnation or resistance?

◆ What were some of your biggest takeaways or ah-ha moments from this chapter?

◆ What, if anything, will you change or adjust about how you lead or behave based on what you've read?

PART I

Turn and Face the Change

Picture this: your company is in the middle of a reorganization. You know this, but you're far enough away from the seats of power that you don't have a strong idea of what's going on.

One day, you receive a request for a video call. You've never met the person on the other side of the screen. They don't even work for your company. They're an outside consultant. *Great,* you think to yourself, *no good news has ever come from an outside consultant.*

You swallow hard. Sweat beads up on your forehead. You put on your best listening face: eyebrows arched, eyes attentive, mouth fixed in that uncanny valley between a frown and a smile.

You're prepared to hear the worst—that your job has been eliminated. That's not the case, the consultant informs you. You're just getting a new job.

Oh, that's not so bad, you think. But before you can breathe a sigh of relief, the consultant twists the knife: you must accept or decline your new role right now.

No documentation. No negotiation. No time to talk it over with your spouse. Right. Now.

You swallow hard and accept. What choice did you have?

A few days later, you receive an official description of your job and responsibilities in your inbox. And that's it. No further communication. No training. No all-hands meeting to discuss the company's new direction. Just an email with your new role and title and a nudge to get back to work.

That's how large-scale change happens in many companies. *And it sucks.*

Now, picture another scenario. The broad strokes are the same: your company is about to undertake a massive reorganization, and you're being reallocated.

But this time, you don't learn the news through a dispassionate video call. You learn it in person, from someone you know, like, and trust within the organization. They sit you down, explain the need for change, outline the company's vision for that change, and describe how you fit into the picture. During the conversation, it's clear that this person took the time to consider you, your role, and how you might respond to the news and then tailor their message accordingly.

In both scenarios, the result is the same: you're getting shuffled around in the company, and the future is a little uncertain. But ask yourself: which company would you rather want to help make that change a reality?

If you said the second company, then congratulations: you have a heartbeat.

This is the premise of *Love as a Change Strategy*.

In Part I, we will challenge traditional assumptions and perspectives on change and then explore the many ways that a culture of love can bring humanity back to change.

CHAPTER 1

Why Change?

As professional change experts, we've mastered the art of making change work regardless of the stakes or circumstances.

We've also mastered the art of failing miserably and falling flat on our faces. To prove our point, here's a brief montage of failure for your reading pleasure.

We'll start at the individual level with Frank. One time, Frank got really into non-fungible tokens (NFTs). He bought one NFT for a couple hundred dollars, and then he got an offer to sell it for over thirty thousand dollars. He declined, certain he'd get a higher bid than that. (Insert narrator's voice: he didn't.)

On the team level, we once changed our project management tools—from smart sheets to spreadsheets and then from spreadsheets to "Oh, sheets!" when we realized the hell we wrought. That "little change" threw a gear in the works for a while. Another time, we spent three years repeatedly redesigning and relaunching our website (Softway.com). They all sucked. In fact, they got progressively worse.

We also have plenty of groaners to share at the organizational level. Like when we tried to implement 8 a.m. standups and no one showed, not even on the first day. Or the time in 2018 when we mandated the adoption of a specific time-logging system. If everyone in the company logged their time just once, we got a pizza party. No matter when you read this book, we still haven't had a pizza party.

There was also that time when Chris tried to make Beyoncé's birthday a company holiday. We're not sure how the failure works here exactly. Did Chris fail Softway for suggesting the idea, or did we fail Chris for rejecting it? He'll tell you it's the latter, but we're pretty sure it's the former. What's the big deal with Beyoncé, anyway? Has she done anything noteworthy since *Destiny's Child?* We don't think so.

Just kidding. We love Beyoncé.

The point is that we have failed at leading change—a *lot.* The organizations we work with have, too, and we're willing to bet that you and your organization have as well.

And look at us: we're all still standing. These failures are nothing to be ashamed of. (Except for those NFTs. Those were a terrible financial decision.) They're lessons to learn from. We're change experts not because we're perfect but because we've dissected our experiences—both the good and the bad—so we can understand what works.

No matter how you slice it, change is hard. It's also unavoidable. The way we see it, you can either build a change-ready organization now or get caught flat-footed when the change bug bites you. Unfortunately, that's not what most organizations do.

Change as Usual Sucks

We live in a state of perpetual and accelerating change. Some organizations lead this change proactively, while others react to it and struggle. In either case, these organizations understand they have a lot riding on the outcomes of these change efforts. For instance:

- Companies that change successfully generate almost twice the earnings before interest, taxes, depreciation, and amortization; create higher shareholder returns; and experience 1.5–3 times the revenue growth.[1]
- Only about 34 percent of change initiatives succeed, with one-third of CEOs failing to achieve their intended outcomes.[2]
- Of the $1.3 trillion spent on digital transformations in 2018, an estimated $900 billion (69 percent) resulted in an avoidable loss.[3]

That's a lot of money spent with very little to show. As if that weren't bad enough, research shows that 50 percent of leaders don't know if their change programs succeeded or failed at their nominal conclusion.[4] So, not only did they spend a lot of money and make a big change effort but they also don't know whether that effort amounted to anything.

To understand how these organizations could be leveraging so many resources with so little to show for it, just ask the employees:

- Thirty-seven percent of employees are resistant to change.[5]
- Two-thirds of employees experience burnout during a change initiative.[6]
- Employees suffering from change-related stress perform 5 percent worse than average employees.[7]
- Seventy-four percent of employees think their organizational leadership needs to make more effort to understand why their teams resist change.[8]
- While 72 percent of leaders say they involved their employees in developing a change strategy, only 42 percent of employees agreed.[9]

Here's what we can conclude from this data: many organizations either attempt or experience change. However, these organizations—as well as their leaders and employees—struggle to change successfully. Just like we learned in our change mishaps and failures, these problems start at the top. Research shows that over a third of executives underestimate their role and require involvement in successful change management, while a third of CEOs are fired for reported poor change management.[10]

So, what are our options? One is to avoid change entirely. Just set your course and try to maintain it as best you can. The other is to improve our understanding and leadership of change.

Naturally, we recommend the latter path. Throughout history, humankind has faced changes in technology, politics, weather, economies, public health, and industry. Through these massive, often involuntary shifts, these people realized the same thing we have: staying the course is neither practical nor tenable.

Most organizations appear to recognize this. In one survey, 79.7 percent of respondents expected they would need to adapt their business in the next five years.[11] Many are already getting started. When we first set out to write this book in late 2024, we found over sixty thousand open positions related to change management. This massive groundswell and demand for change will fundamentally alter every organization, no matter its size.

In such a reality, the question isn't *why* you should change or *if* change will come for you but *how* you will effectively lead change when it is necessary.

To answer that question, first, we must examine our understanding and assumptions about change. Rather than view change as a force we must respond to, we must learn to embrace it as an opportunity to lead *through*.

What Is Change?

Change doesn't happen overnight because people don't change overnight. In fact, most of us resist change when we're not called or compelled to do so. Before Jeff addressed the elephant in the room and challenged our complacency during our leadership meeting (see "The Elephant in the Room"), we resisted our own change effort—even though we had conceived, planned, and *initiated* that change!

We resisted this change partly because it's human nature to fear change. Although we had learned a lot about pivoting an organization in the preceding years, we had never considered the nature of change and how to lead it successfully. Here's what we understand now that we didn't understand then.

CHANGE IS NONLINEAR

One day, Frank decided to go vegan. He preached to everyone who would listen about the virtues of veganism—and how tasty the food was. Had they even *tried* the Impossible Burger? Five stars. Would recommend.

Frank's evangelism lasted about a week. By week two, he quite literally walked into a meeting with a bucket of KFC in his hands and a giant grin on his face.

So, what happened? Why did Frank fall off the vegan wagon so quickly?

Frank would chalk it up to several reasons. First, while he had good intentions, he wasn't intrinsically motivated to change. He had some initial energy for the idea, but eventually, that energy burned out. When faced with challenges, his desire to change was put to the test. Was he willing to sacrifice and change his habits when it got a little bit uncomfortable? Turns out, the answer was no.

Second, Frank hadn't anticipated the big bump in his Whole Foods bill. Going vegan was expensive—at least the way he was doing it. Frank certainly could have overcome this challenge if he had kept with it, but in the short term, that grocery bill shook him off his goals. He hadn't anticipated the practical impact that this choice would have on his wallet.

The more salient reason, however, is that change doesn't happen in a straight line. It restarts, it repeats, it cycles through. It's an on-going effort, not a single decision, episode, or experience.

Viewed in isolation, Frank's attempt to go vegan is a failure. Viewed in the larger context of his health journey, however, it looks like a minor misstep. Sure, this little side quest didn't work out, but Frank's overall change project for his health has been a resounding success (which we'll explore more in Chapter 7). Not every step toward your goal is going to be the right one. But if you take more right steps than wrong ones, you'll get there.

Many leaders—and, as a result, organizations—don't see it this way. They see change as linear, a simple tweak of processes and technology. Set the course, mandate the change, herd your teams up, push them through the gates, and watch as the pieces fall into place. It doesn't work. A study by Prosci found that 47 percent of transformation failures resulted from employee resistance and lack of effective change management.[12]

In other words, ignore the human component of your change initiative at your own peril. Change is messy—like a delicious, all-beef double cheeseburger with all the fixings. Mistakes happen. Surprises crop up. People show resistance when you had assumed they were on board. If you're not accounting for these surprises as you roll out your change initiative, you'll soon get derailed.

People drive change, and people can't be herded in a straight line like cattle. Even smart, well-intentioned people can be stubborn, fearful, set in their ways, or otherwise resistant to change. Combine that with the fact that surprises do happen, and suddenly, you find yourself with many variables that you hadn't accounted for in your initial plan. In a change-ready culture, this unpredictability isn't a bug. It's a feature. When your teams are bought in and empowered to find solutions, the day-to-day change effort may take some steps forward and some steps back, but your overall trajectory will remain right on course—and it will be far more likely to succeed. According to *The Future of Transformation Is Human*, organizations taking a people-centric approach to their digital transformation saw a 73 percent success—compared to a 28 percent success rate for the organizations that didn't.[13]

CHANGE IS NOT A BURNING PLATFORM

In 2015, Softway almost went bankrupt. The fault wasn't in the company's products or services. It was due to the company's toxic leadership. It was a painful experience that we brought on ourselves. Still, we're grateful to it for its function as a much-needed catalyst for change. If Softway hadn't nearly collapsed, our founder Mohammad would never have had his epiphany and embraced Love as a Strategy. He'd still be the same cranky, mistrustful, unforgiving, nasty gram–sending leader he always was. And we probably wouldn't be a company anymore.

This kind of adapt-or-die catalyst is what many in the business world refer to as the *burning platform*. The term itself stems from a real tragedy that happened on an oil rig off the coast of Scotland. One night in 1988, an explosion rocked the Piper Alpha oil rig. As the rig burned, many crew members remained on the platform, hoping to be rescued. However, at least one man, Superintendent Andy Mochan, jumped into the freezing water below to save himself. Andy knew he'd made a dangerous choice, but as he explained later, he felt it was his best choice. At least in the water, he would have a fighting chance.

Miraculously, Andy survived, and his story became a metaphor for how many organizations approach change: you're in a fight for your survival, and you must take action to save yourself and your organization.[14]

Softway has endured plenty of our own burning platform scenarios—first in 2008 when the financial crisis rocked Wall Street, then in 2015 when our toxic culture almost ran the company into the ground, and later in 2020 when the COVID-19 pandemic hit and we lost millions in anticipated revenue on a single day. Existential threats have a funny way of propelling us into action without allowing us to think too hard or long about how or why we should do something. However, while we acknowledge that burning platform scenarios exist, we must also recognize that many are artificially created to create a sense of urgency and drive change. In these instances, leadership will manufacture a burning platform scenario by misrepresenting the situation or exaggerating the stakes.

That's not an effective way to lead change.

Yes, it might work. When you manufacture a sense of urgency, many on your team *will* respond accordingly. However, this strategy is fundamentally born out of fear, which is not the most effective basis for rational decision-making. Worse, it's poison to organizational culture and an environment of innovation. If you anchor your case for change in fear, you might create some short-term success, but you will torpedo your culture in the process.

Artificial burning platforms have no place in a culture of love. If the burning platform is real, then yes, communicate the situation's urgency and get to work solving it. However, if you aren't experiencing a real burning platform scenario, then don't invent one.

CHANGE REQUIRES HUMAN ADAPTATION

How do you lead change for humans? How do you change human behaviors? How do you help humans adapt to new circumstances?

In March 2020, large segments of the global population went into lockdown due to the growing COVID-19 pandemic. This was one of many responses to the large and complex challenge of minimizing exposure to the virus while trying to keep the world running. We were also asked to mask up and stand six feet apart from each other if we needed to venture into the public, to avoid visiting loved ones who were considered a greater health risk, and to get vaccinated as soon as one was available.

These policies and practices had varying degrees of success but only addressed a small sliver of the disruption we faced. Lockdown appeared to be a reasonable solution for the problem of limiting exposure, for instance, but it brought a new challenge: how would people keep working or students keep learning if they were expected to stay home?

Like many organizations, Softway was forced to adapt to this new challenge overnight. As an international company with offices in Houston, Texas, and Bengaluru, India, we had always relied on remote collaboration tools to some degree. However, our Houston and Bengaluru teams largely worked out of an office. When the lockdown hit, we quickly thought about how to get and keep everyone online, paid, fed, and happy. It was a big task that required us to find our own answers as we worked through it.

Today, the urgency of the pandemic might have faded, but many of the adaptations the business world implemented remain—perhaps none more significant than the move to remote work. Before the COVID-19 pandemic, only 4.7 percent of the workforce was remote first. At the height of the pandemic, that number grew to 61 percent. In 2025, 16 percent of all companies are fully remote, 24 percent of all workers are remote first, and 16 percent choose a hybrid approach.[15] That's a significant shift—one that has had implications in other parts of our lives as well, such as how we view and approach shopping for goods and groceries, dining out, watching movies, and showing up to work.

The COVID-19 pandemic is an example of an *adaptive challenge*: a nuanced, dynamic problem set that defies quick-fix solutions. Often, when you first encounter an adaptive challenge, the problem appears straightforward. Quickly, however, you recognize the situation's complexity and find yourself struggling to address it. Eventually, you will emerge from an adaptive challenge, having either solved the problem or weathered it. However, the person, team, or organization that emerges on the other side won't be the same; they will be changed fundamentally.

Adaptive challenges are often a key driver of organizational change. Unfortunately, these challenges are often mistaken for *technical problems*—known issues with known solutions. For instance, whenever your internet goes out and you unplug your router and then plug it back in, you are solving a technical problem. Some technical problems aren't as easily solved, but in every instance of a technical problem, you will have the tools and the knowledge to resolve it.

When organizations mistake an adaptive challenge for a technical problem, rather than solve their problem, they often make it worse. This dynamic is a fundamental reason why 78 percent of all change initiatives fail to reach their goals. The solution appears straightforward, but in reality, it's complex, nuanced, and human-driven.

For instance, when we implemented our time-logging system and rewarded adoption with a pizza party, we thought we were solving a technical problem; we didn't have enough insight into the profitability of our projects, and a time-logging tool would solve that. With a little bit of incentivization to drive adoption, we figured we'd have the insights we were looking for in no time. Easy peasy, lemon squeezy.

Except that's not how it works. We're a people-first organization, but we forgot that people were the end users of that time-logging system. And if those people hadn't internalized a reason and desire to adopt that system, they wouldn't. Internal marketing and incentivization programs didn't help either. Sure, they focused on behavior change, but they were still attempts to apply technical solutions to an adaptive problem. So, despite countless emails, funny GIFs in chats, and endless town hall reminders, we have yet to have that celebratory pizza party.

Technical solutions solve technical problems. However, organizational change is *never* a technical problem, but rather a process of preparing humans to adapt to change and unpredictable circumstances. To successfully drive change, even one as basic as adopting a time-logging tool, you must lead your teams on a journey so that they internalize the change. Recognize the problem before as complex, nuanced, and adaptive, and take a human-first approach to addressing that challenge.

CHANGE STARTS WITH YOU

"Wait, are you expecting me to change and do things I'm uncomfortable with?" Ron crossed his arms, glaring at Ben from across the room. We were leading a workshop as part of our work with a large, multinational organization. The meeting had barely even started, and already Ben was seeing stark division in his team. Some seemed receptive to the organization's planned change. But others, like Ron, were entirely resistant.

Ben could have expected this outcome. After all, he was only six months into his tenure as the head of his company's global sustainability team. His job: to convince the twenty-five-year vets on his team that it was time to change how they approached their jobs. This mandate proved to be a hard sell. An adaptive challenge. Each of Ben's team members was excellent at what they did and had the kind of deep, nuanced organizational knowledge that many businesses only dream of. They'd toiled for years to build up their expertise, and now Ben expected them just to throw it away?

Yes. Ben's planned changes would reduce the time spent on certain tasks from ten hours to ten minutes. He appreciated his team of experts, but he wanted them to concentrate their skills on more important challenges, not rote, time-consuming work.

Unfortunately, Ben didn't frame it that way. He didn't focus on the people at all; he focused on the changes. Feeling ignored and lacking the proper context, Ben's team was scared. They knew that, to change with the organization, they would also have to change themselves. The problem was that they didn't fully understand why they should.

The writer Leo Tolstoy once said, "Everyone thinks of changing the world, but no one thinks of changing themselves." Our boy Tolstoy was onto something. We've seen this dynamic in action firsthand. When we first meet leadership teams like Ben's that are preparing for a big change, they inevitably externalize their effort. "How do we get our employees to change?" they ask. "How do we make it stick this time?"

Our answer usually surprises them: don't focus on your employees to create lasting change within your organization. Instead, focus on yourself. Examine how your behaviors affect your environment, whether for good or bad, and ask how to change those behaviors to better align with your goals.

We forgot to do this as we planned our big reorg in 2023. We all loved and trusted each other as high performers to get our work done. However, we never stopped to ask what that change meant to *us*, whether we were on board with it, and what parts of ourselves had to change to accommodate the plan. Because we ignored this critical step, we also ignored the work. And as the uncompleted work piled up, so did the tension.

Eventually, Jeff forced the issue when he stood up, levitated above the conference room table, and used his formidable super-truth-telling powers on us to help us see the light. In so doing, he invited us to explore how we *really* felt about our reorg. We soon discovered that each of us had some personal issues that we needed to work through before committing ourselves to the project.

In a change-ready organization, everyone has agency and can help bring about change. But to do that, you must see yourself as part of the change. Only then can you consider your people and your teams change ready.

This begs the question: how do you know if the people in your organization are truly change-ready and willing to embrace whatever change you're pursuing?

Simple: watch how your teams react when the leaders aren't around.

For example, one day during a group exercise with Ben's team, Ben got an important call and had to step out of the room. We could have continued the exercise without Ben, but no one wanted to. They all believed that because Ben was the leader, only *he* could effect change, which meant he needed to be in the room for any change-related exercise. This belief wasn't true. The exercise was intended for the team, not for Ben. However, because the team held this mistaken belief, they were unwilling to move forward. Sure, some individual players on Ben's team were curious about the new direction their team was headed, but as a group, they weren't yet change ready.

If You Could Wave a Magic Wand . . .

One exercise we perform with organizations is the "magic wand" exercise. The premise is simple: standing in front of a big white-board, we ask each team member what they would change or how they would fix a certain problem set if typical constraints like money, resources, people, and so on weren't a problem. If you could just wave it all away, what would you change?

The answers tell us a lot about the state of that team's culture and change readiness. Instead of presenting solutions, teams often use the exercise to air their grievances.

For instance, when we conducted this exercise with Ben's team, one person literally wrote, "Slow down and don't change."

That's right: with an imaginary magic wand that could fix *any-thing*, that person's best idea was to keep everything the same.

Think about that. Think about the overwhelming fear this person was experiencing just *considering* the idea of change.

When you approach change from a place of fear, no one wins. Your teams will either reject the change entirely—as Ben's teammate did—or cling to that fear to sustain them through the change effort. Neither is a winning path, neither is particularly healthy, and both are utterly deflating. It's the burning platform all over again: do nothing and be consumed by fire, or make a leap in terror and pray that everything works out.

No one should have to choose between fire and ice. An organization practicing Love as a Change Strategy would never intentionally put its people in such a situation. Lasting change, whether on a team, as an individual, or at the organizational level, is intrinsically motivated. Each member is bought into leadership's vision and ready to dig in and do the hard work to make it a reality. They aren't scared about what *might* happen; they're inspired by what *could* happen.

So, how can Love as a Change Strategy help create a culture of change readiness? We'll answer that in Chapter 2.

Why Change?

- ◆ Have you ever participated in a change effort that eventually went sideways? If so, what do you think was the root cause of the failure?
- ◆ Have you ever been on a team where leadership manufactured a burning platform scenario to compel action? If so, how did that feel? Was the change effort successful?
- ◆ Think of a change effort you were a part of. Did you feel like you had a personal stake in that effort? Did you consider what part of yourself had to change to make that change a reality?

- When thinking about your own organization, how would you describe its readiness for change? What signs indicate whether your teams are truly change ready?
- Change is described as nonlinear and messy. Can you share an example from your experience when change didn't go as planned but still led to valuable outcomes?
- The chapter warns against creating a burning platform out of fear. How can leaders inspire intrinsic motivation for change without relying on fear-based tactics?
- Thinking back to the magic wand exercise, if you had the power to change one thing about how your organization handles change, what would it be?
- What were some of your biggest takeaways or ah-ha moments from this chapter?
- Share a moment of self-awareness about your leadership after reading this chapter.

CHAPTER 2

Why Love Is Necessary for Change

In 2015, Softway experienced its darkest day. Desperate to survive, we cut our workforce by a third—in the coldest and most inhumane way possible.

Cue the existential crisis. We felt lousy about both our organizational prospects and our performance as people. After over a decade in business, Softway had become driven by a toxic, dysfunctional culture. Misbehavior was rampant, disengagement was high, and productivity was low. Mix those ingredients all together, and it was a recipe for disaster.

Reeling from our mass layoffs and worsening prospects, Mohammad, our founder and CEO, undertook some soul-searching. Where did he go wrong? What did Softway's failure say about Mohammad as a leader—or worse, as a person? Given all his rampant misbehaviors, did Softway even deserve to continue?

Mohammad's answer came in the most unlikely of places: an American college football game. After witnessing an improbable comeback win by his alma mater, the University of Houston, Mohammad learned something shocking about the team's culture. The Cougars hadn't won on raw talent (they weren't the most talented team in the conference). They won because of the strength and resilience fostered in a culture of love.

Mohammad first heard about this culture of love during a postgame press conference with the team's rookie head coach, Tom Herman. As Coach Herman described it, the Cougars were invested in each other's success, honest when needed, and supportive no matter what. They were focused on building an all-star team rather than enabling a team of all-stars.

Hearing Coach Herman describe this culture of love, Mohammad was inspired and committed to transforming himself and his organization. Soon after, Love as a Strategy was born. Slowly and tirelessly, Mohammad and Softway's leadership grew their own culture of love, working from both the top down and the bottom up to change their ways and aspire to something better. No more nasty grams about refrigerator etiquette. No more harassing team members if they were a minute or two late to a meeting. No more cattle-call layoffs and security escorts out of the building. The old Softway had failed. The new Softway would thrive by bringing humanity back to the workplace.

Love as a Strategy saved Softway. In just three years, we went from a −15 percent earnings before interest, taxes, depreciation, and amortization or profit to a +28 percent, our average client contract grew from six figures to seven, and our client retention rate improved from 60 percent to 90 percent. In short, our clients stayed with us longer and paid us more.

At first glance, these numbers didn't make sense. None of our transformation efforts were client-focused; they were all focused internally on treating each other with respect and compassion as human beings. Then it hit us: we succeeded because we treated our clients the same way we treated each other. We made them feel good because we made our employees feel good.

To be clear, we made our employees feel *really* good. The numbers we're most proud of during that time are the ones that show our improved retention rates. From 2016 to 2019, employee regrettable attrition shrank from 30 percent to 12 percent. As we write this book in 2025, our attrition rate is down to 4 percent. Where once Softway was characterized by its toxic culture, today, today the vast majority of our employees actually *like* coming to work.

As our relationships with our teams grew, our relationships with our clients grew, too. Thrilled to work with such engaged teams, they began asking for our secret sauce. How could they replicate our success within their organizations? Soon, in a turn of events that still surprises us, we found ourselves leading workshops and transformation programs worldwide through our Culture+ offerings. Today, we have guided thousands of leaders in a variety of organizations representing a wealth of different cultures and nationalities around the world. And we're just getting started.

We documented this change journey in our first book, *Love as a Business Strategy*. If you're interested in a culture transformation-focused book first before taking on the messy work of leading change, we recommend you start there. In this chapter, first we will share the core framework underpinning Love as a Strategy. Then, we will expand the conversation to show how this framework can be applied to successfully lead change in your organization.

The Love as a Strategy Framework

Let's start at the top with our secret sauce: the Love as a Strategy Framework (see Figure 2.1). Go ahead and bookmark or dog-ear this page. We're willing to bet you'll be coming back to this one.

The Love as a Strategy framework begins with *behaviors*—representing the bottom of this graphic. Behaviors *are* culture. A culture of love cannot flourish unless as many people as possible in the organization practice introspection and develop self-awareness. They must be both aware of their behaviors and conscious that a gap exists in all of us between how we *think* we're coming across to others versus how we actually are. The smaller that gap, the more self-aware a person is. When you can leverage your self-awareness to master your behaviors—including your mindsets, attitude, and communication—you begin to foster a *culture of love* within your organization.

A culture of love is built by embodying our six pillars of love: inclusion, empathy, vulnerability, trust, empowerment, and forgiveness. We'll refer back to these pillars throughout this book. However, you will find a more in-depth exploration in our first book, *Love as a Business Strategy*.

We like these pillars because they're easy to understand and spot in action . . . or inaction. Whether you choose to uphold or ignore these six pillars, your culture will reflect those behaviors. For instance, Softway 1.0 genuinely believed installing biometric scanners in our Bengaluru office was a good idea. It wasn't.

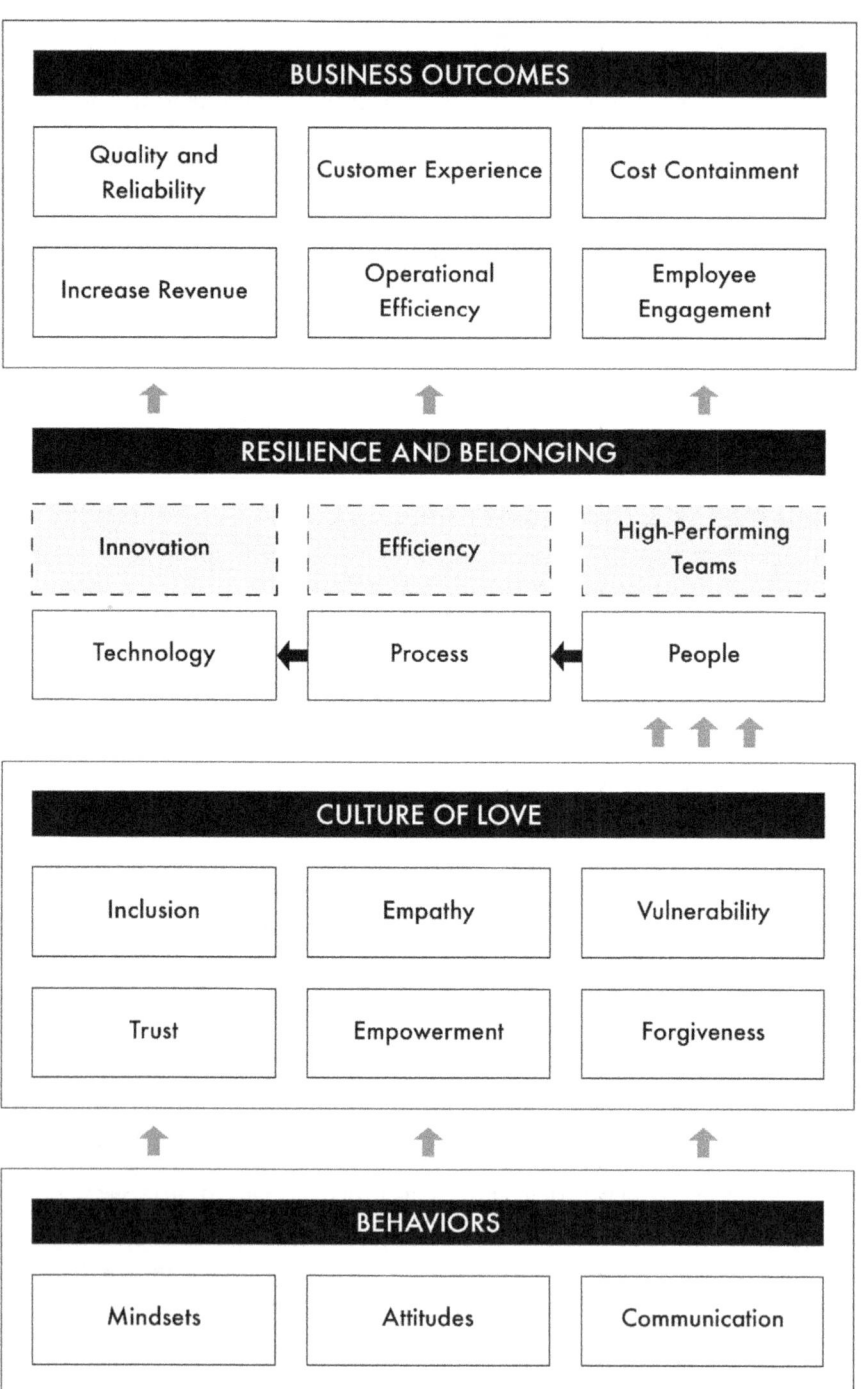

Figure 2.1   The Love as a Strategy framework

These systems only amplified our culture of mistrust. Almost immediately after they were installed, we began using them to track the comings and goings of our employees and penalize them for tardiness. Without organic trust, it doesn't matter what processes or systems you implement. Leadership will find a way to abuse them. As a result, everyone in your organization will feel untrusted, unsafe, and excluded.

However, when an organization *does* practice the six pillars, employees often experience profound *resilience and belonging* through their work and interactions with others. This is the *vibe*, for lack of a better word, that our clients picked up on. They could see evidence of the psychological safety our team members experienced in a thousand small ways—in the way they brought their authentic selves to the workplace, in the way they shared feedback and ideas without fear of humiliation, and in the way they brought a sense of ownership and accountability to everything they did.

Finally, when your employees consistently experience true belonging in the workplace, they will be primed and ready to achieve any *business outcomes* you set your sights on. Want to increase revenue or improve employee engagement? They'll make it happen. Just state the goal, give them the context and support they need, and then let them cook.

When you lead change through the Love as a Strategy framework outlined here, the work becomes—dare we say it—*fun*. Yes, it's still hard work—change always is—but there's a difference between challenge and hardship. Most people are willing to dig into a challenge when they're change ready, aligned with organizational objectives, and bought in.

What Is Love? (Baby, Don't Hurt Me)

In Chapter 1, we explained why an artificially created burning platform is antithetical to Love as a Change Strategy. A burning platform is inherently rooted in fear, which is not a healthy motivator. Love as a Change Strategy replaces that sense of scarcity with a sense of opportunity. In a culture of love, everyone believes they can be the catalyst of change. Here are the key drivers that make love such an effective change strategy.

LOVE PUTS PEOPLE AT THE CENTER

Humans are not evolving or changing as fast as the world—whether in terms of technology, the environment, culture, or any other criteria you might devise. Try as we might, we cannot adapt as quickly as we would like to. As change continues to accelerate, this challenge will only grow more pronounced. We must learn to maintain our inherent humanness and center ourselves in the change process to increase our ability to embrace and adapt to change.

This idea runs counter to how most organizations approach change. Typically, when an organization's back is against the wall, it chooses either process or profit as the truest way to overcome adversity, meet goals, and define success. Just like we did in 2015, they will sacrifice their people to protect the profit or processes established by legacy.

This sort of behavior isn't a winning move. Your organization could have a clear idea of which direction it wants to take, which tools it intends to adopt, or which reorganization strategy it wants to pursue. However, you will most likely fail if you don't consider your teams' mindsets when enacting that change. Even if the change succeeds superficially, very few people will be enthusiastic about it—or commit to sustaining it.

People are an organization's most sacred asset—the first thing it should fight for when its back is against the wall. Love your people, put them at the center of your business, and the process and profits will become easier to correct or transform.

LOVE CALLS BS ON MASLOW'S HIERARCHY

You may have heard about Maslow's hierarchy of needs before. First published in 1943, this well-worn model argues that human needs can be divided into five tiers: physiological, safety/security, love/belonging, esteem, and self-actualization. Because we humans are fundamentally focused on survival, Maslow argues that our basic needs (physiological, safety/security) must be met before our higher-order needs, like love and belonging, self-esteem, and self-actualization. This concept is so frequently repeated that most of us accept Maslow's model as an indisputable fact.

It's not. In fact, in her book *Neuroscience for Organizational Change*, change expert Hilary Scarlett argues that our sense of love and belonging is our most fundamental need. According to Scarlett, humans evolved from all other primates because we learned how to socialize, be together, and create more safety. In other words, we realized that if we operated as a society, we could produce more food and create greater safety for ourselves and our loved ones. Without love and belonging, we couldn't meet our physiological needs or develop a sense of safety and security.

Here's a little-known secret about Maslow and his research: he had plenty of evidence that his theory didn't quite work. The Siksika (Blackfoot) people he spent several weeks living with told him so directly. The foundation of Siksika culture was community—prioritizing values like love, belonging, and mutual support. They couldn't imagine a society where someone didn't have their basic needs met. Unfortunately, while it's clear the Siksika shared this perspective with Maslow, he ultimately chose not to include these findings that challenged his own hierarchy.[1]

You can see this dynamic at play in industrialized society as well. For example, consider the high burnout rate reported during the COVID-19 pandemic. Forced into solitary lives and disconnected from regular human connection, many of us lost our sense of love and belonging. As a result, we began to feel more burdened by our work and responsibilities than we would have if we felt more connected to others around us. Weak social connections lead to lower resilience and a higher rate of burnout. (Ask us how we know.) Stronger connections create greater resilience and expand our capacity to pursue higher-level needs.

This is the core belief of Love as a Change Strategy: we can't effectively embrace change without love and belonging. In the absence of love, we default to fight-or-flight mode.

LOVE CHANGES THE CONVERSATION

Think about a time in the recent past when you didn't want to change, but you did anyway. Maybe you wanted tacos on family pizza night. Maybe you didn't want to adopt that new time-logging software HR had mandated. Maybe you didn't want to move your family across the country for a new job opportunity.

What made you change your mind? What led you to go through with it?

It's easy to think of all the reasons we don't want to change. Maybe you'd never tried pho and weren't sure you would like it. Maybe you didn't see the value of a time-logging system and were worried it would eat up too much of your time. Maybe you weren't that excited about that new job opportunity. But here's the thing: even when those reasons are rooted in legitimate concerns—moving your family is a big decision, after all—ultimately they're little more than a fear response.

Through the lens of fear, we see change as vague, painful, uncertain, and potentially costly. However, through the lens of love, we see change as an *investment*, a chance to fundamentally improve ourselves, our teams, or our organization.

The path to improvement can be meandering and scary. However, fear will only limit your understanding of the problem; you'll see it as a technical challenge with a technical solution. On the other hand, love will help you embrace and understand the full extent of that challenge, even if you can't see the twists and turns ahead; you'll see it as the complex, adaptive challenge it is and that any path forward is fundamentally rooted in addressing human behavior.

Love as a Change Strategy begins with the assumption that people are an organization's greatest asset and that any change must reinforce the love and belonging we have so carefully built. Starting from that context, we wouldn't design or lead any change effort in which we would knowingly harm people. In fact, we wouldn't lead any change effort by issuing a mandate to change. Instead, we would reframe the conversation by changing our focus—not on the change itself, but on building and sustaining a culture of *change readiness*.

Change readiness is the willingness to adapt to challenges, embrace discomfort, and ultimately embrace change. A culture of fear cannot produce change-ready teams. It can only produce frustration, unforgiveness, indifference, false narratives, burnout, intellectual arrogance, and cynicism—outcomes all antithetical to love. A culture rooted in love, however, builds and strengthens the six pillars of love that are essential to creating and leading change-ready teams. When you have a relationship with the person sitting across from you, you will empathize with the adaptive challenges they face and work with that person to overcome that challenge and move the organization forward.

Of course, nobody—and no organization—is perfect. We're all guilty of mistaking an adaptive challenge for a technical problem from time to time (as you'll see in nearly every chapter of this book). It's why we couldn't get the time-tracking initiative to stick, or why Frank couldn't stick to his plan to go vegan. But we don't beat ourselves up over these misses, and we don't try to slap a bandage on the problem afterward. Instead, we dig deeper, examining the mindsets, beliefs, and attitudes preventing us from being truly change ready.

This is the power of Love as a Change Strategy. Love fundamentally changes the conversation so that we're not focused on our fears, shortcomings, or what we stand to lose, but instead on what we stand to gain if we get the change right. When viewed in that light, all the hard work of change feels less like a burden and more like an opportunity—a chance to shed the unhelpful aspects of who we are and embrace the best aspects of who we want to be.

How Do You Measure Change Readiness?

How do you measure a culture of change readiness? How do you measure the impact of love on that culture? Do you measure perks and benefits? High-fives per day? Or, is it simply how well you treat each other?

Introducing Culture Counter, the world's first culture and change readiness measurement tool. Culture Counter offers an unparalleled understanding of your organization—from the overarching company culture down to specific team dynamics.

Culture Counter achieves this by measuring ten key behaviors and attributes that link directly to how we show up at work: inclusion, forgiveness, empathy, empowerment, vulnerability, trust, mindsets, attitudes, communication, and psychological safety. Then, combined with seven change readiness attributes, we deliver an accurate, actionable measure of your culture and change readiness within your organization.

A stronger culture leads to stronger business outcomes. When you focus on improving your culture, every aspect of your business benefits—from increased productivity to enhanced employee satisfaction. For more information, visit CultureCounter.app.

Are You a Victim or a Victor?

Picture two different people.

Person A sees change as something done to them. They are the victim.

Person B sees change as inherently positive, as something they should embrace and pursue.

Now, send Person A and B the exact same email. How do they react?

Most likely, Person A feels attacked or threatened, and Person B sees an opportunity for growth and connection.

So, which kind of person are you: Person A or Person B?

That's a trick question. No one is entirely Person A, and no one is entirely Person B. One day, you might go full Person A and lose your mind when you learn that Taco Tuesday has been canceled (on whose authority, we don't know). The next day, you might be the epitome of Person B when you learn of the wonders of Waffle Wednesday. (Which is totally a thing, way cooler than what you think it is, and very much rooted in love. Ask AI to tell you about it.)

Now that you're hungry, here's the point: how you receive change is up to you. You can be the victim, or you can be the victor.

You decide whether to embrace change or complain about it. *You* determine your outlook. *You* choose how the change will affect you.

Most important, you decide whether to lead change with love or fear.

Changing an organization is hard, but changing people is even harder, and changing yourself is harder still. Most change fails because the leaders who drive it don't put in the work. Instead, they lead by fear, mandating that others change without first examining (or changing) themselves.

In a culture of love, you cannot influence others to change unless you are willing to change yourself first. That's what we learned when Jeff finally addressed the elephant in the room, and that's the secret sauce to our success as change leaders.

We don't always get change right. Sometimes, we fail in dramatic (and occasionally comical) fashion. But we've succeeded more than we've failed because we see ourselves as the victors of change, not the victims. Rather than swim against the change, we've learned to roll with it.

So, what about you? How will you define yourself on your change journey: as the victim or the victor?

Why Love Is Necessary for Change

- ◆ Do you love yourself enough to change for the better?
- ◆ Do you love your team enough to change for the better?
- ◆ Have you been, or are you, part of an organization that's failed repeatedly on major change initiatives? If so, how has that influenced your view of change?
- ◆ How do you see the relationship between a culture of love and achieving tangible business outcomes? Can you think of an example from your own experience?
- ◆ This chapter highlights the importance of self-awareness in fostering change. How do you work to develop self-awareness in your own leadership or team?
- ◆ What role do the six pillars of love (inclusion, empathy, vulnerability, trust, empowerment, and forgiveness) currently play in your organization's culture? Where do you see opportunities for growth?
- ◆ When fear drives change, it often creates burnout and resistance. What steps can you take to replace fear with love when leading change in your organization?
- ◆ Love changes the conversation about change, focusing on opportunity rather than loss. How might this shift in mindset affect how your organization approaches change?
- ◆ How do you personally balance the discomfort of change with the opportunity it presents?
- ◆ Are you more likely to view yourself as a victim or a victor of change? How does that perspective influence the way you lead or respond to change initiatives?
- ◆ What were some of your biggest takeaways or ah-ha moments from this chapter?
- ◆ Share a moment of self-awareness about your leadership after reading this chapter.

CHAPTER 3

Change Starts with You

People are static, one-dimensional characters.

People are only the sum of their parts—smart or dumb, competent or incompetent, honest or dishonest. Nothing more, nothing less.

Whether by design or ineptitude, people are nothing more than train wrecks in slow motion. They will only let you down.

Better to guard your heart so it hurts less when they do.

For years, Jeff formed a whole galaxy of beliefs based on these thoughts. They followed him into every relationship, every job, every family gathering. He wasn't born with these beliefs, of course. They didn't start to take root until his junior year of college.

Jeff was about twenty at the time, enjoying the student life a few hours from home in Austin, Texas. But when he saw his sister calling, he immediately knew something was wrong.

"What's up?" he said casually.

She got right to the point: "Dad cheated on Mom."

What the hell? The voice in his head screamed. Jeff had always looked up to his dad. Like many Chinese American fathers of his generation, he wasn't the most outwardly affectionate type. Jeff's dad showed his love primarily by working hard and focusing on being a good provider. But he was a steady, calming presence, and Jeff enrolled in college thinking he would follow in his father's footsteps and become a civil engineer (even if he didn't really understand what that was).

But after hearing his sister's words, Jeff's image of his father was shattered. The person he thought he had known was a lie.

Jeff took a deep breath and returned his focus to his sister. "That sucks," he said, trying to sound unfazed. "But they're all adults. They can make their own mistakes however they want to."

For a while, that was all he said on the matter. He didn't need to play emotional referee for his family. He just needed to live his life without all this drama and distraction so he could finish college and get on with his life.

And that's exactly what he did—with one caveat. As cool as he'd played it on the phone with his sister, his father's infidelity and eventual divorce from his mom was like a poison pill for Jeff's belief system. For years after, he was prickly at work, difficult to get close to, and distant from the people he loved the most. Convinced that every relationship was only one mistake away from ending, he chose not to invest much emotional capital into building and sustaining them.

Flash forward to March 28, 2016, when Jeff's first child was born. For the past several years, Jeff had essentially cut his dad and the rest of his family out of his life. But a new child was still a big deal, and feeling the pull of familial obligation, Jeff invited his father to the hospital to welcome his grandson into the world.

Then, a funny thing happened. As Jeff saw his dad cradling his grandson, his face beaming with warmth and love, Jeff saw his dad in a new light: as a new grandfather. From there, it was as if the layers unfolded in front of Jeff to reveal a father, a man, and finally a human, fallible and real. Just like him.

Jeff stayed on the thought, allowing his mind to extend to the future as his son slowly grew to adulthood and became his own man. A whole montage flashed before him, every bit as beautiful and captivating as the opening scene from *Up*—and with just as tragic of an ending. The montage slowed and settled on a single, heartbreaking scene. Jeff and his son were in a fight, the kind of no-holds-barred shouting match that could be heard two counties over. In the end, Jeff's son kicked him out of the house and said he never wanted to see him again.

The thought that his son might one day hate him broke Jeff's heart. No matter what wrong he might have done in his life, he wouldn't want that. And, he realized, his dad probably felt the same way about him, even if he didn't know how to show it.

Jeff's life did not magically change from that day forward. Like his father, he is still helplessly and irreversibly human. However, that day did mark the beginning of Jeff's change journey. If he could see his dad for all his different facets—father, grandfather, husband, coworker—then he could see others for all their facets as well.

Getting there, however, would take some work. After all, Jeff had built up years of harmful thoughts and behaviors by this point. It would take some time to recognize and shed all mindsets, beliefs, and attitudes that got him here. If he hoped to create a better future than the one he'd imagined, Jeff knew the change he wanted to see must start with him.

Here's the core truth of change: you can't lead change unless *you* change, and you won't change unless you first identify, interrogate, and dismantle the harmful adaptations you've developed over your life that no longer serve you.

These harmful adaptations can be broken down into three areas: mindsets, beliefs, and attitudes. We humans engage with the world primarily through either a growth or a fixed mindset. The former focuses on opportunity, while the latter focuses on scarcity. Over time, our mindsets and experiences combine to form our beliefs—specific conclusions we have drawn about the world around us and our place within it. Eventually, we externalize those beliefs through our attitudes or how we show up in different situations.

You can see this process unfold through the progression of Jeff's story. First, he received the news of his father's infidelity through a fixed mindset, which helped form his belief that people were only train wrecks waiting to happen. Jeff then externalized this belief through his attitude at work: don't get too close to anyone, avoid group projects, get your job done, and go home before anyone can let you down.

Is this a healthy way of living? Perhaps not, although it was a useful adaptation when Jeff was young and faced a dynamic challenge he didn't fully understand. Today, he recognizes that these adaptations only held him back as he stepped into adulthood. But, in a way, he was right about one thing: you can't change other people.

That's their job. All you can do is change yourself. Of course, to do that, first, you must be willing to take a good, long look at yourself.

Aware of Self-Awareness

Self-awareness is the difference between how we think we're perceived and how others experience us. When the gap is large, our self-awareness is low. When the gap is small, our self-awareness is high.

Here's a classic example of a big self-awareness gap. Mohammad fancies himself a bit of a comedian. He loves cracking jokes, and he's certain those jokes are incredibly funny—even if no one else seems to think so. As a comedian, Mohammad lacks self-awareness. A huge gap exists between how he thinks others perceive him and how the rest of the world actually experiences him.

These kinds of self-awareness gaps aren't exclusive to Mohammad. We all have a more positive outlook about certain aspects of ourselves than is sometimes warranted. Maybe Frank thinks he's the best singer in the carpool, putting James Corden to shame. Maybe Jeff fancies himself the next coming of Messi on the soccer field. Maybe Chris thinks his scratch-made, wood-fired pizzas are to die for when, in reality, you might literally die if you eat them.

Similarly, in our jobs, we sometimes operate under the illusion that we are better than we are. This is a natural phenomenon but a hindrance to change readiness and long-term growth. We must understand ourselves if we ever hope to move forward, which we can accomplish through two key tools:

◆ **Introspection** is a way of looking inward to understand why we act and react the way we do. This differs from reflection, which only asks us to consider how we might improve. Introspection helps us understand the *why* behind our behaviors. Why did Mohammad feel so triggered when Jeff made a relatively harmless observation during the meeting? What narrative was going through his mind that caused him to feel that way? Through intentional introspection, Mohammad can answer this question, understand himself better, and then take steps to address his behaviors.

◆ **Feedback** enables us to see ourselves as others do and ask ourselves whether that's how we want to be perceived. For instance, if Frank cracks what he thinks is an all-time banger of a joke, but the rest of the room interprets it as a personal attack on Chris, then Frank needs to hear that feedback to introspect and recalibrate his humor. Perception is reality.

Both of these tools serve the same goal: keeping the focus on you to help you build your self-awareness muscle. To change *anything* successfully, you must maintain a state of mind where you are aware of your own thoughts and behaviors. Don't worry about your neighbors. Don't worry about your boss. Don't worry about your family. Don't worry about anyone else. Just worry about yourself.

Finally, as you build your self-awareness muscle, remember that intent is not enough. You can act with good intent and still cause harm in the process—just like Frank did with that awful, awful joke at Chris's expense. It happens to all of us one way or another. However, by cultivating a stronger sense of self-awareness, these moments will become less frequent, you will be able to recognize them more quickly, and you will know how to take appropriate actions to resolve them.

We Mean It: Start with Yourself

Some of you may have read our discussion of introspection and thought, "That's spot-on! I wonder how I can get my team to do this."

Nice try, but we're talking to *you*.

We repeat: if you want to influence others' behavior, start with yourself.

And if you're not always perfect at practicing introspection, that's okay. Give yourself some grace. This is foundational work—easy to understand but difficult to execute consistently. There's no on/off switch for this, no certification you can broadcast to your LinkedIn followers. Only daily effort will make you better.

Mind the Mindsets

Okay, let's recap: to lead change with others, first, you must lead change in yourself. To lead change in yourself, you must develop strong self-awareness through introspection and feedback. As you set out on your self-awareness journey, your first stop is Mindset Manor—and at Mindset Manor, mindsets matter. Why? Because they fundamentally determine how we receive and interpret a given change. For example:

- Is your sales team pushing for higher targets with better incentives? Your mindset dictates whether you see that as an opportunity or a failure in the making.
- Is your supervisor pushing you to the limit of what you thought you were capable of? Your mindset dictates whether you seize that opportunity to learn or to make that person the villain. (And if you are being pushed too hard, your learning opportunity might be to practice honesty and self-advocacy.)
- Are you being asked to accept a role as a role player when you used to be in a leadership role? Your mindset dictates whether you see that as an insult or an opportunity to improve your skill set.

To borrow psychologist and thought leader Carol Dweck's terminology, you can interpret any of these scenarios with either a growth or a fixed mindset. People exhibiting a growth mindset see opportunity in any situation. They are unthreatened by change and focused instead on what *could* be. People with a fixed mindset are the opposite—threatened by change and more interested in defending the status quo.

Here's the important part: we're not preprogrammed at birth to have either a growth or fixed mindset. Very few people have one mindset all the time. Throughout a day, week, month, or year, we all receive some information with a growth mindset and others with a fixed mindset. That said, through self-awareness and introspection, we can become more growth-oriented in our daily lives.

For instance, before seeing his father holding his newborn son, Jeff had defaulted to a fixed mindset, which served as the basis for a persona he now refers to as *Divorce Jeff*. Divorce Jeff followed Real Jeff into all his interpersonal relationships, whether at work or in his personal life. It also affected how he viewed and performed his work. If everyone was just a failure in the making, then so was Jeff. If Jeff was already bound to fail, then he shouldn't bother trying in the first place. So, for several years of his adult life, Jeff *didn't* try. He coasted along at a comfortable clip, taking no real risks, avoiding tough conversations, and experiencing little growth.

Jeff would have been content to carry that mindset with him to the grave had it not been for that moment in the hospital between his father and his son. Suddenly, Jeff understood that people and human relationships weren't cast in stone; they were mutable.

Through this mindset shift, a new, growth-oriented Jeff emerged. We'll call him *Papa Jeff*. Papa Jeff approached everything differently, from relationships and work to travel and family. Today, with everything he does, Papa Jeff understands that we're all a work in progress and that everybody makes mistakes. We must learn to forgive and work past our mistakes, not define people by them.

Belay Those Beliefs

Asians are bad drivers.

The woman's role is to manage the household.

You can't be successful without a college degree.

Beliefs like this are culturally ingrained in us. The most common ones become the kind of cartoonish—yet false—cultural stereotypes we've listed here. But while these stereotypes are easy to scoff at, we all have beliefs like this, and they all combine to form complex, unique belief systems that inform how we receive and react to the world.

On their own, the beliefs we hold are neither good nor bad. They just are. We adopt and discard different beliefs throughout our lives, depending on whether they serve us and how we choose to respond to an adaptive challenge. For instance, for years, Jeff's belief that everybody would eventually let him down served him well in his goal of protecting his emotions. But when he saw his father holding his newborn son in that hospital room, this belief system was suddenly challenged: did he ignore the heartwarming moment unfolding before him and maintain his belief that his father was fundamentally unreliable, or did he dismantle that belief and replace it with something new?

Jeff chose to do the latter, creating a new belief that we humans aren't merely flawed but multifaceted (which makes us all the more wonderful). Of course, Jeff didn't realize that's what he was doing at the time. Our belief systems are often invisible to us, operating in the background without us giving them a second thought. Unless we pause to introspect, we never consider how they guide our actions. For instance, Jeff didn't walk around every day consciously thinking that he kept people at a distance because he believed everyone would eventually let him down. He had unconsciously internalized that belief over many years and experiences, which in turn influenced his future behaviors. And, when he saw his father holding his son, he unconsciously confronted and dismantled that belief.

Like Jeff, we unconsciously adopt and apply our own belief systems on an organizational level as well. These silent beliefs are often the greatest obstacle to creating lasting, meaningful change. Recognizing and dismantling those belief systems to move forward isn't a distraction from the work—it *is* the work.

For most of its existence, Softway has operated under the belief that the Indian members of our organization couldn't contribute in certain fundamental ways. For example, they weren't allowed to work in creative or customer-facing roles, and their leadership opportunities were limited. We never made this a formal company policy. However, we all knew how Mohammad—our Indian-born founder who still has family in India—felt about the issue, and no one thought to call out this obvious contradiction.

Unsurprisingly, our Indian teammates saw this contradiction all too well, and they had never been happy about it. They rightfully believed they were just as capable as their American counterparts. Most of them even cited the very opportunities we were denying them as aspirational goals for how they wanted to grow in the company:

I want to be client facing.

I want to learn how to sell.

I want to learn how to manage projects.

I want to be trusted by clients and present to them directly.

Whenever a conversation like this arose and we denied them these roles and responsibilities, we were quick to rationalize our beliefs. *Of course, Indian employees can't be in leadership,* we'd say. *We're a Houston-based company!*

Our reasoning wasn't particularly compelling, but we believed it—and that belief led to horrible structural inefficiencies. For instance, because we believed that Indian employees couldn't be client facing, we put two managers on every project—one American for the customer-facing work and one Indian for the backend work. Not only did this ill-informed team structure create a lopsided workload distribution and an information-sharing nightmare but it also didn't make sense. Some of our client contacts *were* Indian; surely they wouldn't mind talking with a fellow countryperson. What did we gain by enforcing these arbitrary constraints?

In hindsight, we see clearly how damaging this oppressive belief system was, not just to our bottom line but also to our people. We also understand how these uncomfortable and harmful beliefs often lie just below the surface of a so-called rational business decision. We now see beliefs like these as our greatest obstacle to growth and have built our entire reorganization effort in part with the intention of flushing them out and dismantling them.

An Aptitude for Attitude

Our final stop on our self-awareness train is Attitude Alley. If mindset is the lens through which we view the world and our beliefs are the legacy of those mindsets, then attitude is how we act on those views.

It's also part of our base programming. Any new change creates an environment of uncertainty. And when there is uncertainty, there is fear. And, arising from this fear, we have three biological responses: fight, flight, or freeze.

In the modern world, the fight, flight, or freeze response can feel a little dramatic; most of us haven't experienced the thrill of being chased by a real-life bear. But to our instinctual minds, uncertainty is uncertainty is uncertainty. We receive the idea of a change in our jobs in much the same way as we receive the idea of being chased by a bear. When we cannot predict the future, we default to our flight, flight, or freeze mode.

This is exactly what happened to Frank when Mohammad told him he would lead the initiative to grow our creative capacity among our Indian team members as part of our reorganization effort. This news sent Frank into full-on flyer mode. *Holy crap, what does this mean?* He asked himself. *What does this look like? WHAT'S EVEN HAPPENING RIGHT NOW?!*

Frank wasn't proud of his reaction. After all, he'd fought hard the past several years to adopt a more growth-focused mindset. But he couldn't square this idea. In fact, he didn't even think it was possible—which is precisely what he told Mohammad.

Mohammad patiently listened to Frank's objections until his friend ran out of steam. Then, calmly, he said, "You're the right person for this."

"How?" Frank said. "*No one's* the right person for this."

"We'll figure it out. But I want you to be the person in charge."

And that was that. Soon, despite Frank's initial impulse to run screaming from this bear of a new assignment, Frank was all-in on our initiative to build a world-class Indian creative team. And that's exactly what he delivered.

Even a growth-oriented, change-ready organization will revert to fear when confronted with the unknown—at least at first. A culture of love has the tools and self-awareness to fight through this initial response. Love as a Change Strategy means showing up and creating space for tough conversations. It means sharing your experience with this change and how you confronted your own mindsets, attitudes, and beliefs to understand and embrace the change.

What Are You Going to Do Now?

Frank grew up in North Carolina. His parents divorced when he was two, and his mom remarried when Frank was seven to an unemployed, drunk, and abusive veteran. As the sole breadwinner, Frank's mom didn't earn enough to support her husband's many addictions, care for Frank, and maintain a household. This abject poverty they experienced would soon prove to be the catalyst for years of abusive behavior at the hands of Frank's stepdad.

Frank doesn't remember much from this period, and the memories he has aren't good. For instance, he remembers the time his mom came running into his room with a black eye, unable to hide her terror but insistent that she'd had it coming. Or the time his step-dad threw her down a flight of stairs, standing menacingly atop the landing as his mother lay curled up in agony at the bottom, apologizing for some perceived transgression. Memories like that don't just fade away. In fact, they follow us everywhere we go.

Given this environment, it's no surprise that Frank spent much of his time hidden in his closet, quietly reading through Shel Silverstein books like *Where the Sidewalk Ends* and *The Giving Tree*. Without a TV, many personal possessions, or even food to eat in the cupboards, Frank didn't have much else to do. The care and creativity Frank found in those books became his only comfort.

Eventually, after the family was forced to flee to New Braunfels, Texas, due to her husband's lawlessness, Frank's mother began to understand this life was untenable. So, one night, she called Frank's biological father, who lived a few hours away in Houston, and said, "If you don't come to get your son, he's going to die."

The next day, on Frank's eleventh birthday, Frank's dad arrived to quite literally save his son's life. Carefully, he scooped Frank into his arms, put him in the front seat of his car, and drove him back to Houston.

Frank would never live with his mother and stepfather again, but the shockwaves from those experiences would follow him well into adulthood. For years, Frank had lived in a world where no one cared for him. Even when he lived with his father and his new (and very young) family, where he was physically safe and well provided for, he still felt like Cinderfella: always on the outside looking in. Frank's father and new stepmother loved Frank, but Frank was also a reminder of his father's past mistakes. This distance between them prompted Frank to move out on his eighteenth birthday. Better to be out on his own as quickly as possible than continue to be the de facto maid and babysitter in someone else's story.

By twenty, Frank had married. For the first time, he experienced the warmth and love of a healthy family. His father-in-law, in particular, embraced Frank and welcomed him into the family without hesitation. To this day, every time he is with his mother- and father-in-law, Frank hears his whole body say in unison: This *is how family is treated*. This *is what love is*. And in experiencing this love, he has been made whole.

Of course, that doesn't mean Frank doesn't bear the scars of his childhood in the form of unconscious mindsets, attitudes, and beliefs. Frank's tendency to be a *yes man* is the most obvious of these. When he first came to Softway, Frank would say yes to just about everything and everyone. Every day, in every aspect of his life, he'd show up and do whatever was asked of him for fear that others might push him away.

Frank's acute impostor syndrome also compounded these yes-man tendencies. Because he lacked a four-year degree, Frank believed he would never grow past a certain point in any job. Worse, he feared people would judge and reject him when they found out he didn't hold at least a bachelor's degree. To protect himself, he decided to go on the offensive, adopting a "judge or be judged" mindset that still dogs him to this day.

Eventually, thanks in part to Jeff, Chris, and Mohammad's constant supportive nudging, Frank learned to share all of himself and to *be* himself. If he didn't, he realized, he would never truly belong anywhere. As he changed his mindset, attitudes, and beliefs about himself, a funny thing happened: he started to create the same space for others that he had made for himself. If he deserved to belong, *everyone* deserved to belong.

Frank will be the first to point out that dismantling these mindsets, attitudes, and beliefs didn't change who he was or his past experiences. Instead, this act created greater awareness of this part of himself by enabling him to examine those experiences and how they informed his personality and behaviors. Today, he understands that just because these experiences happened, he doesn't have to let them trigger him. He can recognize those triggers and choose how to lead in the moment.

For instance, when Frank feels triggered, he recognizes that there's still work to be done in that area of his life, and he now considers that others on his team or within the organization may have had similar experiences. Like him, those experiences inform how they react and why they might be resistant to change. Further, if they are triggered into a strong reaction, Frank knows that this person still has some processing to do on their own growth journey and that he has an opportunity to help them get there. This understanding gives him more options for influencing change with empathy and authenticity.

True motivation is intrinsic. Frank wasn't ordered to introspect, challenge his beliefs, and learn to trust others with his full self. He *wanted* to do this to improve himself both at work and home. He *wanted* to break the generational curse of poverty, abuse, and neglect that has plagued his family. He *wanted* to repay the love that his father, wife, children, and in-laws had shown him.

More important, Frank wanted to share his story in this book. Even though writing it out for the first time made him afraid. Even though it still hurts him to think about this story. Even though sharing it might hurt his chances of reconciliation with his mother and stepfather.

Why? Because Frank doesn't let fear guide his decisions anymore. He's replaced that mindset with grace and forgiveness, adopting the belief that he can affect others through conscious, everyday choices. Frank is a person of faith, and his faith has taught him the value in finding forgiveness for everyone in his life—even for his mother and stepfather, and even though reconciliation is still a work in progress and far from guaranteed.

To Frank, the axiom "hurt people hurt people" rings true. He knows that his mother and stepfather never consciously chose to inflict trauma on him or each other. He also knows the generational trauma that his stepfather, in particular, experienced as a child and young man, and he understands that his stepfather was just living out that trauma when he came into Frank's life. Like Frank, his stepfather had built a mindset, beliefs, and attitude that helped him survive, even if it no longer suited him later in life.

That was the story of family that Frank learned as a child, and that story was pervasive until he met his in-laws. When he saw and felt their love and how they expressed it as a constant, daily presence, it was like nothing he had ever felt. Experiencing this, Frank realized he had a choice: perpetuate the cycle of fear and generational trauma he had been raised in or create something different—a family rooted in love, grace, and compassion.

Frank chose the latter. His children will never experience the pain of poverty or abuse. They will experience things he never got to—and he will share those experiences with them with a sense of childlike wonder. When his kids built their first Lego kit, for instance, it wasn't just a first for them—but for him. Through experiences like this, Frank chooses daily to greet the world with optimism, a belief that every day is a gift, and an attitude that he is on this earth to share, love, and give grace. Joy is a choice. And every day, Frank chooses not to stay in his hurt, not to stay in his unforgiveness, but to stay in love.

Your experiences probably aren't the same as Frank's. Nevertheless, they have informed and shaped the person you are today. No doubt, many of those mindsets, attitudes, and beliefs are ones you would like to maintain. Others, however, could be explored, understood, and dismantled so that you can become the person you *want* to be rather than the person you are by default.

Frank and Jeff decided to change themselves, starting with the mindset in which they receive the world, which then filtered into their beliefs, and then finally into their attitudes. Both of their stories are still ongoing, and both have challenges that remain unresolved. However, both of their journeys became more bearable when they were able to find love along the way.

As you've considered our change stories in this chapter, hopefully, you've seen the love that can exist even inside the messy, often dark, tangle of our lives and relationships. Jeff and Frank changed because they were able to see the love available to them, adapt to new needs, and use that energy to chart their own course. In your own way, in your own life story, *you* get to do the same thing. *You* get to decide what to do with the bad things that have happened to you. And that choice does not have to be driven by fear.

Now, here's our challenge to you: what will you do with this realization? How will your new understanding of yourself inform you and the way you show up to work?

Leading change begins with uncovering your true self and then carefully choosing what stays and what goes so you can learn to change your behaviors to positively influence others. This is an on-going process, but it's also the crucial first step in creating a change-ready organization, which is the focus of Part II of the book. If you are unwilling to take this first step and work on yourself, then the people in your organization will also be unwilling—and your organization will never be ready to accept the idea of change as an opportunity rather than as a threat. Change yourself first, so that others may follow from your example.

With that said, a warning: If this chapter made you feel uncomfortable, if this chapter made you unsure whether you are truly capable of changing yourself to pursue larger organizational change, then buckle up. In Chapter 4, we're diving headfirst into discomfort.

The Change Starts with Me Journal

To kick-start your personal change journey, we've created the Change Starts with Me Journal. This guided journaling resource helps you identify a mindset, attitude, or belief that no longer serves you, and helps you walk through steps to challenge and shift it.

For a free download, visit www.loveasastrategy.com.

Change Starts with You

- ◆ Think of a situation in which you felt frustrated or misunderstood. Then, ask:
  - How does this apply to me?
  - What else could be true?
  - Who can offer me a perspective of myself that I might not be seeing?
- ◆ What beliefs may hold you or your organization back?
- ◆ What beliefs cause you to resist change?
- ◆ Fill in the blank: "I want to be a millionaire, but _____."
  Now, read your response. Is that an example of positive or negative self-talk?
- ◆ Jeff's mindset shaped his beliefs and attitudes for years. What mindsets have shaped the way you see the world?
- ◆ How can feedback help close the gap between how we see ourselves and how others experience us?
- ◆ Have you ever had a belief that once served you but now holds you back? How did you recognize it?
- ◆ What role does mindset play in how we interpret and respond to change?

(continued)

- ◆ Frank struggled with impostor syndrome. How have past experiences influenced the way you see yourself at work?
- ◆ This chapter talks about moving from a fear-driven mindset to one rooted in love. What's one way you can apply this shift in your personal or professional life?
- ◆ Change starts with you. What's one belief, mindset, or attitude you want to work on to be more change ready?
- ◆ What were some of your biggest takeaways or ah-ha moments from this chapter?
- ◆ Share a moment of self-awareness about your leadership after reading this chapter.

PART II

The Six Principles of Change

"You'll never change. You can't, and you won't."

Sounds like a line from the climax of a bad rom-com, right? Don't worry, we know the formula: everything will work out in the end. After this scene, this mismatched (but still madly in love) couple will go their separate ways, progress through a soul-searching montage set to popular music, find it in their hearts to change, and then find their way back to each other in some grandiose and improbable fashion. Cue more popular music, show the couple smooching, and then roll the credits.

Doesn't it just warm your heart?

We like to poke fun at the world of rom-coms, but the truth is, they're onto something. As we showed in Chapter 3, changing who you are is hard. And in the real world, we don't have the power of montage to get us through it. Instead, we have to introspect in real time—and the results are far from guaranteed.

Knowing this, it's no wonder that many organizations don't even bother trying to help their teams navigate the human side of change. Instead, they introduce change methodologies that put a set of rigid processes in place to avoid the hard work of telling people that a necessary part of change is behavior-based.

But processes are brittle, and they've been known to break due to an unexpected stressor, a change in the environment, or a "harmless" tweak gone awry. When that happens, what do your teams fall back on to guide their behaviors and solve the problem? More processes?

Not if you want to lead with love—and not if you want to create a culture of change readiness within your organization.

If you truly want to change yourself, your teams, your department, or your entire workplace, you must be okay with not having all the answers or not knowing how things will play out. There can't be a process, or a training module, or a role-play session for everything. Sometimes, the best you can do is point your ship in what you believe is the best direction and let the currents take you where you need to go.

So, how can you be confident that you've pointed your ship in the right direction? We follow a set of clearly defined operating principles—our *six principles of change*. These principles help us make informed choices about how we show up, how we operate, how we behave, and how we make decisions when we find ourselves in situations we've never encountered before—which, in the context of change, only happens every single day. Here are our six principles, in a quasi-particular order:

1. Embrace discomfort.
2. Prioritize relationships.
3. Practice empathetic curiosity.
4. Experiment.
5. Wield your influence.
6. Be effective.

Real talk: we had trouble deciding how to order these chapters in a way that would best guide you through this section of the book. Understanding one principle isn't a prerequisite for understanding another; each is part of an interdependent system that feeds off of and into each other. For instance, you must prioritize relationships to practice empathetic curiosity—but by practicing empathetic curiosity, you will almost certainly strengthen your relationships. Or, you must prioritize relationships to embrace discomfort, which helps you better prioritize relationships.

We chose this order because the first three principles (embrace discomfort, prioritize relationships, and practice empathetic curiosity) are all more relational and behavior-focused; each helps us diagnose and understand the adaptive challenges we might be encountering and to uncover the beliefs preventing us from moving forward. The latter three principles (experiment, wield your influence, and be effective) are all more tactical; they focus our attention on creating the new experiences that change our beliefs—and in a culture of love, experiences *follow* behaviors.

Reading these chapters in the order we've laid out here will give you the most comprehensive understanding of these principles, how they relate to each other, and what they look like in action in the real world (in a word: messy). In practice, however, you don't need to follow any rigid process or order. As long as you focus on the core intent of these principles and practice applying them in a way that inspires change both in you and those around you, then you're doing it right. It really is that simple—even if, as the stories that follow show, it's rarely easy.

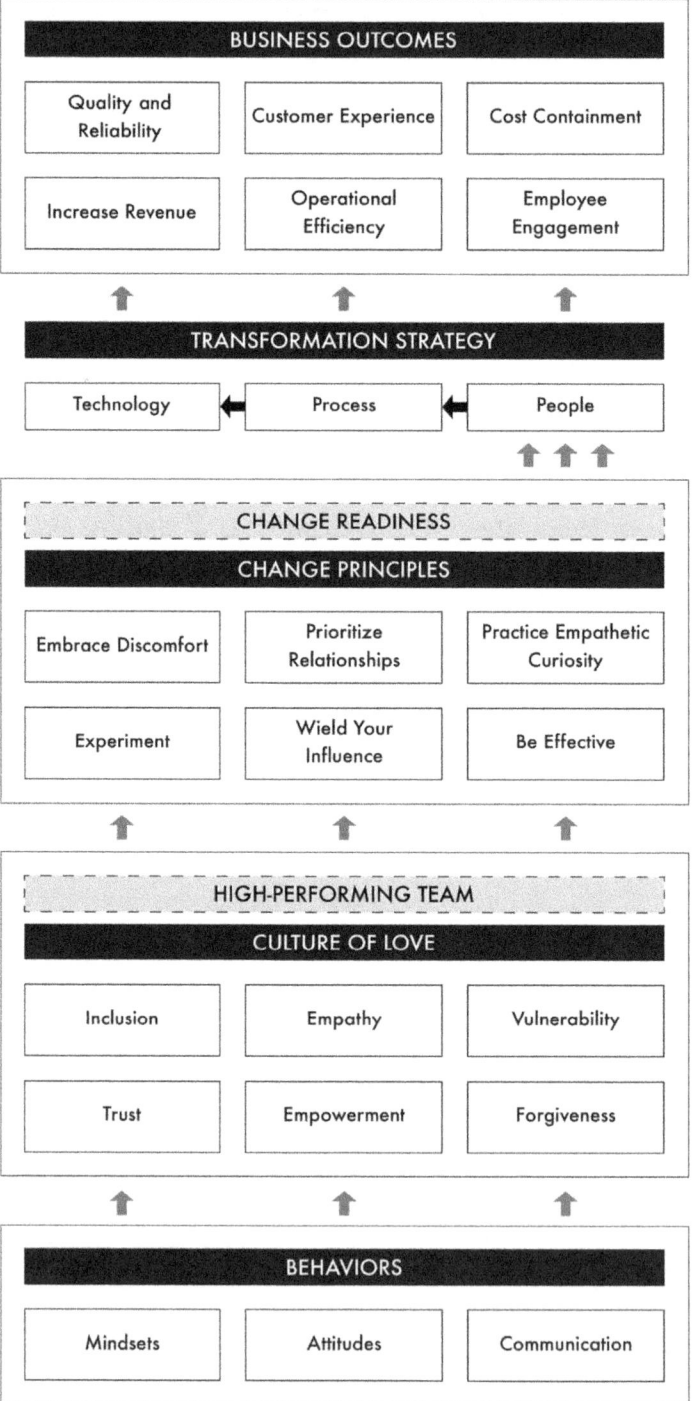

CHAPTER 4

Embrace Discomfort

"Okay, this is some *Love and Hip-Hop* reality TV BS," Imani said. "I'm going home!" Then, she stood up, collected her possessions, and walked right past us and out the conference room doors without saying goodbye.

We looked around at the gathered leadership team representing a large, metropolitan school district. Everyone was staring at us, their eyes searching for clues about what just happened. Was this a test, another one of our off-beat exercises designed to help the group experience discomfort? What kind of crazy schemes had we cooked up with Imani as her leadership consultants?

Unfortunately, this was not a planned activity. Yes, we were the consultants on record, but we were just as surprised as everyone else.

"Chris, I think we blew it," Mohammad whispered. Chris nodded, feeling especially guilty about what had just happened. Not only had Chris insisted on the specific activities that led to Imani's departure but also he had been pushing everyone in the room hard all day in the hopes of surfacing all the deep-seated feelings that the team had been struggling to address. Just when he thought they were on the verge of a breakthrough, instead, they collapsed.

Assuming we had just lost our contract with our first education client—we started packing up our stuff and getting ready to head back to the airport, our heads hanging low like that sad Charlie Brown gif.

Then Chris's phone rang. It was Imani.

"Hey, guys," she said. "That was a moment for me, but I really do appreciate what you all did. Yes, I'm disappointed with my team. That's their problem. You all did a great job facilitating!"

We were relieved to receive the call and hear that she appreciated us, but we were also skeptical. Was she just practicing love as a firing strategy?

As it turned out, no. Imani (we're using an alias here), the district's superintendent, was sincere in both thanking us for our work and taking her team to task. During the workshop, she had made it her goal to flush some of the deep operational, behavioral, and identity-related divides among the leadership team to the surface. Even though we had approached these discussions with love, Imani had always known they would be tense. However, as the day went on, she didn't feel like the team was making headway.

We felt the same way. We saw how different members of the leadership team were rude or evasive to each other, particularly in the way conversations would break down in tears or misbehavior before any meaningful progress could be made. We kept pushing the team to break through, but our efforts were met with the same resistance Imani had encountered. When Imani stood up and left, we took it as a sign we had pushed them too far.

Fortunately, we hadn't. Imani's dramatic-but-necessary exit had turned the heat up to the exact right temperature for the team to experience a much-needed breakthrough. After the initial shock of Imani's exit, the leadership team hadn't collapsed into anger and name-calling. Instead, these leaders began to reflect on what just happened and share their experiences openly and directly—precisely what we and Imani had been pushing for all along.

As we would learn later while interviewing members of the district's leadership team about the incident, this wasn't the first time Imani had deployed such a bold tactic. Imani saw that her team had become too "Imani-centered," and she was trying to move the group past that mindset. She didn't want to be seen as the person who initiated all activity, broached the hard conversations, or solved the group's problems.

So, she had begun strategically deploying a powerful leadership move: she took herself out of the equation so that others would feel comfortable stepping out of her shadow and playing a larger role in important conversations. During video conferences, other team members would notice how Imani either held a neutral facial expression or shut her video off entirely during certain contentious moments. Other times, Imani would directly "name the thing," as their leadership team came to call it, saying something to the effect of, "I'm leaving y'all to do this because you're supposed to do it. Once you've done it, come back to let me know or get my buy-in."

So, when Imani declared that the leadership team was getting into some "reality TV BS," she wasn't quitting on them. She was challenging them to do better. Her team recognized this and rose to her challenge. "We all knew what our teammates were doing, and we didn't say anything," one attendee said later of that galvanizing moment. By removing herself from the equation, Imani forced her team to snap into the moment, introspect on their role in the conflict that had plagued the district's leadership team, and then work to make it right.

We're glad this story has a happy ending, but it was pretty uncomfortable in the moment. Good. As the name of this chapter suggests, we're big fans of discomfort, running headfirst into it whenever we recognize the opportunity to do so.

In that way, you could say we're just like the buffalo.

When cows sense an approaching storm, they try to outrun it by moving in the same direction as the storm. Anyone can understand the impulse: something we don't like is coming, so we had better run away from it. But this impulse is counterproductive; by running in the same direction as the storm, cows spend more time in the storm than if they had simply stayed put. When buffalo sense a storm, however, they don't run from it. Instead, they turn around and run head-on into it. As a result, the storm is both on them quicker and over quicker.

This is how we think of discomfort in a culture of love: run headlong into it and get it over with. Once you're through it, you're through it. It's not fun, but it's better than running from it and prolonging your misery.

This isn't an excuse to be reckless. While a healthy dose of discomfort can lead to incredible breakthroughs, too much discomfort can lead to breakdowns. In this chapter, we'll explore the many nuances of embracing discomfort in a culture of love and the lessons we learned from some particularly uncomfortable moments on our change journey.

Get in the Growth Zone (and Stay There)

How comfortable are you with public speaking?

Discussing politics at a family function?

Accepting a reassignment at work?

These are just a sampling of the questions we ask in our Culture Practice workshops to help attendees consider their own discomfort in certain scenarios. The responses are invariably different. Some people are quite comfortable with public speaking, while others feel surprisingly good about giving team members feedback. (No one is comfortable talking politics at family events, though.)

Ultimately, that's the point of the exercise: each of us has different areas that make us uncomfortable. The more time we spend in these areas—what we call *growth zones*—the more growth we will experience. Why? Because we generally don't learn much doing things that make us feel comfortable. However, by leaning into the uncomfortable moments and adapting to the challenges they present, we learn more about ourselves and the challenges we're made to confront. As the saying goes, growth begins where comfort ends.

You've probably experienced this before. Maybe you didn't want to give that presentation because public speaking makes you super uncomfortable. However, after working through your discomfort and learning to calm your nerves and present confidently, you realized you had a previously undiscovered gear you could shift into when necessary. Congratulations: you've just successfully navigated the gauntlet of the growth zone!

As illuminating as this experience was, it almost didn't happen. Why? Because we don't like feeling uncomfortable. Instead, we default to the biggest growth killer around: avoidance.

We all know what avoidance is, but sometimes, we don't recognize it when it occurs. To stay in the growth zone—in other words, to stay *uncomfortable*—we must learn to recognize how avoidance disguises itself in the workplace.

Train Your Sights on Work Avoidance

Raise your hand if you've ever done one or more of the following:

- You failed to speak up during a meeting because you were waiting for someone else to say what you wanted.
- You rationalized your behavior when a teammate called you out.
- You deflected responsibility or blamed someone else for not doing their part.
- You weaponized your incompetence and avoided the work by saying you were "still learning" or "no one told me what to do or how to do it."
- You prematurely made a joke to lighten the mood.

Each of these is a type of work avoidance. That last one, in particular, is a doozy—and Frank's specialty. There's never been a tense moment in the office where he wasn't screaming inside to tell a joke to cut the tension. Sometimes, the jokes are genuinely funny. All the time, they're an attempt to divert attention from the discomfort. The pullback toward comfort is *strong* in this one, folks.

But here's a type of work avoidance you probably haven't considered: training.

That's right, training. That universally valued practice that all companies want more of, yet none seem to know what to do with. We like training too . . . when it's necessary. Too often, though, training is used as a stalling tactic to implement a planned change, delaying and belaboring the experimentation and discomfort required for genuine, fruitful growth.

Training is, by definition, a program of mandatory reorientation designed to be enacted without any agency given to the trainee. It's designed to circumvent the kind of conflict that could arise from asking for team input (we'll take a closer look at conflict avoidance in Chapter 5). Where's the collaboration? Where's the kind of deep learning that can only come through experimentation? A little bit of training to help people understand the basics is fine. A six-month training program might sound rational, but in reality, it's an elaborate stalling tactic designed to avoid the discomfort of giving people the agency to learn (and make mistakes) on their own.

So, what's the alternative? Get the affected teams involved in the change as quickly as possible. For example, in one of our more successful change efforts, as soon as we knew we needed to face the ongoing artificial intelligence revolution head-on, we initiated a four-day hackathon to allow team members to participate in and shape our adoption efforts, helping them feel loved and connected to the company as part of the change strategy. By the end of the four days, the team had a deeper and more nuanced understanding of the tool than any training could have provided (for the full story, see Chapter 7). If we're being honest, we should have embraced this approach sooner. And speaking of honesty, that leads us to another sneaky form of avoidance . . .

Choose Honesty over Harmony

Think of one of your most cherished relationships. Why is that bond so strong?

Rarely is the answer that you've just had a comfortable, happy time together for the duration of your relationship. More likely, if you trace the lines back long enough, you'll stumble on some awkward and painful moments, embarrassing ordeals, and tough, deep, and meaningful conversations. None of those experiences were fun, but they were essential for helping that relationship grow.

Like personal bonds, the strongest professional bonds are forged not by placating coworkers but by embracing discomfort and getting real with each other. You cannot lead change with love without being willing to create and experience pain and grow from the experience.

To implement this belief, we follow a simple principle called *honesty over harmony*. This principle follows from the unattributed quote: "Honesty without kindness is brutality. Kindness without honesty is manipulation. Honesty with kindness is integrity." Or, as we like to say at Softway, honesty with kindness is *love*.

Let's break that statement down.

First, "Honesty without kindness is brutality." We've all experienced brutal honesty, where someone just lays into us with no filter in the name of being honest or direct. It doesn't feel good. It's one thing to experience discomfort, but it's another to be hurt by someone's statements. Yes, the point was made, but not in a constructive or loving way. This leaves no space for accountability or relationship, just a swift punch in the face.

Second, "Kindness without honesty is manipulation." Honesty is the willingness to say the things that often go unsaid. When you feel a certain way, you share those feelings to be honest with yourself, your intent, and your feelings. However, honesty isn't just speaking without lies. It's speaking the full truth. You can say a series of kind, accurate statements but still be dishonest to yourself and those you're accountable to by what you leave out.

To give an example, say that Frank is giving a presentation. Jeff appears on the edge of his seat the whole time, nodding along to every slide, quip, and pop culture reference. Jeff appears to support Frank's position through his body language, but in fact, he thinks Frank's whole presentation is nothing more than the ravings of a madman. Jeff is being kind and harmonious in the moment, but he's not being honest. He's avoiding the problem to preserve comfort. In doing so, he's manipulating Frank, leading him to think he's doing a good job when, in reality, he's bombing.

That's neither helpful nor kind. It's false harmony. If you allow your teammates to bomb their presentations without providing meaningful feedback, your organization will eventually bomb something much larger and more important—like a cross-functional transformation effort, for instance.

Many organizations believe they practice honesty when, in fact, all they do is reinforce false harmony. You've probably experienced these "nice" cultures before at organizations where no one is argumentative or even pushes back on each other. On the surface, there's nothing wrong with these teams. They sincerely want to do what's best and right for each other, the organization, and those they serve. However, everyone is so concerned with preserving the peace that they actively resist efforts to improve, change, or rock the boat. If someone raises an important question, they're often immediately (and very politely) swatted down. "We're all good here," someone might say. "Why are we making this so uncomfortable?"

Here's why: because making things uncomfortable is *good*. Discomfort is where the magic happens. It's the secret sauce of real, lasting change. Conflict isn't interruptive, unproductive, or harmful to team unity. It's essential.

This brings us to the last part of the statement: "Honesty with kindness is love." No one gets honesty over harmony right 100 percent of the time because it requires us to live up to our highest ideals of ourselves. To adapt a popular meme, in each of us are two wolves. One wolf is our default position, the person we're accustomed to being and have naturally developed into throughout our lives. The second wolf is the person we aspire to be.

Frank's default wolf chooses harmony above all else. If, during a meeting, he sees Mohammad get triggered and shut off his camera, he knows what he *should* do. He should say, "Hey, Mohammad, I recognize that something has triggered you, and you're shut down. Can we talk about it?" But does he always embrace discomfort and say the hard thing? He does not. The call ends, back channel conversations ensue, and the team grows farther apart rather than closer together.

This struggle between our two wolves is precisely why we must practice standing in our growth zones and working through our discomfort rather than avoiding it. If we fail to practice honesty over harmony in the small moments when nothing more is at stake than bringing a cranky Mohammad back into the fold, we will fail to practice it in the big moments when more is on the line.

Luckily, once you're aware of the harmony trap, spotting it and breaking free is easy. The next time you think your team is dancing around the elephant in the room, pull a Jeff. Say, "I feel like we're being harmonious. I would like for us to be honest." There you go: clean, simple, and effective. Honesty can be that easy.

Just remember, permission to be honest differs from permission to be a jerk. Discomfort is temporary. Conflict is temporary. Don't let something temporary damage or destroy your relationships—ultimately, your organization's greatest asset.

Feedback Sandwiches Taste Like Crap

Since we're in an honest mood, we need to get something off our chest: the feedback sandwich is just awful. It's merely another way to avoid discomfort—one that everyone can see right through.

You've almost certainly received or delivered a feedback sandwich before. If not, the process goes like this: say something good the person is doing, say the bad part that makes you uncomfortable, and then close out with another good thing.

This approach might sound good in the abstract, but it's just a conversational crutch in practice. At best, it unnecessarily prolongs feedback conversations. At worst, it superficially addresses important issues, making them far less likely to be addressed.

To break yourself of this useless habit, here's our best advice: prioritize relationships (see Chapter 5). When you know and value the person in front of you, you might still feel uncomfortable delivering feedback, but you will respect that person enough to do right by them and share hard truths with kindness and empathy.

Oh, and be self-aware and open enough to hear direct feedback from others. This is a two-way street, after all.

Say No to the Frozen Middle

Many change management programs are designed to keep leaders feeling comfortable and in control. They shouldn't. No leader should feel comfortable when transformation programs experience an 84 percent failure rate globally. These failures aren't the result of a bad team. They're the result of leadership being overconfident in their plan and unwilling to listen to real criticism.

Leaders should always feel like they have a stake in the change. They should be able to see and experience the same amount of discomfort as their employees. Experiencing discomfort leaves you vulnerable, making you open to receiving feedback. Feedback enables you to adjust based on what's happening in your organization. When both sides understand the stakes, they are committed to success—working together, communicating frequently and honestly, and making adjustments as needed.

Unfortunately, most organizations end up in the *frozen middle*. They make their plan, create their documents, dive into execution, and then get stuck. Why? Because, to borrow a phrase from Imani and her team, they didn't "get in the rumble" with their teams. Getting in the rumble means putting yourself in the center of uncomfortable conversations, calling attention to unspoken problems, and creating space for hard conversations between teammates—all with the trust and understanding that everyone is working toward the same goal.

When Imani initiated a change project to bring Love as a Strategy to their district, she expected pushback—and she got it. At the outset of the transformation, the team held weekly all-day meetings to work through their change project's many practical and logistical challenges. During these meetings, no one was on the same page about anything—worse, no one was honest. They would say one thing to the group and then say something else entirely to Imani in private after the meeting.

This kind of doublespeak is common in organizations that lack a culture of love. Without trust, many team members don't feel comfortable sharing their true feelings with their team. On this particular leadership team, certain members of the team felt more comfortable with certain people than others, and this clique-ishness resulted in a leadership culture that often chose harmony over honesty. A few leaders frequently found themselves holding ideas back during meetings that could have helped move the group forward. Because no one was willing to embrace their discomfort, get in the rumble, and work out their issues, crucial work wasn't getting done—and the problem was beginning to affect their students.

"At the end of the day, the work wasn't getting done effectively, efficiently, and in excellence for our scholars," one of the district's leaders told us. "We could have been moving the ball faster and further if we could just figure out how to trust, how to rumble without being in our feelings too long."

Recognizing this misbehavior, Imani started calling attention to the issue, both in individual and group settings. Imani primarily walked her team through these issues through candid feedback intended to help them grow as leaders and work through their fears and doubts. Imani didn't always like how her team behaved, and they didn't always like what she had to say. Still, by continuing to get in the rumble with her team daily, Imani demonstrated that she wasn't leaving her team to work through this transformation alone. She was right there in the middle with them.

That's what embracing discomfort and leading change look like in action. If leaders want to see change, they must be the change they want to see. Even more, they must be the first group to change so they can embody the change they want others to see. Then, they must build a bridge for others to come across to the other side, practicing empathetic curiosity to understand how people are struggling, what's causing their struggles, and how they can work to embrace their discomfort, lean into their growth zones, and overcome their adaptive challenges together.

Transformation Awaits on the Other Side of Discomfort

Working with friends can get emotional and tense. Saif and Mohammad grew up together. They've known each other since they can remember, and Saif's background in software development made him a natural fit for Softway, where, in 2021, he was named vice president (VP) of technology. However, just when Saif thought his prospects couldn't be any better, Mohammad came along with his big reorganization plan and shifted Saif from his VP role into a new role as director of technology consulting.

Mohammad saw this move as a tremendous opportunity for Saif. Technology consulting was a brand-new part of our business and long-term growth plan, one that would open up Softway to an entirely new client base. Mohammad chose Saif for the role because he had the technical and leadership skills to make this new department his own. And, as with all role changes we planned at Softway, his salary wasn't affected. He still enjoyed the same pay and benefits as he always did.

Perhaps, more than that, however, as both a boss and a friend, Mohammad wanted to give Saif an opportunity to grow as an individual, as a consultant, and as a leader. Saif was excellent at what he did, but, from Mohammad's perspective, he had hit a bit of a dead end in terms of growth opportunities for his career. That's not what Mohammad wanted for him—and he suspected that's not what Saif wanted for himself either, even if he was unable or unwilling to see it.

At first, Saif wasn't able or willing to see this perspective. He liked what he was doing, he didn't particularly feel like being uncomfortable in a new role, and, when he first heard the news, he couldn't help but see this move as a demotion—even worse, as an insult. It wasn't easy for Saif to sit with this discomfort, especially when he had so many questions. Why didn't Mohammad trust him in his VP role anymore? What did his career path at Softway look like now? What if this new role didn't suit him?

That last question lingered in his consciousness the most. As Saif shared when we interviewed him for this book, it wasn't the title change that bothered him but the shift in function. He had spent seventeen years at Softway working on a team that he loved, but now he was being asked to do something he wasn't as experienced in, he wasn't passionate about, and he didn't enjoy. That was scary. That was unknown. That was unwelcome.

And that is exactly what he told Mohammad on hearing the news: "I don't want to do this." Mohammad listened to Saif's concerns and resolved to work through these issues with him—not through a superficial, one-and-done conversation, but through a series of focused and intentional conversations over several months.

During their first sit-down, the mood was tense and uncomfortable. Saif was still very much in his feelings, unsure why he had agreed to these conversations in the first place. If the decision had already been made, if no amount of discussion could create a different result, then what was the point of relitigating the decision and dragging everything out?

At the core of this anger was a sense of betrayal. Mohammad and Saif had always enjoyed a strong relationship. Historically, when Mohammad had to make a big decision involving Saif, he engaged his coworker in dialogue about the decision *first*. This time, though, Saif felt dictated to; all he had was Mohammad's decision, with no insight into the thought process that led to that decision. With so many unanswered questions, it was natural for Saif to feel angry and resentful. Sure, Mohammad was making the effort to engage him *now*, but it was too little, too late. Saif wasn't sure he wanted to open up.

Still, he gave it a shot. If Mohammad was willing to sit on the hot seat, Saif might as well turn the heat up for him. Over the next hour, Saif did his best to hold Mohammad accountable. Why had he made this decision? Why hadn't Mohammad brought him into the decision-making process earlier? What had Saif done wrong? Did Softway still see him as valuable to the company? Did he still have a future at Softway?

Saif could see that Mohammad was trying to answer these questions as best he could, but he didn't find Mohammad's responses particularly compelling. As the conversation wrapped, Saif felt they had made little progress—and he wasn't particularly interested in continuing to try. "Let's be done with this for now," he told Mohammad. And for a while, they were.

The professional world is inescapably resolution oriented. If someone is upset, the leader or manager's goal is to move that person to closure as soon as possible and then carry on as if everything is hunky dory after that. But that's not how discomfort works. It's a process, a journey of uncertainty that must be embraced and explored before true resolution can be had. Rushing through this process will only exacerbate whatever issues exist.

Mohammad understood that his dialogue with Saif would take some time, but that didn't mean he liked it. He didn't like that he had upset such a trusted and valued member of the team. He didn't like that he had not approached and communicated this decision as well as he could have to start with. And he certainly didn't like that Saif might very well decide that Softway no longer provided the opportunities he was looking for.

Still, while these thoughts made him uncomfortable, Mohammad had to be okay with it, to trust the process, and to trust that Saif would find his way back. He couldn't just wave his hands, resolve the issue, and expect Saif to get back to work. Not only would that be unrealistic, but it would be an insult to Saif. Adaptive challenges take time to work through.

Eventually, the pair reconvened and tried to talk through everything again. But from Saif's perspective, Mohammad still wasn't getting it. All Mohammad wanted to talk about was the importance of this move to the organization, which Saif understood and didn't object to. He didn't want to know why they'd created this role and new department; he wanted to know *why him*. For the past several months prior to his reassignment, Saif had watched as the technology team struggled to enter its next era of software development, and Softway's customer experience had stagnated as a result. He had been right in the middle of solving this challenge when the rug was pulled out from under him. He was committed to and excited by that work and wanted to see it through.

"It's not about the title," Saif reiterated to Mohammad. "If you had called me vice president of technology consulting instead of director, I'd still have the same problems with the decision. I can help the company more by improving our engineering capabilities and transforming our customer experience."

"You can help the company by doing that, and if everything goes according to our plan and we meet our revenue goals, I'd be happy to see you return to that work," Mohammad said. "But right now, those aren't our biggest needs. We need new clients, and your greatest value to the company is to build this department so we can find and serve those new clients."

The mood on the call changed. Saif still wasn't fully resolved, but they were finally speaking the same language. He let out a sigh of relief and told Mohammad he was looking forward to the next call.

During that next conversation, Saif could see that Mohammad had heard his concerns and adjusted his focus. Carefully, Mohammad detailed the thought process that had led him to consider Saif for this new role. It was a careful, considerate, and rational explanation. For the first time since this whole saga started, Saif felt *heard*. Mohammad deeply understood Saif's desire to contribute as a software developer and had assigned Saif this new role *because* of that desire, not despite it. Once Saif understood that, he began to see this change not as a detour but as a new path full of opportunity.

By the end of the call, Saif was ready to move forward. Not because Mohammad told him to deal with it. Not because enough time had passed and he eventually caved in. But because Mohammad stayed in the discomfort with him—and in so doing, demonstrated that he trusted, valued, and supported him.

By the end of the year, Saif was thriving in his new role and had experienced tremendous growth as a leader. This growth didn't come easy, and Saif was resistant to it at first. But, personal feelings aside, Saif never wavered in his commitment to his work or to supporting his new team. He recognized that, like him, they were on their own journey of discomfort, and he wanted to be a good leader to them even as he navigated his own path.

This sort of leadership is *precisely* why Mohammad chose Saif for this crucial role. By his very nature, Saif can't help but lead. He led when he was unhappy, he led while working through his discomfort with Mohammad, and then he doubled down once he understood the growth available to him on this journey. This wasn't the path Saif ever expected to be on, but now that he was, he was determined to lean into his discomfort and make the most of it.

Imagine two people standing side by side. Both are looking at the same roller coaster and feeling the same butterflies. However, while one person can't wait to get on, the other wants to run away screaming. Why? Fear and excitement are both expressions of discomfort. The difference is in our perception. Sometimes, we like to push ourselves out of our comfort zone; other times, we'll do anything to stay inside it.

Most change management methodologies are designed to do the latter, to limit discomfort and bring teams back to equilibrium as quickly as possible. We take the opposite approach: sit with your teams in discomfort long enough to make the effort productive—if not transformative.

Saif's transformation was possible only because he and Mohammad worked together to embrace discomfort and open dialogue. Without dialogue, team members don't have communication with each other. They have speculation. And all speculation leads to is a case of the *uns*—untruths, unresolved issues, and unforgiveness. Once Saif and Mohammad could reestablish communication, Saif felt open and able to express his concerns and find a path forward.

And, much to Saif's delight, this new path proved to be reinvigorating, allowing him to nurture other strengths like networking and relationship building. He loved connecting with new people both inside and outside the company, and that feeling of connection helped him to understand and embrace his new mission. By shifting to a growth-oriented mindset, Saif began to see all the avenues for him to leverage this change into new growth opportunities both in his role and in his career.

This is how we learn. This is how we change. This is how we become change ready.

We remain in stasis when we are comfortable and grow when we are uncomfortable. Clinging to comfort leads to fixed thinking and viewing change in good/bad binaries. However, the individuals, teams, and organizations that allow themselves to experience real discomfort are far more likely to accomplish true transformative growth. Stay in discomfort long enough, and you will arrive at innovative solutions to adaptive challenges in ways that those who play it safe cannot and will not.

This is what happened to Saif. For most of his career at Softway, he had been inclined to work on projects he was passionate about and implement skills he already possessed. His previous role had been comfortable but stagnant—and he knew it. Once he became receptive to the change being asked of him, he began to discover new things about himself, to thrive in areas he might never have experimented with previously, and to lean into discomfort and have the hard, necessary conversations essential to moving forward. Where once Saif tended toward stasis, now Saif embraces discomfort—and he now understands the importance of our next change principle: prioritizing relationships.

Embrace Discomfort

- How do you react to moments of discomfort at home and at work? How would you like to react in moments of discomfort?
- What areas do you consider to be in your comfort zone, and what do you consider to be in your learning or fear zones?
- What's an example of a time where discomfort led to personal or professional growth for you?
- The chapter compares embracing discomfort to how buffalo run into storms. How can this mindset help in leading change?
- Work avoidance can disguise itself in humor, rationalization, or deflection. Which forms of avoidance do you see most often in your workplace? Which type of avoidance do you use?

- How does choosing honesty over harmony improve relationships and workplace culture?
- What were some of your biggest takeaways or ah-ha moments from this chapter?
- Share a moment of self-awareness about your leadership after reading this chapter.
- What, if anything, will you change or adjust about how you lead or behave based on what you've read?

CHAPTER 5

Prioritize Relationships

Human behavior is often discussed within the framework of *problems*. We encounter an adaptive challenge, we experience the discomfort that comes with it, and we do what we can to make that problem go away.

Never is this more apparent than in moments of interpersonal conflict, when we messy humans default to our most basic programming. We're not trying to misbehave or hurt anyone. We're just trying to return to comfort, and the other person keeps getting in the way.

So, what's the solution? In a word: *relationships*.

Leading change with love means putting people at the center of the transformation. Prioritizing relationships enables you to do that by creating the space for solution-focused experimentation and empowering people of different mindsets, beliefs, and attitudes to come together and solve large, complex challenges. That's the ideal, anyway. But to help you understand what a change-ready, relationship-forward team looks like, we first need to show you what it does *not* look like. After all, if part of the work of change is prioritizing relationships, then we must learn to recognize when we're not living up to this principle and address it in a way that produces lasting, meaningful, and transformative growth.

In the following tale of conflict, there are no victors, and there are no villains. There is just Chris and Greg, two people working toward a common goal—and butting heads every step of the way.

The Three Types of Conflict

Greg joined Softway as director of account services. Not too long into his tenure, he interviewed and hired Chris to be the director of strategic planning. Greg saw how talented Chris was and knew that he would immediately bring value to Softway. So, their relationship began on an incredibly positive note.

Still, although Chris and Greg both worked within the sales and account services teams, their work didn't often overlap, and they were essentially coworking strangers in the early going. One day, Mohammad, who, like Greg, quickly saw Chris as a rising star in the company, asked Chris to evaluate whether the sales team's method-ologies aligned with the company's new customer relations goals. It seemed like a simple enough request at the time, but in hindsight, it was the catalyzing event in a yearslong struggle between the two high performers. And with each new squabble, the two worked their way through the following three types of conflict.

TYPE 1: TASK CONFLICT

Almost immediately after he began poking around the sales team and learning about their sales approach, Chris saw that it was no longer in alignment with Softway's new strategic planning goals. So, since sales was part of Chris's background, he designed and imple-mented a new sales plan—failing to run it by Greg first.

Greg was furious, and rightfully so. That was his sales plan Chris was replacing, and he should have been part of any change to that plan.

But rather than tell Chris how he felt, he went to Mohammad.

"*This* is how I sell. It's what I do, all I know, and it works," Greg said. Then, he chucked Chris's new sales plan aside, retrained his sales team, and led with his preferred approach.

Escalation achieved.

This opening salvo in what would eventually become Greg and Chris's Cold War represents what is known as *task conflict*. As its name implies, task conflict is characterized by disagreements on the task level, such as how the task is being done, allocated, and so on. Task conflict is the easiest to name and address because it enables interpersonal, transactional interactions. Chris wants the sales team to operate one way, and Greg wants it to operate another.

When a task conflict arises, most teams treat it as a technical problem (see Chapter 3). This is what Chris did when he replaced Greg's sales plan, and what Greg did when he saw that replacement plan. Neither Chris nor Greg liked what they saw, so they discarded it in favor of their preferred approach.

Sometimes, task conflict really is nothing more than a technical problem. But sometimes, as was the case with Greg and Chris, a greater conflict lies just beneath the surface.

TYPE 2: RELATIONSHIP CONFLICT

Over the next few years (yes, *years*), Chris and Greg disagreed on various projects, processes, and policies. Sure, there were niceties and professional collaboration. But there was also a deep, pervasive tension that threatened to spill over into the rest of the company at any moment.

Each managed their frustration in a different way. Chris would play nice in public and then say everything he *really* thought in private, indirectly implicating Greg in all his "constructive" feedback. Greg said what he wanted to say in the open, appearances be damned. As for the rest of us, we sure didn't want to take sides. Instead, we played the role of neutral countries in an effort to help Chris and Greg maintain peace.

But here's the thing: it's impossible to be neutral when two key people in your business are locked in a Cold War. As the political historian Howard Zinn once said, "You can't be neutral on a moving train." We *did* take sides, each in our own way—and even if we weren't aware we were doing it.

Mohammad was especially guilty of this—in fact, he created the conditions for this Cold War to ignite in the first place. As the CEO, he set the tone. He decided who sat in what seat, how we were expected to treat each other, and that we would get our work done. In such a situation, you can't help but take sides—and more often than not, he took Chris's.

Now, Greg is no fool. He saw what Mohammad was doing every step of the way. He saw that Chris was undermining him. He saw that Mohammad chose to privilege Chris's previous sales experience over Greg's deep knowledge of Softway's sales operation. He saw the way Mohammad alternated between coming down hard on him or shutting him out entirely. So, when Mohammad eventually waved his hand and made Chris the new head of sales, Greg couldn't help but laugh. *This* is Softway's idea of a culture of love?

It wasn't. Mohammad wanted to be better, but he still hadn't figured out how to have tough conversations while leading with love, and so he chose not to have *any* conversations with Greg at all. He never expressed his concerns about the sales team's performance. He never solicited Greg's input on how to improve. He never told Greg why he decided to move him from his position as head of sales. For all his talk of prioritizing relationships in a culture of love, Mohammad had clearly deprioritized this relationship.

Here's the thing: even if sales dramatically improved under Chris's leadership, their behavior was inexcusable. But sales *didn't* dramatically improve; they more or less stayed the same. Chris's approach wasn't markedly any better, and the sales team never fully accepted his authority. They still came to Greg for support. Imagine how that must have felt for Greg. He'd been told he wasn't doing a good enough job to stay in a certain role, and yet he was still left to perform many of the duties of that role because the sales team was still counting on him to do them—even if he wasn't getting any credit for the effort. After all this smoke and shade, the only result was more smoke and shade. And, as Greg told us later, "It's hard to be the bigger person in that scenario."

The Cold War escalated, every day bringing more slights, tit-for-tats, and passive-aggressive attempts to ruin reputations. Chris would work behind the scenes to undermine Greg's authority and credibility, while Greg chose not to go out of his way to have someone's back who clearly didn't have his. Neither put much thought or reflection into why their relationship had become so strained. At this point, neither really cared. All they knew was that they didn't like each other and weren't willing to give the other any grace.

Meanwhile, the rest of us continued to tiptoe around the problem. Whole policies were built around this relationship conflict. Entire teams and meeting structures were carefully planned just to keep these two from ever being in the same room. Every time they were, the aggression and escalation were too much to bear. Sometimes Greg would have it in for Mohammad, sometimes Chris would have it in for Greg, sometimes Mohammad would have it in for Greg, and so on. We could all see what a toxic, embarrassing problem this had become, but no one thought they had a part to play in resolving it—not even Mohammad. Reflecting on this moment, Greg noted, "Imagine if someone actually had the nerve to say, 'We're not leaving this room until we have an open discussion and you guys figure it out.' That's all it would have taken. But it never happened."

But embarrassing problems aren't just embarrassing problems. They are strategic liabilities. During this time, many of Softway's strategic decisions came down to Mohammad, Greg, and Chris. The best way to make those decisions is to get everyone in the same room so they can hammer everything out. But because of this Cold War, getting everyone in the same room was the *last* thing anyone wanted. So, all decisions followed some version of Mohammad and Greg meeting together, followed by Mohammad and Chris meeting together, followed by a check-in with Greg, and so on. The whole thing was neither efficient nor effective (see Chapter 9).

Even after all this drama, even though he was constantly playing middleperson between Greg and Chris and couldn't make any decisions in a simple, direct way, Mohammad *still* didn't recognize or understand the part he played in incubating and exacerbating this Cold War. Sure, he knew he took Chris's side more often, but he also genuinely valued Greg and saw him as an essential part of the company. But if that's how Mohammad felt, he certainly made no effort to communicate it. On several occasions, Greg almost gave up on us entirely and accepted an offer somewhere else. Had that happened, (1) it would have been *our* loss, not Greg's, and (2) we might never have fully understood how this conflict had grown so out of proportion, because he wouldn't have been there later on to set the record straight—and to finally help Mohammad realize the part he played in this story.

TYPE 3: VALUE CONFLICT

As part of his role, Chris tried to understand and embody Softway's Love as a Strategy ethos—its mindsets, behaviors, attitudes, and so on. This wasn't just a posture; he genuinely believed in what Softway stood for (and still does). He was certain that leading with love would help us grow stronger as an organization and build better relationships with our clients, and he worked to steer the company in that direction.

Greg subscribed to these values, too—they're a major reason he never took another job elsewhere—but he also recognized when they weren't being upheld. For all our talk about trust, for instance, he could see that Chris certainly didn't trust *him*.

So, what was the core of their value conflict? It's not that one is more of a team player than the other. Both are fiercely independent people with high standards and expectations, and both would sometimes rather take extra work on their shoulders than trust someone else with it. The difference, as Greg saw it, is that Greg believes Softway is in the business of serving customers, while Chris believes that Softway is in the business of taking care of people. While Greg thinks in terms of finance and strategy, Chris thinks more in terms of making sure each individual is taken care of. Neither is right nor wrong, and neither are perfect practitioners of their own values, but when two groups are unwilling or unable to see a situation from any lens other than their own, conflict is bound to arise.

The problem with value conflict is that people rarely realize when they're engaged in it. In so-called professional environments, we tend to reduce everything to task conflicts because it's uncomfortable to go further than that. That's why Greg escalated to Mohammad when Chris rewrote the sales plan, and why Chris always focused his criticisms of Greg on performance rather than values. Rather than stand in their discomfort and practice honesty, they chose harmony—albeit a flimsy, messy, in-name-only sort of harmony.

And the result? Neither Chris nor Greg understood the other's core issue with each other. Chris didn't know how Greg interpreted his rewriting of the sales plan because Greg never told him. Greg never understood why Chris couldn't support him publicly, even though, despite their differences, Greg would often provide cover for Chris (but not always).

When two people are engaged in perpetual conflict without practicing empathetic curiosity to understand the other's side (see Chapter 6), that's unhealthy, unsustainable, and bad for business. Imagine working in a sales team where you're expected to operate from a different playbook depending on who you spoke with last. When your mandate isn't clear, you're left guessing as to how you should behave in any given moment.

Eventually, this uncertainty resulted in a massive lost opportunity for the company. A couple of years back, an up-and-coming, venture-backed company working in the retail and biotech industry (focused on consumer health profiling) wanted to work with us on a branding and digital transformation project. The nature and scope of the project would have been any creative's *dream*. It was the kind of project Chris had been lobbying for on behalf of Softway's creatives for months—the kind of project creatives had frequently stated was a key reason why they chose to stay or leave Softway in exit interviews. It would have been intellectually and creatively stimulating and looked great in both our and our creatives' portfolios.

To secure the deal, all Softway had to do was fly its team out to Los Angeles and address a few minor things to finalize everything. Greg set up the date and invited Mohammad, a few other directors, and a key lead creative.

The creative got cold feet—citing an internal meeting that could have been rescheduled—and Chris didn't push the creative to reconsider. Because the team couldn't get aligned on their basic goals and priorities, the deal was lost. Had Chris and Greg just been able to align on their priorities and put the necessary support in place to make their proposal sing, the contract would have been a huge win for Softway. But they couldn't, and instead Softway suffered the worst kind of loss: a self-own.

Clearly, we couldn't go on this way as a company. This wasn't just a petty grievance. This was our livelihood. Something had to give.

Prioritizing Relationships Transforms Conflict

At this point, it's worth clarifying that not all conflict is unhealthy. After all, conflict is just the interpersonal manifestation of discomfort, and embracing discomfort can lead to profound personal transformation. But Chris and Greg weren't interested in transforming. They were interested in winning the next battle in their eight-year-long Cold War.

That's right. We said eight years. *Eight*. The Big Ocho. Turn it on its side, and you have infinity.

Finally—mercifully—the dam broke. In January 2024, Mohammad established an executive team called *the integrators*—effectively a C-suite or executive team composed of everyone at the company who reported directly to Mohammad. Since both Chris and Greg reported directly to him, Mohammad put both of them on the team. Together. In the same room. Doing the same work.

We like to call this particular power move *pulling an Imani*. Finally, at long last, Mohammad decided he was tired of all this *Love and Hip-Hop* BS and pulled the executive equivalent of dropping an entire pack of Mentos into a two-liter bottle of Diet Coke. Here were two personalities who couldn't be any less integrated, yet Mohammad saw fit to have these men lead a task force on integration as part of our reorganization. Oh, the irony.

Mohammad wasn't just creating a potentially volatile situation because he thought it would be funny. Instead, he saw the newly formed integrators team as an opportunity for Chris and Greg to finally move their relationship forward, which is exactly what he told Chris and Greg when he announced his decision.

"You both need to figure this out," Mohammad said. "This has gone on long enough." (Understatement of the decade, and made without a hint of self-awareness.)

That's right, Chris thought, seeing victory in sight. *It's about time Greg was held accountable for all his issues*. Chris put some time on Greg's calendar for a one-on-one and prepared to bask in his coworker's apologies.

Thankfully, Chris never showed up to that meeting with that attitude. Call it divine intervention.

That weekend, Chris heard a powerful sermon from his pastor, Pastor Phyllis. At the end, she asked the gathered congregation, "Now, ask yourself, Who are you holding unforgiveness toward?"

The first (and only) name to pop into Chris's head was Greg's.

The rest of the day, Chris engaged in some serious introspecting about his relationship with Greg and the many trespasses he had been guilty of over the past eight years. Was it possible that he had antagonized the situation just as much as his counterpart? Could it be that Greg wasn't out for Chris's head and was just trying to do his job? The more he considered his behaviors, the more he realized how much he had contributed to the problem.

At least Chris was right about one thing: this meeting *would* be an apology session. But he'd be the one doing the apologizing. It was time to transform this conflict into something a little healthier.

Here's the problem with task, relationship, or value conflict: they're rarely addressed in the workplace. Most typically, as was the case with Chris and Greg, they're outright avoided. Greg would raise an issue, and Chris would table it for another day. Chris would raise performance issues about Greg, and no one would act on them because they knew Chris was just trying to weaponize his role. The rest of us would literally go out of our way to make sure the two sat on as few meetings together as possible. None of us was leaning into our discomfort. All of us were practicing harmony over honesty. And *nothing* was being solved.

In another organization, someone might look at our ability to avoid an out-and-out war as a win—as an example of our impeccable "conflict resolution skills." But we weren't resolving anything. For years, we were just kicking the can down the road.

To create true resolution, we must instead work toward what author John Paul Lederach calls *transformational conflict*. In transformational conflict, instead of avoiding the issue or only addressing its symptoms, the parties in conflict work to resolve the deeper-seated misunderstandings or differences that led to the conflict in the first place.

Chris and Greg were able to begin the process of transformational conflict when the two sat down for their first one-on-one. Chris still intended to share his truth and describe how his interactions with Greg had made him feel, but in the spirit of true dialogue (see Chapter 6), Chris entered the meeting ready to be *changed*—and to commit for the first time to making real progress in their relationship.

The conversation began with Chris stating his goals for the conversation and their relationship. "Greg, this is really uncomfortable for me, but I recognize that we have been at each other's throats for a long time, and I recognize that I've played a significant part in that." Chris paused for a moment. Greg remained silent. "I want to get better, and I want this relationship to get better, and I want to overcome this. But it will take some discovery on my part to get there. Are you willing to do that work with me?"

"Yes," Greg said tentatively.

Then, for the next hour, the two proceeded to carefully unload and examine all the baggage they had been holding onto. Chris didn't like Greg's decision-making processes and thought he should include others more often. Greg felt like Chris never had his back—even when it was obvious he was right. They both acknowledged where they had room to grow, and slowly, they began exploring the nuances of some of these issues.

"If you're making a decision I disagree with, I still won't pretend to have your back in those moments. But I promise to talk to *you* about it instead of implying that you have performance issues." Then, Chris smirked. "Just so you know, I *do* go to bat for you sometimes when I think you're right. I just make sure you never find out about it."

"Well, that would be nice to know from time to time," Greg said, his posture relaxing. "And just so *you* know, I do the same. Differences aside, I've learned a lot from you and think you do good work."

And so it went. At the end of the conversation, Chris and Greg didn't magically become best friends. But they had transformed the conflict into something constructive, something they could build on going forward. The pair agreed to be intentional in how they collaborated and communicated, and they committed to continue their one-on-ones as part of an ongoing effort to improve their relationship.

Today, Chris and Greg still disagree on things, and they're still working on treating each other better. But that's the key difference: *they're working on it.* Even in conflict, you can prioritize relationships. Doing so keeps the conflict healthy—making it a place to embrace discomfort and learn rather than close yourself off and settle in for war. Instead of trying to hurt or undermine each other, Chris and Greg now approach their conflict with an open mind and an eye toward supporting each other and making each other better.

Change causes conflict, whether in life or the workplace. Sometimes, we see conflict as an opportunity to learn and grow. However, when that conflict often goes unresolved, it becomes externalized in our relationships with others. This also leads to change—just not the kind of change that anyone wants.

Your mindset and beliefs determine how you react to conflict and what kinds of attitudes you take as a result. Sometimes, those attitudes will be constructive, and sometimes they will be destructive. Through the lens of transformational conflict, you can ask how you can end the destruction present within the moment and how you can be future focused instead of stuck in the present. Transformational conflict doesn't just ask what you can resolve now but how you can lean into your discomfort to create something better for tomorrow.

The Conflict That Never Was

Within the realm of conflict, there's a special sort of beast: the conflict we make up in our own minds. Whenever we anticipate discomfort in a future conversation with someone, we often tell ourselves stories about what will happen. Typically, we dote on the negative outcomes from conflict, not realizing that the opposite has just as much of a chance of being true as our imagined woes.

Sometimes, these stories are accurate enough. But more often, they're pure fantasy, filled with preconceived notions, imagined grievances, and assumptions about a person's innermost thoughts. Frank, in particular, will sometimes craft entire conversations in his head, imagining the specific things a person might say, and then their response. He's not alone; many of us tend to decide about someone else and their expected behaviors before giving that person a chance to react authentically. As a result, we invent ways to avoid the interaction altogether, convinced that in doing so, we're saving everyone a world of trouble.

This is just another kind of avoidance—and the opposite of empathy, connection, and accountability.

Worse, it usually doesn't work. When we remove someone else's agency, like Chris did when he rewrote Greg's sales plan, we typically create more animosity. Avoiding hard conversations damages relationships, no matter our intentions or how much better they feel in the moment.

And besides, even if you're a master storyteller, you never really know how someone will react until you give them a chance to do it. We humans are full of surprises.

Avoidance Is Conflict, Too

So far in this chapter, we've focused on a particular kind of relationship and a particular kind of conflict—that of two peers in leadership positions who were engaged in a particularly nasty interpersonal struggle (and stoked on by their CEO). But how does conflict affect relationships when the power dynamic is different? What happens when a leader is in conflict with their team? What happens when a leader has no relationship to lean on with that team and make things right?

To examine this, we will explore another story involving Greg. We promise we're not trying to pick on him. (We had many productive conversations with him while working on this chapter.) But it's a revealing story, and we promise it has a happy ending.

Like many stories, Greg's story begins with a belief: "The people on the tech services team are incapable of delivering what I need."

Sounds harsh, right? But before we leap to judgment, here are two things to keep in mind.

First, as Greg put it to us as we interviewed him for this chapter, "I have high standards—and I'm hard as hell on everyone." Sometimes, these high standards have been a useful trait in his life; they're what make Greg the rockstar at Softway that he is. However, when people don't meet that standard, he can be pretty rough on them. Didn't format that slide deck consistently? Greg noticed. Didn't run your report through even a basic spell-check before sending it off? Greg noticed. Didn't deliver something to a client on time and hold your commitment? Oh, you'd better believe Greg noticed. Greg's well aware of his tendency to be hard on people, and he's working on it. But sometimes it's a struggle: When you have the ability to make a person feel either ten feet tall or ten inches tall, how do you wield that influence responsibly? (We'll explore that question more in Chapter 8.)

Second, he was genuinely trying to make things work with the tech services team. But there were challenges. For instance, 90 percent of the team worked in India, creating an array of practical challenges in terms of communication, coordination, and review. He'd prioritized relationships with many of these team members—forming especially strong bonds with many of them during the COVID-19 pandemic—and he knew how to wield his influence with his Indian team members when the need arose.

High standards mixed with unforgiveness make for a dangerous cocktail, and Greg was struggling to get the results he wanted while still leading the team with love. Every time tech services missed a deadline, the reason was the same: he was doing his part, but the rest of his team was failing him. Little did Greg know, but the tech services team felt unsupported as well and struggled to get their concerns heard.

It was clear that Greg and his team were facing an adaptive challenge, and blaming, punishing, or attempting to mandate change wouldn't solve it. To move forward, the team would have to embrace their discomfort and prioritize their relationships to hear and understand each other.

As fate would have it, plans were already in motion to accomplish just that. In February 2024, we flew all the American members of the leadership team to India to kick off our reorg rollout with a series of workshops and team-building experiences (see Chapter 12). After sharing our plan to get him as much face time with his Indian team members as possible, Greg committed wholeheartedly to the effort.

The more Greg interacted with his team in India, the more their relationship grew, and the more Greg began to understand their experience in their roles. Greg's team was *ambitious*. They didn't want to just be the best technologists at Softway; they wanted to be the best technologists at *any* company. The problem, they explained, was that they had several impediments to completing their work, including gaps in the communication chain, unclear expectations, work not being sent to them on time, you name it. The Indian team didn't like these impediments any more than Greg did, but they had been hesitant to speak up because they didn't want to see anyone get in trouble. (Which, by the way, was a classic example of conflict avoidance on their part. But we digress.) Through conversations like this, Greg and the Indian members replaced an unhelpful belief with a true, genuine relationship.

No other moment exemplifies this transformation than Greg's epic reveal of "the shirt." On the final day of the trip, as he was wrapping up with is team and preparing to head back home, Greg casually stood up and began to speak about how much this trip had meant to him. Slowly, as if he were Clark Kent transforming into Superman, he unbuttoned his shirt to reveal . . . a jersey for an *Indian* cricket team!

If you're an American reader, you probably have no idea why this was such a big moment. Let's get you up to speed. Greg, an Australian, is a huge cricket fan. And, as anyone who follows cricket knows, there is no greater rivalry than the one between Australia and India, whose teams are constantly vying for dominance in the Cricket World Cup.

This rivalry is *deep*. Think Coke versus Pepsi, Starks versus Lannisters, Yankees versus Red Sox. People build whole identities around these fandoms.

So, when Greg revealed his jersey, it was an absolute shock to his Indian team members. An Australian wearing an Indian cricket jersey? Is this real life?

"This is how much you mean to me," Greg said. " I'm here to support you. I'm all-in on Team India."

Quickly, Greg moved to back those words up with action. Back at work, Greg became his team's greatest advocate. When a deliverable was stalled out, he went out of his way to ensure everyone had all the resources they needed. When workloads crept up, he shielded them from burnout. When his American team got raises, he made sure his Indian team did, too. Whatever they needed, he made sure they got it—and then some.

Six months later, Greg was back in India for some more deep work with his team. This time, on the last day of the trip, during the farewell gathering in the final all-hands meeting, the reporting managers all excused themselves and left the room. When they returned, they were all wearing Team Australia jerseys—custom-made Team Australia jerseys (they don't sell Team Australia merch in India), and with Greg's last name on the back! In less than a year, the very same people who had fears, concerns, and major trepidations in reporting to Greg had now become his biggest fans.

We are happy to report that there wasn't a dry eye in the room.

This is the magic of authentic relationships: not only are they the gateway to all the best outcomes but they also feel *really good* to be a part of.

When Greg committed to building a strong relationship with his Indian team, all of the tech services department's challenges were transformed. They didn't go away, of course, but now Greg saw them differently—and he saw his Indian team as allies in helping to solve them. By changing his beliefs, Greg changed his attitude. By changing his attitude, Greg changed his behaviors. By changing his behaviors, he and his team were able to create better results *together*. None of this work was easy, but Greg has done a phenomenal job not only in challenging and changing his beliefs but in becoming the best leader the tech services team could have hoped for.

There's a perception about work culture and work relationships that it's a waste of time. We're all here to do a job, this belief goes, so that's all we should focus on. We believe that prioritizing relationships *is* the job. Better relationships lead to better communication, consistency, coordination, and efficiency, which enhances the quality of your work environment and output.

Does this mean we should build a workplace where we're all parked around a conference table, singing "Kumbaya" on an acoustic guitar? No. Remember: honesty over harmony. Prioritizing relationships is not the same as prioritizing a "nice" culture where everyone is afraid of rocking the boat.

In any organization—and especially in any change effort— discomfort *will* happen. People *will* get triggered. People *will* say things that they might later regret. It happens. We're human. But rather than view conflict and discomfort as something to avoid, we see it as something to embrace. That's how accountability in the face of conflict is formed, that's how real relationships are built, and that's how Love as a Change Strategy takes root.

Once you've had that breakthrough, keep going. Prioritizing relationships is a never-ending project. Approach every relationship, conflict, and moment of discomfort with empathetic curiosity. Ask yourself how you're contributing to the problem, and commit to leaning into the hard moments.

It's not always easy, but it's always worth it.

Weekly Relationship Ritual Planner

Chris and Greg now have a standing one-on-one so they can continue to prioritize their relationship. For a calendar-based tool to help you prioritize *your* relationships, see our Weekly Relationship Ritual Planner. This tool includes small weekly actions (e.g., gratitude texts, check-in questions, shared wins) designed to help strengthen key work relationships.

Download this (and all our other resources) at Loveasastrategy.com.

Prioritize Relationships

- ◆ The chapter discusses how people often prioritize harmony over honesty. Can you think of a time when you or your team avoided addressing a conflict? What was the outcome?

- ◆ What are some signs in your workplace that a task conflict might actually be rooted in a relationship or value conflict?

- ◆ Think of a recent workplace disagreement. How might things have changed if both sides had leaned into discomfort instead of avoiding it?

- ◆ What relationships at work feel strained or cold, and what responsibility might you have in contributing to that dynamic?

- ◆ Have you ever been caught between two colleagues in conflict? How did that affect your own behavior and work?

- ◆ What are some real (or imagined) conversations you've avoided because you were afraid of how the other person might respond?

- ◆ What beliefs about certain coworkers, teams, or roles have you inherited or adopted without realizing?

- ◆ What does transformational conflict look like in your organization—or what would it look like if it were practiced?

- ◆ What's holding you back from building stronger relationships at work?

- ◆ When discomfort arises in a team setting, how do you typically respond—and how might you respond differently if relationships were your guiding principle?

- ◆ Who on your team or in your organization do you want to understand more deeply—and what's stopping you from starting that conversation?

- ◆ What were some of your biggest takeaways or ah-ha moments from this chapter?

- ◆ Share a moment of self-awareness about your leadership after reading this chapter.

- ◆ What, if anything, will you change or adjust about how you lead or behave based on what you've read?

CHAPTER 6

Practice Empathetic Curiosity

"Just go with it."
"Trust the process."
"It'll be okay."

Leaders often make comments like this when communicating with employees—no one's immune to it. In fact, Mohammad made these exact same statements a *lot* when he tried to get us to adopt Sortd as a daily productivity tool (see if you can find them all in the opener to Chapter 9).

But really think about these statements in your mind. Their intention might be good, but they're hollow. They aren't collaborative. They aren't reassuring. They aren't empathetic. They're merely commands packaged in soft language. All they do is sow distrust and pushback, creating change resistors instead of change adopters. Statements like this close off dialogue, discouraging team members from sharing their concerns or perspectives. This is the decision. It's already been made. You're expected to comply. That's that. Discussion over.

So, when Saquib was confronted with language like this after learning he would be shifting roles as part of our reorg, he was rightfully upset. He deserved better; our job as change leaders was to move Saquib toward change readiness by practicing our six pillars of change. Part of this work is to have hard conversations on the individual level so everyone feels heard and seen as part of the change effort. With Saquib, we failed to do that, and now, instead of leading change, we had to deal with unintended fallout.

Since you probably don't know Saquib, let us paint you a picture. Saquib is egoless, mild-mannered, and really good at what he does. Any leader would love to have a team full of Saquibs, which is precisely why Mohammad asked him to cofound Softway in 2003. For the first twenty years of Softway's existence, Saquib did whatever the company needed. He custom-built all our systems to collect and understand our key financial, operational, and business metrics. He grew our team in India at a key moment in our history. He did whatever was needed of him because that's who Saquib is, and that's what Saquib does.

So, when we won a particularly large and important account, we needed Saquib to work his magic as that account's lead consultant. Hands down, Saquib was the best man for the role. Not only did he intimately understand our business and our particular way of managing client relationships but he was also incredibly well-respected among our Indian team members, who would play a crucial role in delivering this project. We needed someone with a proven track record of both boots-on-the-ground and interpersonal excellence, and we knew Saquib was our man.

There was just one problem. To put Saquib on this account, we would need to put him in a consultant role, which would recategorize him as a level 4 employee on our new org chart. That's just one level above entry level—quite the demotion for a cofounder with twenty years of experience in the company.

To any rational person, such a move would feel like an insult, and we knew it. In a culture of love, the right thing to do to honor and prioritize our relationship with Saquib would be for Mohammad to engage Saquib in conversation about this change, sit with him and his discomfort, and show empathy for what he was feeling.

He didn't do that.

Like we said at the beginning of the book, change is messy, and mistakes are often made. Our failure to lead Saquib through this massive change with love is one of our biggest blunders of our reorg journey. Instead of communicating openly with Saquib, Mohammad made the decision in a silo without letting Saquib know it was coming or otherwise soliciting feedback. Then he had someone else communicate the change to Saquib, expecting everything to be fine.

But it wasn't fine, and Saquib rightfully made his displeasure known.

Here, it might be helpful to break the chain of communication down. First, for context, Saquib's reassignment is related to Saif's and Greg's. Saif became the director of technology consulting and reported to Greg (see Chapter 4), and Greg became vice president of technology (see Chapter 5). In his new role as a level 4 consultant, Saquib reported to Saif and Greg. Since Saif and Greg were now Saquib's immediate bosses, Mohammad had them handle the initial communication with Saquib. The conversation didn't go well. Realizing they were the wrong messengers—and seeing that many of our team members who had recently been assigned to the newly formed tech consulting team also had questions, Saif and Greg set up a follow-up meeting between Mohammad and the team.

In the days between the initial communication and the follow-up meeting, Saquib felt his anger and frustration at the situation growing. He wanted more details but couldn't get a straight answer from anyone other than "Wait for the alignment meeting." It all felt so corporate and anonymous, and Saquib worried that the group setting would make open dialogue difficult.

The day of the meeting came. After so much buildup with no answers, Saquib walked into the room looking for any reason to be mad. It didn't take long to find one. Mohammad entered the room, spoke in more detail about the planned changes and how they aligned with the organizational vision, and then said, coldly, "These changes are set in stone."

Great, Saquib thought to himself. Here he was, a cofounder of the company—the person who had *created the tool that had driven this company* for so long—and he wasn't even given a say in his fate. Saquib felt betrayed and unfairly separated from his fellow cofounders. And he wasn't wrong. *At the very least, Mohammad should have talked to me before this presentation*, Saquib thought.

His anger peaking, Saquib stood up and spoke his mind. About how much this change pissed him off. About how he was being placed in a near entry-level position after playing such a crucial role in the organization. Then, pointing directly at Mohammad, he said,

"How would you feel if you were demoted to the same level as a new employee?! This isn't right, and I'm not going to take this sitting down."

Oof. Two misses in a row—first with Saif, and now with Saquib. Mohammad had to make this right. He knew it. We knew it. And Saquib definitely knew it.

The question was: how? With so much damage already done, how could we restore Squib's faith in Mohammad and the leadership team? How could we show him this decision was made *because* of his unique talents, not despite them? If Mohammad was to repair his relationship with Saquib, he would need to practice *empathetic curiosity* like never before and really listen to what his longtime colleague had to say.

Empathetic curiosity is the practice of suspending judgment and listening to somebody without rationalizing, interjecting, reassuring, or dismissing. By genuinely showing curiosity for the other person and their point of view, you create space for that person to explore the mindset, beliefs, and attitudes underpinning their feelings and, if appropriate, to help them challenge and dismantle the unhelpful beliefs that shaped their experience. Once the adaptive challenge is more clearly understood, you can work together to address it fairly and transparently.

With its goal of creating dialogue and understanding, empathetic curiosity is an essential tool for leading change with love, putting others' thoughts, needs, and feelings front and center. However, empathetic curiosity is by no means a passive process. As an empathetic listener, you're not there just to humor someone as they unburden themselves just so you can turn around and say, "Trust the process. It'll be okay." To facilitate change in others, you must be willing to change yourself, consider new information, and examine your role in the situation.

Eventually, Mohammad and Saquib were able to engage in a successful dialogue to understand and address the adaptive challenges that the pair faced, and both emerged changed from the experience. But it wasn't easy, and the outcome was far from certain. In this chapter, we will examine the methods Mohammad and Saquib used to reach this understanding in our typical trademark fashion: by showing you all the ways *not* to do it.

Debate Versus Dialogue: A Battle for the Ages

What do you think about working from home versus working from the office?

We say working from the office is better. You get more work done, you're free from all your little at-home distractions, and you have better opportunities for chance conversations that can move big ideas forward. Yep, we're on team work-from-the-office all the way.

How are you feeling after reading that? Are you nodding in agreement, or are you ready to throw this book across the room?

Please don't throw any books—especially if you're reading a digital copy on an expensive device. We're actually a very workplace-flexible organization. We just took a side on this question to prove a point: debate is rarely an effective way to communicate change. Why? Because it forces people to take sides—and when people are focused on defending their position, they're far less interested in hearing the other person out or changing their own mind.

Instead, as our vehicle for practicing empathetic curiosity, we're big fans of dialogue. Dialogue encourages participants to listen for understanding of what might be correct, true, and insightful about what others have stated. Unlike debate, the goal of dialogue isn't to win but to transform through mutual growth. Rather than stake out a fixed position and defend it, participants prepare to hear the other side clearly and be open to differing views and experiences.

To draw a contrast between dialogue and debate, we will follow Mohammad and Saquib's story down two paths, using common debate tactics as our signposts.

Down the first path, the path of debate, Mohammad 1.0 will be your guide. A classic business bruiser, Moh 1.0 *loves* finding all the wrong, incomplete, or flawed elements in his opponents' statements and then systematically exposing and dismantling them until he has emerged the victor. Sure, it's a lonely life at the top of Debate Mountain, but at least he can rest easy knowing he's right and everyone else isn't just wrong, but a fool.

Down the second path, the path of dialogue, Mohammad 2.0 will join you. Moh 2.0 represents the real-life Mohammad who actually showed up to these conversations with Saquib. As you'll see, he doesn't always get things right, but he's committed to his duty as an empathetic listener and genuinely wants to understand Saquib's very valid concerns.

Now, with that out of the way, let's get to debatin'.

TACTIC 1: YOUR POINT OF VIEW IS SUS

At the beginning of the first discussion between Mohammad and Saquib, Saquib came out swinging. "You only set up this meeting because I've been making my feelings known around the office," he said.

Notice how Saquib started with the absolute *only*. In a debate, this is all the excuse Moh 1.0 would need to dig in against Saquib. "Don't be ridiculous," Moh 1.0 says. "How can you even say that about me?" In the back of his mind, Moh 1.0 knows Saquib is right, but since he's here to win, he'd never acknowledge even this most basic of points. Here's a chance to shut down the conversation and claim an early victory.

Fortunately, that didn't happen. Instead, during their real-life discussion, Mohammad 2.0 tried to focus on creating a dialogue by acknowledging the truth of Saquib's claim. Just like Moh 1.0, he also noticed Saquib's use of absolute language. The difference is in how he responded to it. Instead of hearing *only* as a launchpad for an attack, Moh 2.0 saw it as an indicator of a deeper problem. Recognizing a chance to lean in and learn more, Mohammad said, "Yes, that's true, but I also want to hear what you have to say, including your frustrations."

See what he did there? Mohammad's role as an empathetic listener was to remove his perspective and put himself in Saquib's shoes—especially if Saquib was critical of Mohammad (which he was, and rightfully so.) At the outset of this discussion, Moh 2.0 was successful in remaining neutral and asking to hear more.

TACTIC 2: WRONG SPOTTING

Moh 1.0 is a hawk with eagle eyes and bear claws—the most feared of all imaginary predators. So, the moment Saquib says something that's not completely accurate or misses the point, Mohammad uses that as leverage to dismiss the whole argument. "Clearly, you don't understand this reassignment," Moh 1.0 says. "So why are you even wasting my time with this?" Just like that, now the two men aren't debating on the merits, but on whether they should be debating at all. Score another underhanded point for the sinister Moh 1.0.

Unfortunately, Moh 2.0 did the same thing during the actual dialogue. Mohammad listened to Saquib's complaints for a while, but eventually he became impatient. "This isn't the real problem," Mohammad said. "You're thinking about this in a superficial way."

And just like that, the dialogue was shut down. Sorry, folks. Moh 2.0 is still working out a few bugs. We'll address this one in the next update.

Maybe Mohammad was correct in his observation, or maybe he wasn't. In the context of this dialogue, Moh's right- or wrongness is irrelevant. It's his accusational wrong spotting that's the problem. Mohammad's job wasn't to editorialize but to listen, which he failed to do consistently.

Introspecting on this conversation later, Mohammad realized his mistake. He'd *wanted* to be an empathetic listener, but in the moment, he found it difficult to suspend judgment. Softway needed Saquib to help build this strategic account. It was far and away the most important thing he could do for the company. Why couldn't Saquib see past his small-picture objections and see the opportunity here? If Mohammad couldn't create the space for Saquib to share fully, then he would never know.

TACTIC 3: DEFEND ASSUMPTIONS

"You let me down by choosing not to dialogue with me ahead of time," Saquib said. "What were you thinking there? Were you worried I would say no?"

Mohammad and Saquib were back at it in another dialogue session, and once again, Mohammad could feel Moh 1.0 banging at the doors to be let out. Like any leader, Mohammad had a lot of assumptions about what proper communication protocols should look like—including who needed to know what, when they needed to know it, and who should deliver that information. Moh 1.0 wanted to cling to those assumptions as if they were the absolute truth— probably pulling rank to do it. "I'm the CEO. It's my right to share decisions however I please, and I know how to communicate in a way that's best for the company."

Fortunately, Moh 2.0 was back in the game. He recognized his impulse to defend, let that impulse pass without acting on it, and then refocused his thoughts on Saquib's perspective. From that vantage point, Mohammad listened as Saquib explained the feeling of being shut out of a decision-making process that significantly affected his role in the organization. He understood that he couldn't necessarily sway the decision. Still, he wanted Mohammad to understand that he felt hurt the way he received this information and believed he should have been brought into the conversation earlier.

Hearing Saquib clearly this time, Mohammad felt embarrassed. *Saquib is right*, Mohammad thought. *Why hadn't I been the one to deliver this news one-on-one and walk Saquib through this decision?* Slowly, Mohammad began to change his mind, which flies right in the face of our final debate tactic . . .

TACTIC 4: NO CHANGING YOUR MIND

Saquib's other big concern wasn't with the work he would be doing—he understood that part—but rather with his rank in the organization. If building this new client account was so important, his new position should reflect his value to the company. A level 4 position didn't do that. "There should be a bigger difference in levels between someone like me and newcomers to the organization," Saquib said.

His decision made, Moh 1.0 would just stick with whatever he'd already decided. "I hear you, but I don't care," Moh 1.0 says. "You're going to do whatever the organization needs you to do."

Raise your hand if you've ever heard that one. Heck, we just heard the actual Moh say his decision was "set in stone."

It might feel good to dig in like this in the moment, but anyone on the receiving end can see it for what it is: plain old stubbornness. Deploy this classic tool of debate, and watch as the conversation is once again shut down before it can even begin.

Luckily, Moh 2.0 was already coming around by this point, and he could see that Saquib was right. He and the leadership team hadn't considered this perspective when they planned the reorg, and now he saw clearly that this part of the new org structure didn't make sense. So, Mohammad changed his mind and committed to tweaking the org structure on Saquib's behalf, adding a level 6 to the org chart. Saquib would still be level 4, but he could now serve in a supervising role to any level 5 or 6 employee if the need arose, clearly separating him from an entry-level position in terms of both duties and authority.

Reflecting later on his conversations with Mohammad, Saquib said simply, "It was a relief." Yes, all these drawn-out discussions could have been avoided if Mohammad and the leadership team had looped him in sooner and solicited his input. That said, he was grateful that he could share his true feelings in detail without being shut down, gaslit, or dismissed. He could see by the outcome of the conversion that Mohammad had sincerely listened to what Saquib had to say. And, as the cherry on top, he was proud that, by sharing his truth, he could create better circumstances for himself and others in the organization.

After several weeks of grief, anger, and uncertainty, Saquib, Mohammad, and the leadership team were finally aligned. Not because we dismissed his objections. Not because we told him to suck it up and that everything would be okay. But because Mohammad listened to him with empathetic curiosity, the pair was able to work together to chart a better path forward.

Was everything magically set right between Mohammad and Saquib afterward? No—just like it wasn't between Mohammad and Saif in a similar situation, and just like it wasn't between Chris and Greg after they confronted eight years of Cold War. Love as a Change Strategy isn't a round of "Kumbaya," and we mean it when we say honesty over harmony. Change happens gradually and intentionally. It takes only a moment to betray someone's trust, but it takes weeks, months, or even years to build it back. At the very least, Mohammad and Saquib were back on that path, and Saquib went all-in on our reorg.

That's the power of empathetic curiosity for you. Now that Saquib understood the intent of our reorganization and his role within it—and now that he saw that he still had agency and influence over what happened at Softway—he became one of our most vocal champions. Traveling to India, he personally met with different team members, listened to their concerns, and shared his experience. "I wasn't sure about this reorganization at first either. If you know my story, I strongly opposed it," he told the group. "But if I can adapt, so can you. And I sincerely believe this is a big opportunity. If we embrace it, no person or time limit will stop us from going to the next level."

The Dialogue Versus Debate Cheat Sheet: A Quick Guide for Better Conversations

When navigating change—especially the kind that challenges deeply held beliefs—how we talk matters just as much as what we say. That's where the Dialogue Versus Debate Cheat Sheet comes in.This resource helps you quickly identify whether you're engaging in a debate (trying to win) or a dialogue (trying to understand).

If you'd like to build your skills as someone who encourages and facilitates dialogue, we've created a handy downloadable resource, available at LoveAsAStrategy.com.

Dialogue Takes Practice

Dialoguing takes only a moment to grasp but a lifetime to master. Most of us are used to engaging the world with our beliefs and attitudes turned up to eleven. It feels uncomfortable and unnatural to hit the mute button, suspend judgment, and listen. As you master the art of empathetic curiosity and learn to engage in true dialogue, here are some common pitfalls to look out for.

GROUP HUGGING

Don't weaponize compliments in a dialogue. While it might feel helpful, these are just premature attempts to return the conversation to comfort before achieving true understanding.

Recently, we were leading a dialogue session with the leadership team of a large school district, and a woman we'll call Lee volunteered to share an adaptive challenge for her and the group to work through. During the dialogue, Lee shared how she felt like an inferior member of a team she served on, where everyone was an assistant superintendent except her. As she shared her experience, she said, "I don't feel like my voice matters on this team, so I just keep to myself."

It was a great moment of vulnerability—that was instantly squashed by a cascade of compliment bombs.

"Lee, you're so smart."

"Lee, you're awesome!"

"Aw, don't think that way."

"We love you, Lee!"

As soon as Lee heard all this feedback, she sat back in her chair, folded her arms, and said, "This happens every time. I keep trying to share my state of mind, and no one listens to me."

The other leaders in the room didn't mean any harm, but their attempts at goodwill still shut the conversation down, reinforcing Lee's belief that she couldn't be vulnerable with her team. Because the group chose harmony over honesty and attempted to return to comfort, Lee lost her chance to be heard, and the team lost its chance to change for the better—or at least create a space where change could happen.

JUSTIFYING

This is a big one. Lawyers, in particular, *love* to rationalize, defend, or otherwise justify their behaviors. It's almost like they're litigating their case. To that, we say save it for the courtroom.

Typically, this switch into litigation mode happens during an attempt at paraphrasing. The listener will start okay—"Here's what I heard you say"—and then they offer a reasonable summary. But they don't stop there, adding, "But let me tell you the problem with that . . ."

To be fair, it's not just lawyers who do this. For instance, Lee's supervisor, who was also in the group, was a big rationalizer. Smart guy. Great boss. Cares about doing a great job. But when he was supposed to be dialoguing with one of his employees, he couldn't help but slip into justification mode.

Here's what happened: a team member expressed concern about being moved into a smaller space in the basement. It wasn't a nice space—no windows, no conference room, and no joy whatsoever— very *Severance*-esque, but not nearly as well-lit or mid-century-modern hip. The superintendent heard all this, paraphrased the woman's concerns, and continued, "But don't you realize I moved you to this space because you need to learn to collaborate better?"

And just like that, the conversation died.

But it was also a great teaching moment. After Mohammad pointed out what this supervisor had just done, his eyes lit up. "Oh, this is *tricky*," the superintendent said. "I thought this was going to be easy."

It *is* easy to understand—but much harder to master.

PROBLEM-SOLVING

Similar to justifying is problem-solving. We've all heard the adage that to understand someone, first walk a mile in their shoes. We're big believers in this principle and spoke extensively about it in our first book. But this saying only works if you genuinely consider how another person might respond. If you're just inserting yourself into the situation and otherwise still thinking and acting like yourself, you've missed the point entirely.

So, if, during a dialogue, you catch yourself about to say something like, "Here's what I would have done," shut that thought down. You might have a chance to share that perspective later, but it has no place in this kind of discussion.

Again: easy to understand, hard to master. All leaders get the urge to play problem-solver—and doing so in the right context is very useful for any business. But it's not useful when your goal is mutual understanding. All it does is invalidate the person on the other side of the table trying to share their perspective with you.

EMPATHIZING

Yes, this whole chapter is about practicing empathetic curiosity in a culture of love. However, empathetic curiosity is a different behavior than *signaling* empathy—which is little more than expressing sympathy without a corresponding action. Resist the urge to say things like "I feel so bad for you," "I'm so sorry," or "You poor thing!" It's nice, but it's not helpful.

Remember: empathy is the position you take. Curiosity is the action you communicate. There's no curiosity in a statement like "That's just not fair!"

You've Got This

Empathetic curiosity can give you tremendous insight into the complex, tangled human experience at the center of these challenges. But to gain and benefit from that insight, you must first learn to shut up, listen, and embody the mindset (empathy) and the behaviors (curiosity) necessary to make these discussions work.

Again, that's not easy, but it is essential to creating change-ready culture. When we're engaged in dialogue, we often feel triggered or upset by what the other person is saying and are eager to react and correct the person. Those are natural feelings and worthy of examination. But to succeed, you must be willing to choose the hard work of sitting with your discomfort rather than acting on it.

That said, know it *will* get easier and come more naturally as you practice it—and that the rewards are worth it. We shudder to think what would have happened if Mohammad 1.0 had hijacked his conversations with Saquib and fought tooth and nail to win rather than to understand. Thankfully, Mohammad 2.0 arrived in the spirit of dialogue, suspended his judgment, and worked to understand Saquib's perspective.

Because both men were willing to put in this work, they gained greater empathy for each other and were changed by the experience. Mohammad realized he had been wrong in restructuring the organization, and Saquib secured a crucial change that benefitted him and his coworkers. Because neither person was trying to win but rather to understand, in the end, they both won.

But they had to work through some discomfort to get there—and they had to be honest not only about the facts but also about their feelings. Debate-focused organizations typically want to "keep it professional" and "focus on the issue." However, change is inherently emotional, and communicating change is even more so. Love as a Change Strategy argues that ignoring our emotions isn't professional; it's negligent. Change-ready organizations embrace honesty over harmony, share how they're feeling, and address those feelings as part of the solution.

It's messy (love often is), and you will make mistakes along the way—just like we do with every one of our six principles of change. But it's what you do *after* a misstep that matters most. Do you shut out dissent, justify your actions, and demand everyone move forward? Or do you slow down to listen and learn about what you might have missed?

Unless you're superhuman, you almost certainly missed something. Give yourself the grace and the time to learn from those misses. Put yourself in the shoes of every person affected by the change. Invite their input. Be open, honest, and vulnerable. Let people know that they can come forward, that you will listen, and that you will adjust when needed. Lead with love.

And remember: you've got this. Not because you're a great decision-maker on your own. Not because you're always the easiest person to talk to. And definitely not because you were captain of the debate team in high school. But because you're empathetic and curious enough to understand how your decisions affect others—and you're willing to be changed by the experience.

Practice Empathetic Curiosity

- ◆ Think about a recent conversation that left you feeling unheard. What could the other person have done to make you feel seen, and how might you do that for others?
- ◆ When you're focused on solving a problem with your team, how often do you engage in dialogue over debate? Be honest.
- ◆ Understanding the difference between debate and dialogue, how will you change your communication strategies to create a space where everybody is focused on finding the best way forward?
- ◆ When you're challenged at work, do you tend to debate or dialogue? What patterns in your communication style might be closing the door to curiosity?
- ◆ Have you ever responded to feedback with justification or problem-solving? What was the result—and how might curiosity have changed the outcome?

◆ When someone shares something uncomfortable or emotional, how do you usually respond? Do you offer comfort, compliments, solutions, or silence—and why?

◆ What assumptions do you carry into conversations with people who challenge your perspective? How do those assumptions affect your ability to practice empathetic curiosity?

◆ How do you typically react when you feel misunderstood? What might happen if, instead of defending yourself, you asked a curious question?

◆ What were some of your biggest takeaways or ah-ha moments from this chapter?

◆ Share a moment of self-awareness about your leadership after reading this chapter.

◆ What, if anything, will you change or adjust about how you lead or behave based on what you've read?

CHAPTER 7

Experiment

"If you don't change, you will end up just like your dad."

It was early 2019. Softway was on the upswing, Frank and his family were happy, and life was pretty good. Except Frank wasn't feeling like the best version of himself. He was overweight, edging upward toward three hundred pounds. Worse, he had no energy. He was barely thirty, and already he felt like a spectator in his children's lives, watching them play from his comfy vantage point on the couch.

So, when he heard this blunt assessment from Dr. Faizun Anwar—Frank's physician and Mohammad's sister—he wasn't exactly surprised. Still, her words cut deep, rattling around inside of him until he could focus on little else.

To understand why this wake-up call hit so hard, here are a few things to know about Dr. Anwar. First, she doesn't mince words. She is as direct and honest as the doctor Hugh Laurie portrays in *House*. Frank knew Dr. Anwar would always level with him, but this time was different. He'd never seen that look on her face before—an odd blend of panic and disappointment.

This brings us to our second point: You never want to disappoint an Anwar. The feeling is worse than disappointing your parents. You feel it in your bones.

The last thing to know is that Dr. Anwar had also been Frank's dad's physician before he died of a pulmonary embolism in 2014 at the age of fifty. Dr. Anwar had done what she could while Frank's father struggled and ultimately failed in his health journey. She knew Frank's history, she knew all the conditions he and his father shared, and she knew that Frank was well on track for his own medical emergency.

Given these facts, Frank knew that Dr. Anwar's candor wasn't merely a scare tactic. She was deadly serious—and legitimately scared for Frank's life. His mind still racing, Frank thanked her for her advice, gathered his things, and left.

On his way to the car, he could only think of one thing: now what?

Frank was embarrassed at how much his health had spiraled in the last few years. He was embarrassed to look in the mirror and see Triple-Chin Frank looking back. He'd tried plenty of different diet and exercise approaches—keto, paleo, fasting, fancy gyms, crappy equipment from TJ Maxx, you name it. Friends and family tried to help him too, offering suggestion after suggestion about how to get on the fitness horse:

"You should get a Peloton."

"You should sign up for a different gym if that one isn't working out for you."

"Why don't you come work out with me?"

"Have you tried this app? It worked great for me."

"You're fine. You carry your weight well and are just big-boned."

Whatever Frank tried, whichever fad he bought into, or whoever's advice he followed, the result was always the same: he'd make good progress for about two or three weeks, and then he'd find himself back on the couch again, rationalizing why this latest attempt hadn't worked.

It would be easy to see this story as part of a sad, frustrating pattern of failure. But let's give poor Triple-Chin Frank credit where it's due: he kept trying.

Sure, Frank wasn't getting the results he wanted, but he never gave up for long and was always willing to try something new. He understood the value of a good experiment.

Research has shown that experience really is the greatest teacher. Like Thomas Edison's repeated experiments as he worked to perfect the light bulb, Frank was learning all the ways *not* to get healthy. The problem was that he didn't recognize his progress for what it was. Instead, he saw each abandoned attempt as a legitimate failure—and the cumulative impact of all these so-called failures was absolutely devastating to his self-image and motivation.

That's not how we view experimentation in a culture of love. Leading change isn't about knowing every step and waypoint on the journey. It's understanding where you are and where you want to go, setting off in that direction, and learning what you need to succeed. Sure, you won't always get it right, and sometimes you'll end up back on the proverbial couch just like Frank did. That's why they're called *experiments*, not *easy wins*. But as long as you learn something from the effort, then you're still moving forward. Let's break down some of the core tactics of effective experimentation by examining some of our favorite recent successes, mixed bags, and mishaps and exploring how they contributed to our understanding of leading change.

Take Your Lumps and Move On

It's amazing how the world always seems to fall apart right around a deadline. Ahead of a key meeting for our newly christened Center of Innovation (COI) team, somehow the entire world conspired to make sure no one could attend. One person got sick. Another's internet was down. Several others suddenly had jury duty. Another was driving through a long, long tunnel and couldn't get cell reception. When it became clear that this team member was never going to emerge from that tunnel (legend has it they're still stuck there today), we knew something was up: no one wanted to show, because no one accomplished anything, and no one wanted to be held accountable for their failure.

Just like that, the COI was no more. Six months of effort and nothing to show for it . . . except shame and frustration.

It wasn't supposed to be this way. The COI was supposed to help us *solve* our delivery problems, not create new ones. It even had a cool and official-sounding name. A center where innovation happens? Sign us up!

And to be fair, people *did* sign up. Lots of them—many of the brightest young up-and-comers in the company, teaming with talent and ideas. They were passionate. They talked a good game. They were fantastic at identifying problems.

And as we would soon discover, they didn't gel at all as a team.

To kick off the project, we presented the COI with an initial set of challenges. Their primary responsibility was to outline the workflows of all our current projects so we could better understand how the sausage was made, so to speak. We saw this task as low-hanging fruit, a prelude to the more involved and innovative work to come.

But we never got to the other work because the workflow documents never materialized—just like the team never showed up to the meeting to present their findings. It wasn't that the people on this team were bad at documenting. It was that everyone had a different idea of how to do the work. With no one willing to step up and lead, the team got caught up in endless debates and false starts. Once we understood this, we took our lumps, acknowledged how we could have supported them better, and killed the project.

Our intentions were good, but in hindsight, we could see the COI was a bad idea. Rather than creating innovation, it stifled it. Once everyone else in the organization learned of the COI and its mandate, they stopped trying to solve problems and innovate within their roles. They weren't lazy; they just didn't want to step on the COI's toes. In the meantime, all our delivery challenges persisted. If anything, they grew worse—the exact opposite of what we'd hoped would happen!

So, what did we learn from this failed experiment?

First, trying to centralize innovation is fraught, to say the least. Our teams knew their challenges best and were best positioned to devise novel solutions.

Second, don't die on hills you don't have to. We could have tried to keep the COI going after that initial failure, but we couldn't bear the thought of anyone getting stuck in another infinity tunnel. Sometimes, it's better just to admit you had a bad idea and walk away.

Finally—and here's the big one—remember that good teams are *balanced* teams. Didn't you think it was odd that we focused so intently on recruiting all our young up-and-comers to the COI? Each of these people was talented, but they were all talented in the same way. In a culture of love, effective teams balance expertise, talents, and strengths. You need the problem spotters *and* the problem-solvers. You need the up-and-comers *and* the seasoned vets. You need the leaders *and* the doers. Without this balance, your team will likely struggle to get off the ground.

Some experiments fail quickly. That's okay. Learn from that failure and apply those lessons to your next round of experiments.

Good Goals Are Worth Fighting For

Real talk: we're good at naming things that don't live up to their names. First, there was the Center of Innovation, which was neither a center of anything nor a driver of any innovation. Then, there was No Meetings Friday—which *didn't* have meetings and *was* on Fridays, but also completely failed to live up to the spirit and intent of its name.

If you're like any of our team members at Softway, hearing "no meetings" combined with "Friday" immediately perks your ears up. Finally, a chance to put on your sweatpants, hunker down in your home office with a nice cup of coffee, and get some real deep work done before welcoming the weekend.

Sounds too good to be true, right?

Well, it wasn't. Actually, No Meetings Friday at Softway was even better than described: if you didn't want to, you didn't have to work at all!

That was the result, anyway, but it wasn't the intent. In 2020 and 2021, mired in the doldrums of the COVID-19 pandemic like the rest of the world, we were experiencing unprecedented rates of both boredom and burnout. Team members were overworked but disengaged, obsessed with boosting productivity but detached from the humanity that typically drove results. Then there were the meetings—so, *so* many meetings. They took root and multiplied like Texas crabgrass, so much so that many of our team members complained that they didn't have any time to deliver their actual work. Everyone was working hard, but no one was getting anything done.

We needed a break—and fast.

Cue No Meetings Fridays. We piloted it in 2022, made it official in 2023, and abandoned it in 2024. Turns out that's not the kind of break our teams needed.

So, what happened? Well, as we intended, our team members *did* get a lot done on No Meetings Fridays. They changed their oil, did their laundry, made grocery runs, fixed the loose board in the backyard fence, and so on. None of this had anything to do with the deep work they were supposed to be doing, but it was valuable to them and freed them up to enjoy more downtime on the weekend.

This was great for our employees. Truly. We don't hold their choices against them at all. But all that important deep work still wasn't getting done. In fact, it was piling up faster than ever. After six months of No Meetings Fridays, it was clear that this experiment was hurting more than it was helping, so, just like the COI, we scrapped it.

Well, not entirely. We were still committed to creating more breathing room in our team members' schedules, and No Meetings Friday inadvertently confirmed how important that breathing room was. Seeing that our employees needed more personal time, we tried another experiment: the alternating four-day workweek. Every other Friday, everyone got to take the day off.

Once again, we thought this policy would be an unqualified hit. It wasn't. The more we experiment, the more we've come to understand that any change will be met with resistance—even two extra days off a month. In hindsight, though, some of the objections *did* make sense: clients would worry about having less time to work with us, and no one wanted to work longer days to make up lost ground.

Both were perfectly valid concerns. However, we also had a perfectly valid response: nothing was getting done on Fridays anyway. This change helped team members manage their personal needs one Friday and then catch up on their deep work the next. It was the Goldilocks zone of time off—not too little, not too much, but juuuuuuust right.

At least, that's the hope. Ask us when you see us how this experiment is going, and we'll give an honest answer. In the Love as a Change Strategy, we fall in love with the problem, not the solution. If it turns out that this particular solution doesn't get our teams in the Goldilocks zone, then we'll try something else.

Promote a Bias Toward Action

Artificial intelligence (AI) is consistently creating new opportunities for innovation, solving some of our most nagging business problems, and revolutionizing how the world gets work done.

Stop us if you've heard this claim before. We certainly know we're not the first to say it.

Still, all sensationalism aside, there is some truth to these statements. AI *does* represent a big change to business as we know it, and every business needs to take stock of how it might affect them—without fear and *with* love, of course.

In early 2025, like many business leaders, Mohammad could see the writing on the wall for Softway: get in front of AI or become obsolete. Some agreed with Mohammad, seeing AI as a tremendous opportunity. Others disagreed, seeing it as a threat. Most of Softway's employees, however, greeted AI with a shrug. They could take it or leave it.

No group was entirely right or wrong. But one thing was clear: as a company, we weren't aligned in our view of AI, and for a time, we weren't sure how to move forward. Doing nothing would upset the pro-AI group, who would worry we were squandering an opportunity. Embracing AI with a mandate to adopt new tools and systems would upset the anti-AI group and fluster the indifferent group, who would have preferred to do nothing at all. No matter our path, we felt like we couldn't win. As a culture, we weren't change ready.

That's when it hit us: why not make an experience out of it? Talking about AI would only draw us into an endless, unwinnable debate. However, *experimenting* with AI in real time with no pressure and no strings attached could accomplish the following:

♦ Change people's beliefs and understanding of what AI could do for the company and for themselves.
♦ Help us understand *how* AI tools might benefit us to increase efficiency and deliver better results.
♦ Reinforce our belief in a *bias toward action*. As the cliché goes, you miss 100 percent of the shots you don't take. If all we did was debate the value of AI without testing our ideas, then we wouldn't get anywhere. Just as our friends from Chapter 4 encourage their teams to "name the thing," we encourage ours to "do the thing."

Excited by the idea, we hatched our plan and scheduled a four-day hackathon. Actually, to make sure we didn't put our whole company on ice at the same time, we scheduled several four-day hackathons—first with US leadership, then with Indian leadership, then with US staff, and then in India by department.

Now, for any of you readers out there thinking about undertaking your own hackathon, here is what we discovered: the first day is most crucial. To set expectations and foster a spirit of experimentation, we dedicated the entire first day to discussing the following:

♦ Why we were there

♦ What was in it for us—both what we stood to gain and what we stood to lose

♦ What AI is capable of and where it's going (This sent shivers of both excitement and panic across our team as we discussed the end of work as we know it and the beginning of work as it would be.)

♦ What we were afraid of—whether on the individual level (fear of losing a job) or the organizational level (fear of making our problems worse)

♦ Which of our most persistent pain points we hoped to solve, from the small, day-to-day paper cuts to the larger project- and systems-wide challenges we'd faced

In the context of our little hackathon, this discussion helped get everyone in a productive headspace. Those who saw themselves as the soon-to-be "obsolete" humans that AI was out to replace now saw themselves as agents in control of their own destinies. Those who already saw AI as a boon now saw the opportunity more clearly and began to focus their excitement on solving our specific business needs. With their fears tempered and their focus sharpened, the team was primed to start exploring.

For the next two days, our elite hacking team got to work doing the thing. While we split the larger team into smaller use case-specific teams—for instance, a team for operations, a team for products and services, and so on—we encouraged a few folks to float between teams to provide feedback, clarity, and accountability. Even though the hackathon portion was virtual—we met in person the first day, virtually the second and third days (thanks, Houston Snowpocalypse 2025!), and reconvened in person on the fourth day—the atmosphere was electric.

In the true spirit of an experimental hackathon, we tracked our victories in a few different ways:

- **Breakthroughs.** These were, of course, great. There's nothing quite like having what feels like a good idea, testing it, and finding out that it works—sometimes even better than you expected.
- **Fail smart.** We could write a whole book on what *not* to do when adopting AI into a business. (Instead, we made a podcast during the hackathon. See the end of this section.) And we are so, so grateful to have learned these lessons in a controlled, consequence-free environment.
- **De-siloing.** Did we mention the atmosphere was electric? It was so much fun to watch sparks fly and silos crumble as teams got out of their comfort zones and truly innovated. People in completely unrelated teams would reach out to each other to learn more about another team's results, and they would be interested in how it could be used for their work and, eventually, for the whole organization.

From one simple experiment—a series of four-day hackathons—we saw unbelievable growth. Naturally, we were encouraged by the outcomes and opportunities for our internal processes. However, the biggest surprise was a set of innovations that we were able to integrate into our core product immediately. More important than the business results, however, were the human results. Through this hackathon, we transitioned from a culture polarized about AI to an organization that embraced it and saw it as a benefit to both the company and our customers.

That latter bit was a happy accident. We didn't enter the hackathon intending to update our core product, but that's what happens when you let your teams cook without dictating the recipe.

What Does AI Mean to Your Business?

Here's another happy by-product of our hackathon: the *Beyond HumAIn Podcast*. In this practical, actionable introduction to AI transformation, Frank walks listeners through a step-by-step framework to adopting AI that actually works.

Here, the focus isn't on the technical minutiae but on the human side of AI—how to dismantle your fears, clarify what it can mean for your organization, and expand your capability to adopt it, and so on. No computer science degree required. Just like you don't need to be an engineer to drive a car, you don't need to be a computer scientist to adopt AI in your business.

To listen, visit softway.com/beyond-humain-podcast (or subscribe wherever you get your podcasts).

What's Your Case for Change?

If there's one big lesson we hope you take from this chapter, it's this: your experiment doesn't have to be successful to be valuable. To paraphrase the Bhagavad Gita, there is no energy wasted on the path. There is only the path itself. If you keep focused on the goal and know *why* you've set that goal in the first place, you'll get there eventually.

That reminds us: whatever happened to Frank and his health journey? Did he find an approach that worked for him, or is he forever doomed to bounce between bowls of kale and buckets of KFC?

Let's check in on Frank right after he left Dr. Anwar's office in early 2019 to find out what happened next.

Back in his car, Frank fumbled with his keys, unable to steady his hands and get them in the ignition. After a few moments, he gave up, sat back in the driver's seat, and allowed Dr. Anwar's words to wash over him. Then, still shaking, Frank called his wife, Megan, and broke into tears. "I've got to change," he said. "I'm not ready to leave you."

That's the day Frank's health journey truly began.

Finally, Frank had found his case for change. He wanted to be in it for the long haul with his family. He wanted to participate fully in his children's lives rather than be a spectator. He wanted to see his kids grow up and get married, and then he wanted to participate in his grandchildren's lives, too.

He could see it all so clearly, and he was determined to make that vision a reality. There was just one tiny problem standing in the way: Frank was about to leave for a few months on a literal world tour with Softway—not exactly the best time to make a major lifestyle change.

He committed anyway, shared his case for change with us, and then we committed to working on it with him. No matter where we were—Singapore, London, Curitiba, or Bengaluru—the four of us made time to exercise. Sure, Chris would show up to the gym a little late and keep to himself (and Beyoncé) on the treadmill, but we were all there every day for every session.

It wasn't a perfect journey from that day onward—but Frank has seen remarkable progress. He was already good at experimenting before that fateful day in Dr. Anwar's, but afterward, he'd found the missing piece of the puzzle: a reason to keep trying and moving forward no matter what.

This mindset—this case for change—has made every health experiment Frank has conducted an unqualified win.

When Frank and his family experimented with going vegan, 99 percent of that experiment didn't work. But 1 percent of it did: they no longer drink cow's milk. Win.

When Frank experimented with twenty-four- and thirty-six-hour fasting programs, he quickly realized that (1) he hadn't prepared enough ahead of time (the caffeine and sugar withdrawals were *brutal*), and (2) it wasn't for him. But you know what was? Intermittent fasting, which helped him lose tons of weight across the board. Win.

When Frank tried jogging for two weeks and quit, joined different gyms and stopped showing up, and tried and quit keto, paleo, and all the other popular fringe diets, he learned important information about what motivated him and what made him feel good. That's right: another win.

Experimenting is hard, and failure is part of it. But if you have a strong case for change, you'll be far more likely to keep going—and to keep experimenting. With all of Frank's so-called failed experiments, he could have given up and slid back into his old bad habits. But he didn't. He kept going for the love of his family.

As we write this, Frank is now six years into his journey and showing no signs of slowing down. In fourteen years, Frank will be the same age as his father was when he passed away. In fifteen years, Frank will be celebrating the rest of his life with his loved ones.

So, what's your case for change? How much discomfort are you willing to feel to create it? And what are you willing to try to make that change a reality?

Discomfort sucks. Most of us have learned to avoid that feeling at all costs. But it's also essential for driving change, even when approached with love. If you're willing to experience the discomfort of change, you must trust that there's some kind of reward waiting for you on the other side. This personal case for change will guide you when you're stuck in the trenches, doubtful that you're making any progress, and wondering how you got there in the first place.

This process will not be easy, but it *will* make you more change ready and capable of leading others through their own transformational journeys.

The Hackathon-in-a-Box Planning Guide

Want to host your own hackathon, but aren't sure where to start?

Our Hackathon-in-a-Box Planning Guide offers a comprehensive tool for planning and executing a successful hackathon like the AI example in the chapter, including the following:

◆ Timeline templates
◆ Team formation strategies
◆ Problem definition worksheets
◆ Facilitation tips for the crucial first day
◆ Methods for tracking breakthroughs
◆ Post-hackathon implementation planning

To download your Hackathon Planning Guide, visit Loveasastrategy.com.

Experiment

- ◆ What's your current case for change? What discomfort are you willing to face to make it a reality?
- ◆ Reflect on a time when something didn't work out the way you hoped. What lessons did you carry forward— and did you give yourself credit for learning them?
- ◆ Do you tend to see your failed experiments as setbacks or as steps forward? How might reframing them unlock your motivation?
- ◆ Have you ever clung to a bad idea or failing initiative too long? What stopped you from letting it go?
- ◆ What's one small, low-stakes experiment you could try this week to test a new idea, workflow, or behavior?
- ◆ What experiments in your life or work have taught you the most—even if they failed?
- ◆ Frank kept experimenting because he had a strong why. What's yours—and how can it help you stay grounded when discomfort or failure shows up?
- ◆ What were some of your biggest takeaways or ah-ha moments from this chapter?
- ◆ Share a moment of self-awareness about your leadership after reading this chapter.
- ◆ What, if anything, will you change or adjust about how you lead or behave based on what you've read?

CHAPTER 8

Wield Your Influence

They don't call him Chris After Dark for nothing.

Overall, he's a lovely person—kind, considerate, and happy to push his next meeting if you've got something important to get off your chest. He's not perfect, of course. His eight-year saga with Greg can attest to that. But his heart's in the right place, and he's the kind of person you want to have in your corner. Unless:

- ◆ You're speaking with him after his regularly scheduled bedtime (10:30 p.m. sharp).
- ◆ You catch him after a rerun of an episode of *The Real Housewives of Atlanta*.
- ◆ You get on his last nerve and don't collaborate effectively on a project.

That's when Chris After Dark comes out. And make no mistake: this version of Chris can throw some weapons-grade shade.

Sometimes, Chris After Dark is legitimately funny. Other times, he's just reality TV show mean and unbearably sarcastic. One day, during what everyone thought was a routine alignment meeting during our reorg, Lacee and Ashley found out just how mean he could be. The meeting started out normal enough. Everybody walked through their status updates one by one, and the results were not encouraging.

This task was behind schedule. That team was dragging. Another team wasn't even sure what they were supposed to be doing.

As the conversation turned to *why* this was happening, Chris had some useful insights. So, he shared them—in as snarky a way as humanly possible. "Well, we're all just trying to get things done and check all the boxes, aren't we? No time to consider people impact at all." Chris paused, then threw his final dagger, "Which, I guess, is what we're all about in this reorg."

Wow. Will the sun ever come back up? Not if Chris After Dark has anything to say about it.

Now, to be fair, Chris had a point. On the one hand, we absolutely needed task-oriented leaders like Lacee and Ashley to help drive this reorganization project. On the other hand, he worried they had become *so* task-oriented that they weren't considering the people, relationships, and emotions involved in the effort. Change takes time, and setting a date for everyone to be "over it" and ready to move on felt a little extreme. The result was that Chris, Lacee, and Ashley weren't rowing in the same direction. Lacee and Ashley were frustrated that nothing was getting done, and Chris was frustrated that meeting deadlines was all that seemed to matter to them.

However, while Chris could have communicated these concerns with love, he chose chaos instead—crashing through the alignment meeting like the Kool-Aid Man and throwing Lacee and Ashley under the bus in front of everyone. Before this moment, they had no idea how he felt because he'd never given them that feedback. Now, *everyone* knew how Chris felt. But because he chose to weaponize his feedback rather than deliver it with kindness, no one was sure how to move forward.

What followed was a lovely game of passive-aggressive corporate telephone. Ashley and Lacee basically ignored Chris, who was unaware of how his shade throwing had made them feel. Chris went about his business considering all the people involved in our reorg— all the people, that is, except for Lacee and Ashley, who decided to take their issues to Mohammad. Mohammad wasn't sure why he was being dragged into this, but he listened with empathetic curiosity to their concerns, and then he went and talked to Chris. Chris wasn't interested. "I'm fine with whatever they do," he said. "They've just got to figure out what their priorities are."

But it wasn't fine. "No, Chris, you need to tell them your concerns yourself and stop playing mind games," Mohammad said. "I'm tired of taking heat for this, and I can't be everyone's therapist anymore."

CEOs often find themselves in the role of confidant and therapist among their leadership team. It's not an official part of the job description—and it's not particularly healthy—but it happens. This time, Mohammad wasn't having it. Everywhere he looked, the leadership team was unfocused and misaligned—siloing themselves in their work, trying to please Mohammad rather than get results or engaged in petty spats that missed the big picture. That wasn't what leading change looked like, and by the time the drama with Chris, Lacee, and Ashley came to a head, Mohammad was at his wit's end.

It was a classic leadership team standoff. From those few shade-laden sentences, Lacee and Ashley felt unheard and unsupported in their efforts to keep the reorg moving forward. Chris felt unconsidered and disregarded in terms of the time needed to listen and engage people who were getting left behind, especially because sales and delivery were competing for the same time. And Mohammad felt like he was managing a preschool where no one could solve their problems for themselves. Moh wasn't wrong. Chris, Lacee, and Ashley had all the tools to remedy the situation themselves; they just didn't realize it. Instead, they defaulted to the person with the power and asked him to make everything better. It happens. We've all done it to Moh (which is why he's so tired all the time).

But while their default behaviors were understandable, they certainly weren't helping—and they certainly didn't reflect our vision of the high-performing team we strive to be. In fact, we weren't behaving like a team at all—more like a collection of representatives assembled to serve our interests and protect our resources—very *Game of Thrones.*

These sorts of problems are common among teams that skip the change readiness phase and dive straight into execution. Underpinning these misbehaviors is fear—fear of change, fear of looking bad, fear of losing resources, you name it. It's the burning platform all over again, which, as we know, is not a healthy basis for creating change readiness.

What you put out is what you get back, so wield your influence with care. If your behaviors reinforce a team dynamic where you withhold or weaponize your concerns, use moderators to solve your disagreements, or otherwise operate without regard for your fellow teammates, you perpetuate an organizational culture where those behaviors are tolerated. However, if your behaviors reinforce the principles we've been discussing here in Part II—embracing discomfort, prioritizing relationships, and practicing empathetic curiosity—then you will see those efforts reflected in your teams.

Leaders in a change-ready organization wield their influence to promote healthy relationships, maintain trust in each other, engage in healthy conflict, and show awareness and appreciation of each other's strengths. More important, they recognize that power isn't centralized or dictated by title or position; influence can come from any person in any corner of the organization. Whoever has the most relevant experience and skills has the authority to lead in a given situation. In this chapter, we'll explore some examples inside and outside Softway's walls to show this principle in action.

Jaya the Awesome

Jaya is awesome—really, really awesome. The head right above this sentence says so. But if that's not enough of a proof point, let us explain why Jaya is so awesome. Jaya, our director of IT operations, doesn't wait for permission to do things if he sees an opportunity to drive business value. With his shrewd ideas, he saves tons of money for our clients and business. Above all else, he takes a people-first approach in everything he does.

Naturally, that last one makes us the happiest, since it drives all the other results we love. Our favorite example of Jaya's people-first approach to work is when he manifested a DevOps engineer, for us seemingly out of whole cloth. One day, a project came up that required one more DevOps engineer than we had in-house. This role, designed to be a bridge between software development and IT operations, was in short supply.

This put us in a bind. The typical move in such a situation was to hire externally—in this case, a new team member from India—but doing so would take some time and add the permanent overhead of a new full-time employee to solve a temporary need. While you can hire new talent in India relatively quickly, your new employee can't immediately start. Instead, they must wait through a sixty- to ninety-day notice period before joining the organization.

Enter Jaya the Awesome. Seeing how urgently we needed someone to fill this role and knowing it would take twice as long to fill it externally, Jaya made a revolutionary suggestion: "Why not just get Sahude certified in Amazon Web Services (AWS)?"

Now, Sahude is awesome, too. He excels at everything he tries, and his growth mindset makes him the perfect candidate for learning new skills on the fly. That said, we never in a million years would have thought to ask Sahude to get an AWS certification—not because he wasn't capable but because he didn't have the kind of previous background that would have stood out in a normal resourcing conversation. Specifically, most people with an AWS certification have a background in engineering. Sahude did not.

But Jaya believed in Sahude and wouldn't let a pesky little detail like an engineering degree stop him. So, he (1) put Sahude up for the role, (2) put up his own money (he was reimbursed later) to bypass the time needed for internal approval, and (3) put Sahude first with unwavering encouragement. Soon, Sahude was crushing it in a role he wouldn't have otherwise been considered for—saving us a considerable amount of hand-wringing in the process.

Such is the value of Jaya the Awesome. He isn't the most senior-ranked person at Softway, but he isn't afraid to wield his influence and create opportunities from within the company. Because Jaya is always pushing those around him to excel and seize new opportunities, he saw a chance to help the company, save time and money, and advance a coworker's career. In so doing, he showed that wielding influence doesn't just change an organization; it changes people's lives.

A Leader No More, or Jeff, You Brought This on Yourself

Remember that story where Jeff chose honesty over harmony, levitated above the table, and kick-started our reorganization effort? As he bravely addressed the elephant in the room, he said these fateful words: "I'm willing to give up my own position if that's what it means to move forward."

And so it was. And Jeff was totally fine with it. For real.

The Jeff of 2025 is not in a leadership position at Softway. He sits on no management teams and has no management responsibilities. No one reports to him. As an individual contributor for the first time in over seventeen years, Jeff can now spend the vast majority of his time playing his favorite game: *Throw Throw Burrito*. Just kidding. He still does tons of great work for Softway, just like he always has.

But the truth is, management isn't Jeff's greatest strength. We have a whole chapter about it (Chapter 6) in our first book, *Love as a Business Strategy*. He wasn't *bad* in his management role—and he *was* getting better—but his skill set wasn't well-suited to help lead Softway through our next phase of growth, and he knew it. That's a big reason why he stood up during that planning meeting and addressed the elephant in the room—to show that he understood his days as a manager might be numbered, to be accountable to that outcome, and to encourage others to practice self-awareness and consider whether they were the best fits for their roles moving forward. Jeff's willingness to move off from his management position opened up the path for someone else to lead who could be more successful and impactful.

But while Jeff's role and title might have changed, his influence within the company has not. If anything—and somewhat paradoxically—his influence has actually *grown* after he dropped his fancy title.

Think of Jeff as our organizational ace in the hole, influencing the leaders of governments and large multinational corporations through his client-facing work. Through his candor and solution-oriented perspective, Jeff helps the leaders he works with to use *their* influence and power. In that way, you could say he has become something of a "leader whisperer."

We've seen this influence at play within our own halls as well. Mohammad, for instance, has always respected Jeff's insights and candor, and he's always known that Jeff's sharp insights have the ability to be the difference maker in any given project, any given conversation. But it wasn't until Jeff stepped away from leadership and into the role of influencer that Mohammad understood the raw impact a "mere" role player could have.

If all this feels a little counterintuitive, it's not just you. Typically, you would think that the most trusted people in the organization are rewarded with high-power positions. However, we've discovered that removing a high-influence person from power can create even deeper levels of trust. Because Jeff departed his leadership position voluntarily, others know that when he speaks, he speaks sincerely, without playing politics or otherwise jockeying for position. He *means it*. As a result, leaders like Mohammad take Jeff's feedback very seriously, and their trust in Jeff has only continued to grow.

Think about that for a moment so we can all appreciate the change Jeff has undergone over the years. Remember the Jeff we shared in Chapter 3, the person who was afraid to build *any* meaningful relationship, let alone a meaningful *work* relationship, for fear of being let down? In the intervening years, he's learned to prioritize relationships, share his immense knowledge and expertise, and walk the walk in everything he does. And the best part is that these relationships and built-up goodwill have been *earned*. People don't know, like, and trust Jeff just because he's been around a long time. They know him because he *puts in the work*.

That work was reflected in the day he stood up and addressed the elephant in the room. In many ways, he was ideally suited to be the messenger. Mohammad had felt the same way as Jeff, but he was the CEO. If Mohammad had been the one to stand up and ask everyone to reconsider their positions and titles—and be willing to give them up—the message wouldn't have hit the same way. At best, it would have fallen on deaf ears or been outright dismissed: "Easy for you to say, Moh. You're the CEO."

Jeff had skin in the game in a different way than Moh. There *was* a real possibility Jeff would lose his leadership position, and he was openly and proudly saying he was okay with that if it moved the company forward—and that everybody else should be okay with that, too. It was the right message, with the right messenger, delivered at the right moment, and generating the right impact. Our reorganization might never have happened if not for Jeff's leadership.

But that's the thing about Jeff: he leads not because he has a title but because he walks the talk. When it became clear that his role within the company would take him out of a formal leadership position, he approached that change gracefully and intentionally. To him, it wasn't just a matter of stepping aside but supporting those stepping in by ensuring they had everything they needed to thrive.

In *The Devil Wears Prada*, when Miranda Priestly is threatened with losing her job, she responds with fear, building a coalition of people who promise to walk if anyone ever tries to replace her. Through this revolt, she ultimately protects her position and consolidates her power. Jeff could have tried something like this. He could have looked at this change with resentment, envy, or jealousy and unleashed his favorite flavor of misbehavior. He could have looked at his other team members and listed all the reasons why they were less capable, had less experience, or were less likely to succeed.

He didn't do that.

Instead, he championed them. He advocated for them. He supported them. In that way, their success became his success. Sometimes, that's what leadership looks like: giving up your own position so that others might thrive.

How Harris Health Leads with Love

Harris Health is a unique hospital system. It's neither a for-profit nor a nonprofit hospital. Instead, it's a "safety net" funded by Harris County, Texas, where its many locations exist to care for those who either lack insurance or are denied coverage through their regular insurance. It's the largest safety net hospital in the state and the fourth-largest in the country, with more than 1.5 million patient encounters each year.

At the helm of Harris Health is Dr. Esmaeil Porsa, who has served as the system's CEO since 2020, about two months before the onset of the COVID-19 pandemic. We first became aware of Harris Health through Mohammad's brother, Siraj, who, at the time of this writing, works at Harris Health as the chief health informatics officer. For months, Siraj had been singing Dr. Porsa's praises, and we believed that Dr. Porsa's vision for Harris Health aligned closely with our own vision for the rest of the business world. So, as we wrapped up work on our first book, *Love as a Business Strategy*, in early 2021, Mohammad asked Siraj to pass along an early draft of the book to Dr. Porsa in hopes that the doctor could offer a blurb and help spread the word. Siraj introduced Mohammad to Dr. Porsa, Mohammad sent him the draft, and then we waited for a response.

We got more than a blurb from Dr. Porsa. We got an ally.

One morning, Mohammad saw a forwarded message from Siraj. "Look what Dr. Porsa said to the company—all ten thousand employees!" Mohammad scanned through Dr. Porsa's message, and then he found the four words that had gotten Siraj so excited: "I love you all."

As far as Sirajj knew, Dr. Porsa had never said that before to his employees. Sure, he clearly believed in some of the pillars of love that we believed in at Softway. But up until that point, he had never had the courage to come out and use the *l* word in a company-wide communication.

According to Dr. Porsa, who spoke with us about this experience while we were writing this book, it felt good to finally write the word *love* in an email—really, *really* good. It felt authentic to both who he was and the mission of Harris Health that he'd been entrusted with.

What we didn't know at the time was that this *l*-bomb nearly didn't come to be. After reading a draft of the message, his human resources (HR) team pushed back hard, claiming the statement didn't meet compliance and backing their viewpoint up with words like *liability, setting yourself up*, and *glass bowl*. They even provided a list of alternative statements Dr. Porsa could try instead that, in their view, conveyed a similar level of appreciation. But none of it sounded authentic, so he pulled his CEO card and sent out his original message anyway.

The result was an HR nightmare of epic proportions.

No, wait. Scratch that. It was (checks notes) a shot in the arm for an ailing hospital culture (puns intended).

Almost immediately after hitting send, Dr. Porsa was inundated with positive feedback from various hospital staff. To this day, whenever he needs a little boost, Dr. Porsa pulls up some of those responses to remind himself why he got into this work: to lift people up.

With that initial email, Dr. Porsa set the tone for how he would wield his influence as CEO to change the culture at Harris Health. No more upholding the status quo. No more fear or retribution. Dr. Porsa would lead authentically and humanely to create a better workplace and better patient outcomes.

Of course, this effort wasn't just about warm fuzzies. Dr. Porsa's actions backed up his message. Day in and day out, he was on the front lines of the Harris Health system, often visiting several sites a day. As one emergency medical technician pointed out, no matter which location her job took her on any given day, when she walked in the doors, there was Dr. Porsa, ready to lend a hand and remove barriers. For instance, during the height of the COVID-19 pandemic, Dr. Porsa repurposed entire wings of the hospital so they would have beds available for anyone who needed it.

As the urgency of the pandemic wound down, Dr. Porsa turned his attention to improving the culture of the Harris Health system from top to bottom. To do that, he worked with HR to develop and institute the "Leading with Love" culture and leadership program.

The scope of the project was ambitious. First, Dr. Porsa assembled the roughly 250 members of upper and senior management and required them to read our book, *Love as a Business Strategy*, along with two other books in an effort to reimagine what Harris Health's culture could be. Then, he had his HR team attend one of our Culture Rise sessions so they could learn from and be inspired to create and run the workshops and experiences for their 250 leaders. With that initial effort underway, HR then rolled out the Leading with Love program to the rest of the organization in waves—from the executive suite all the way to their frontline supervisors.

Look no further than the HR team to see what a tremendous transformation this is. In the span of roughly a year, this team went from a group that blushed at the word *love* to one that was leading a Leading with Love program. (Granted, they initially pitched it as "Lead as One," but we're going to let them have this win.) Of course, that's just one group in a ten-thousand-person organization. Their efforts helped realize a profound culture change on a massive level.

Reflecting on the success of the Leading with Love program, Dr. Porsa knows exactly why it resonated so much. "It kind of shocks you when you first hear it: 'Leading with Love.' It kind of jolts you," Dr. Porsa says. "That's the whole point: it stops you and makes you reflect. And isn't that wonderful that you can have that immediate impact as soon as you hear it?"

To Dr. Porsa, leading change with love is like driving with your GPS on. Sometimes, you make a wrong turn, and the system has to recalculate. But this is why it's so important to clearly articulate your case for change and make that vision a practical reality. How does your organization respond when it has to recalculate? Do your teams collectively throw their hands up in the air and give up, or do they pause, reflect, and keep going? When you lead with love, Dr. Porsa found, your teams are far more likely to keep moving ahead, confident that they're all working toward a common goal.

Still, there's one ingredient to Love as a Strategy that Dr. Porsa taught *us*: accountability.

As Dr. Porsa began implementing the six pillars of love we introduced in *Love as a Business Strategy,* he found that they got most of the way but not all the way. Trust, vulnerability, empowerment, and the like were all great, but without accountability, they were also moot. People must feel free to "name the thing," (see Chapter 4) to wield their influence and hold people accountable for their actions.

Out of the entire Lead with Love initiative, Dr. Porsa's emphasis on accountability met with the most resistance among his staff. Many wondered how they could be "reprimanded" in a culture of love. Whenever he encountered this pushback, Dr. Porsa's response was always the same: "Just because I'm holding you accountable doesn't mean that I don't love you."

That's exactly how teams who love each other work. They wield their influence by holding each other accountable, by actively engaging in the work, and by openly discussing the outcomes they're producing—for better or for worse. While that accountability must come from every corner of the organization, it must be driven from the top.

In many organizations, CEOs are just passengers on the train. At Harris Health, however, Dr. Porsa isn't just a passenger; he's the engineer. He's right there in the front of the locomotive, shoveling fuel into the furnace—driving, embodying, and *owning* the culture of love he wants to create.

Not only does such an effort take energy but it also takes *courage.*

It takes courage to stand up to your (well-meaning) HR team and say you're going to use the word *love* in an official company email. Of all the messages Dr. Porsa could have chosen to promote, of all the ways he could have chosen to wield his influence, he chose love.

It takes courage as the CEO of ten thousand people—a position of tremendous power—to mandate that *everyone* in the Harris Health hospital system wield their influence to create the kind of change that would lead to better outcomes. And in a safety net hospital system, these improved outcomes aren't merely a flashy new set of metrics to paste onto a slide deck. They're real, human lives.

Legitimate power can be a challenging tool to wield. You can use it to create or to destroy, to insulate yourself or to assist others. Dr. Porsa wielded this power in the right way at the right time to create necessary change in a system built to resist it. Sometimes, you have to do the right thing—even if it's difficult, even if there's resistance, even if there are consequences you might not want.

Influence Is a Precision Instrument

As a leader, are you serving others or waiting to be served? Are you aware of the weight or impact on someone when you ask them to do something? Are you willing to be wrong?

Wielding your influence isn't just a principle, but a skill. To sharpen your skills, download the Wield Your Influence Toolkit from LoveAsAStrategy.com.

This Is the Work

The team members at Harris Health weren't the only ones who needed accountability. Back at Softway, Mohammad watched in horror as the members of his leadership team—specifically, Chris, Ashley, and Lacee—were locked in a death spiral. Taking a page from Dr. Porsa's playbook, he called a meeting to hold the team accountable for their misbehavior.

First, he reinforced expectations. No one on the leadership team—or any team—should have to play the role of go-between (especially not him). Teammates needed to practice vulnerability and talk openly with each other. Period.

Second, the leadership team needed to align on its priorities so that we could execute both as individuals and as a working unit. Creating more cohesive, integrated teams was one of the main goals of this whole reorganization effort, after all. If we couldn't get in the rumble and make it work at the top of the org chart, we certainly couldn't scale it to the rest of the organization. Our misalignment wasn't a distraction from the work—it was the most crucial work we could do. Without stopping to create alignment, we would continue to struggle moving forward.

Slowly, the gears of change were set in motion. After Mohammad shared his piece and stressed the need for accountability among Ashley, Lacee, and Chris, everyone opened up about how they felt. Ashley shared how Chris's comments made her feel and the amount of work she and Lacee had put into the plans and support for every leader in the change. Lacee, through tears, shared how her feelings were also hurt and that Chris's comments felt unfair.

Chris owned it. He admitted that he had been part of conversations with team members that he had not shared with Ashley and Lacee. The concerns, fears, and feelings of falling behind were not universal knowledge— because Chris had never shared or surfaced them beyond Mohammad. Now that Lacee and Ashley understood this, they began asking questions to understand how they could shift plans and timelines.

This moment of honesty and perspective brought the heat down. More important, it transformed the working relationship among the three leaders to prioritize upfront sharing, open disagreement, and required dialogue—whether for this or future initiatives that required collaboration. While everyone felt awkward both during and immediately following this crucial conversation, the trio found it easier to get their change plans back on track with transparency and honesty (and without Mohammad).

Further, all parties agreed to change their behaviors in meaningful ways. Lacee and Ashley agreed to account for the relational work necessary to drive our change effort and to make it part of their project management process. These days, they prioritize alignment by asking the following questions:

- Are we philosophically and spiritually talking about the same thing?
- Do we understand what's in each other's heads?
- Do we understand what's happening on the respective front lines?

If the answer is no to any of these questions, the next step is simple: have a conversation about whatever sticking points are present. Communicate. Share. Prioritize relationships. Ensure everyone is aligned before we begin the operational steps of enacting change—and if not, adjust the plan as needed.

For his part, Chris agreed to keep Chris After Dark out of alignment meetings. He wouldn't show up to conversations ready to accuse, defend, or otherwise throw shade. All this accomplished was putting him in an oppositional stance against his teammates. Instead, he committed to show up to those conversations prepared to prioritize relationships, collaborate, stay curious, and find ways forward together. More important, if he had a concern or suspected that he, Lacee, and Ashley weren't aligned, he would come to them directly with his concerns—no sneak attacks in the middle of a meeting and no running to Mohammad to help them sort everything out.

Situations like this are no fun. But they are real—and they *are* going to happen. You can run away from the storm, or you can turn to face it.

The Chris After Dark experience helped reinforce our understanding of what it means to responsibly wield your influence when leading change. Too often, during the early days of our reorganization, we used our influence to emphasize our independence, create interpersonal competition, and get on Mohammad's good side. In other words, we behaved like a team of all-stars trying to earn our gold stars. After this incident, we recommitted to operating as an all-star *team*, using our influence to reinforce our relationships and move forward together.

Does that mean we've solved the problem completely? Absolutely not. Communication among our leadership team could still be improved. Mohammad would still love to officially retire from his side hustle as team therapist. But we know what we want to be, and we know that our influence creates the environment we operate in. Our words and behaviors affect those around us, and we are responsible for leading change by embodying the behaviors we want to see.

Our reorganization effort stalled for months because we had not yet internalized this mindset shift. Instead, we embodied the mindsets, attitudes, and behaviors we sought to dismantle. But rather than let us get away with it, Mohammad chose to join us in the rumble, help us diagnose the challenges we faced, and hold us accountable for finding a way out.

It wasn't where we thought we'd be several months into our reorg. That's change for you: winding, surprising, and nonlinear.

Once you realize that's a feature of change and not a bug, you'll learn to embrace that unpredictability, wield your influence, and lead more effective teams.

Wield Your Influence

- ◆ How do you typically use your influence within your team or organization? Is it intentional, reactive, withheld, or overlooked?
- ◆ Have you ever gone Chris After Dark in a meeting? What triggered it—and how did it affect your relationships or outcomes?
- ◆ Think of a time you avoided giving direct feedback. What held you back, and how might things have turned out differently if you had addressed it earlier?
- ◆ When have you seen influence used to uplift and support others? What made that moment effective or memorable?
- ◆ What do you believe earns someone influence within a team—title, tenure, behavior, or something else?
- ◆ What does accountability look like in a culture of love to you? Can you love someone and still hold them to a high standard?
- ◆ Jaya empowered Sahude to grow into a role no one else had imagined for him. Who around you might be ready for more—if only someone believed in them?
- ◆ What's one way you can wield your influence differently this week to strengthen relationships, encourage growth, or foster change?
- ◆ What were some of your biggest takeaways or ah-ha moments from this chapter?
- ◆ Share a moment of self-awareness about your leadership after reading this chapter.

CHAPTER 9

Be Effective

"Do I have to do this?" Chris asked.

"Yes. It will change your life. Just go with it," Mohammad replied.

"Do I have to set the 'done' column on the left-hand side like you do?" Jeff asked

"Yes. It's the best way. Trust the process."

"I'm not sure this will help my workflows . . . or anything, really," Frank said.

"It will. This is why your life is so disorganized, because you're not doing this yet. All it takes is some discipline. Trust me. It'll be okay."

"I don't have time to set this up and keep it organized," Chris said.

"Yes, you do. You're not too busy. Look at my board." Mohammad then pulled up a digital task board with over fifty items—all for that Monday. It was either impressively organized or the agenda of a madman (or the impressively organized agenda of a madman). "There's no way you're busier than this," Mohammad added. "You just have to commit."

Such was the behavior of Mohammad in the days after he discovered Sortd. For those interested, Sortd is a tool that applies the Agile concept of the *Kanban board* to email (and no, we don't have an offer code for you if you'd like to experience it for yourself). One day, Mohammad tried out Sortd with his workflow and was immediately all-in. Then, Mohammad being Mohammad, he mandated that we all adopt Sortd, too, convinced that it would fundamentally improve our behaviors, discipline, focus, and ability to execute.

Mohammad's heart was in the right place; he wanted to help us become even higher high performers. But while we love us an effective organization, and we love finding new ways to increase our impact, Mohammad was rather maniacal about this tool. He didn't just want everyone to adopt the platform. He wanted all of us to use it in a particular way—*his* way. No customizing to fit our workflows or ways of thinking was allowed. Whole meetings were dedicated to setting up our Sortd boards correctly—and other meetings were cut short if Mohammad suspected we weren't staying on top of our boards. "Didn't you have this video due today? Where's that on your board? I don't see today's meeting on there, either. Where's that?"

You get the picture. The pressure we felt to keep up and keep organized was both overwhelming and counterproductive. Eventually, Mohammad's relentless evangelism backfired. Why? Because he fell for one of the classic blunders of leading change: he believed that a tool and a mandate would change our behavior, even though he knew from experience that, especially in a culture of love, behavior change must come first. We never understood why Sortd was so important, so we never felt compelled to adopt it into our workflows.

Mohammad should have known we would respond the way we did, but it didn't occur to him. The tool had worked so quickly for him, and he was so quickly bought into it that he assumed everyone else would react just as enthusiastically.

Does Mohammad still think everyone should use Sortd? Definitely. He remains convinced that he gets more done during his day because of how well Sortd keeps him organized. But he's no longer a dictator about it. He understands that the key to building effective teams isn't mandating tool adoption but influencing the behavioral changes that will lead to more effective teams.

Today, if he wants us to consider a new tool (Trello is his current favorite), he begins with an invitation: "Hey, I think this tool might be valuable to you. If you want to try it, I can walk you through how I use it and what I've learned." We won't always adopt the tool Mohammad recommends—only two-ish other people on our team still use Sortd—but we're far more likely to accept the invitation and at least give the new tool a try.

As Mohammad likes to say, "You can lead a horse to drink, but you can't make it water." Whenever we focus on efficiency over effectiveness, we tend to stumble—just like Mohammad sometimes stumbles on his American idioms. That's okay. We learn from these stumbles, and these lessons help make us more effective in turn. Through this trial and error (remember: always be experimenting), we are reminded that you can assemble the best team, you can have the best culture, and you can have the best reasons for change. But to lead change effectively, you still have to lead as a human being. Here's how we make our horses water in a culture of love.

Effectiveness over Efficiency

There's a popular maxim in the business world: "This could have been an email." This mindset lies at the root of the entrenched organizational obsession with efficiency over effectiveness. But readers beware: efficiency does not equal effectiveness. Often, the relationship is inverse.

We once worked with an organization that carved out a whole part of the company, spun it out as a separate business, terminated all the employees who worked for it, and then rehired them as contractors to do the same work. This wasn't exactly a stand-up move in any circumstance, but their "efficient" rollout was brutal. After leadership spent months of behind-the-scenes work planning this massive change, employees were given only short notice that they were about to lose all their benefits as full-time employees and return to work as contractors instead of employees without benefits.

That's no way to lead change with love. Plus, it doesn't work. It's not *effective*. Because they prioritized efficiency, the company ultimately needed to pivot again less than two years later because their initial change didn't take. This time around, they hired us to help them better communicate their plans and address their shortcomings. Our first order of business? Host a virtual town hall where senior leadership would finally show accountability for how dehumanizing the previous change effort had been. Only after these employees were able to once again see these leaders as human and trustworthy were they willing to follow leadership through another reorganization.

Stories like these show how organizations get the efficiency-over-effectiveness conversation all wrong. In our experience, effectiveness *is* efficiency. To be more efficient, you need more honesty. To be more honest, you need better relationships. To have better relationships, you need to slow down and build them. Experiential communication honors this process by explaining (1) why a planned change is happening on a human-to-human level, (2) the organizational vision at the heart of the planned change, and (3) what role each person within that change will play, emphasizing how leaders will be participating first.

None of this work happens overnight, but that's the point. To lead change, you must carefully navigate the conversations that will allow that change to take root. It's the classic slow-down-to-speed-up mindset—and emails, all-hands meetings, and training and education won't get you there. Why? Because none of them addresses the human behind the change or attempts to influence that person's mindset, attitude, and behavior. To lead change effectively, do what we've learned to do through many trials and many errors: create memorable experiences. Experiences shape our beliefs, which inform our actions, which get results.

In Part III, we're going to give you an inside look at the experience we created to create a culture of change readiness in anticipation of our reorganization effort: a week-long, company-wide trip to the Indian wilderness. It was a big undertaking, and some might say an unnecessary one. However, we knew that if we were truly going to break down old barriers and point our organization toward the future, our entire company would need an intense, hands-on, and communal experience to reset their beliefs and prepare for the hard work of making that change a reality.

We had only one mandate at the retreat: embrace discomfort. And we designed every experience with that mandate in mind.

It worked. We emerged from that retreat both changed and change ready, united in how we would think and talk about change as an organization from that point forward. Afterward, we spoke the same language regarding mindsets, discomfort, conflict, leadership, and communication. When we encountered a barrier, we tapped into this common language, embraced our discomfort, flushed the issue to the surface, and engaged in open dialogue until we sorted it out. The shift in our culture was monumental.

Had we focused merely on transmitting knowledge, we could have communicated our entire change plan through a single, impossibly long email. It certainly would have been cheaper. But the experience we created wasn't about sharing knowledge and plans. It was about fostering understanding between teams. It was about preparing our people for change so that they would be emotionally ready when it came time to implement that change. It was about slowing down to create alignment so we could be more effective as an organization moving forward.

To be clear, we didn't dive right into implementing our reorg plans afterward. Instead, we spent the next few months letting our planned change take root. From October 2023 to February 2024, we focused on conducting the important one-on-one conversations necessary to ensure everyone was bought into our change program and ready to do their part, which, for many, meant working in a new role and context. When we were sure we had full organizational buy-in, we finally put all our plans into action and hit the ground running.

Experience over Training

Throughout Part II, we've badmouthed training as a practice. It's not that we hate training. It's just that we think the way most organizations approach training is outdated, mundane, and ineffective.

Just because you offer training through Zoom or added an animated gif doesn't mean you've modernized your training practices or made it more efficient. In fact, you're probably wasting everyone's time. It's difficult to engage large groups of people on Zoom. People lose focus, turn off their screens, unlock their phones, and get lost in games of *Candy Crush*. And if they're caught zoning out, they have an easy excuse: "Sorry! Wi-Fi went out. What were you saying?" Are these trainings efficient? Sure, if your only metric is the time spent delivering the training module. However, if you're measuring retention, then these trainings aren't efficient at all—nobody learned anything!

Don't get us wrong; there is a time and place for training. When Jaya the Awesome needed to get Sahude certified in Amazon Web Services, training was absolutely the way to go (see Chapter 8). Sahude had a technical challenge that a straightforward, known solution like skill-based training and certifications would solve.

For most adaptive challenges, however, training is not the solution. Why? Because for everyone but the speaker, training is largely passive.

It's one person (or a small team of people) dictating a monolithic perspective on the whole. It's teaching people how to set up their "done" columns on the left in Sortd when no one understands why they should be using this tool in the first place. It's knowledge divorced from the kind of experiential learning that makes that knowledge *mean* something.

This is why we opted for an interactive hackathon to address and understand the potential uses of artificial intelligence (AI) at Softway. Recognizing that AI represented an adaptive challenge rather than a technical problem, we invited our members to be the heroes of their own journeys, encountering unexpected challenges, coming on strange and unusual characters along the way (mostly Frank), and working together to unite the realms of man against the evil forces of Sauron. Wait, that last part was *Lord of the Rings*. Scratch that.

The result? We went from a workforce that largely resisted this new technology to one that did the following:

- ◆ Embraced AI across the board
- ◆ Produced a more streamlined and effective workplace
- ◆ Developed brand-new products and services that increased revenue

The change in mindset in just a week's time was nothing short of remarkable. On day one, everyone shuffled into the Airbnb rental with the excitement of having to get a tooth pulled. By day four, the space was literally vibrating with excitement when we saw how these tools could supercharge our efforts. Jeff was so inspired he saw sounds and heard colors.

Should a hackathon be our go-to substitute in lieu of training for all situations moving forward? Absolutely not. Every adaptive challenge is different and requires a different set of experiences to solve them.

For a company like Interface, a publicly traded carpet tile company, a hackathon would have done little to help create buy-in for CEO Ray Anderson's goal to get the company carbon zero by 2020. For years, Anderson had tried to make this dream a reality, but he could never get enough people at the organization on board. He'd tried mandates and announcements, but his employees just waved him off and called him a crazy tree-hugger—and the stock market punished him by devaluing the price of his company's stocks.

Undeterred, Anderson tried a different approach: a celebratory sales reward and executive leadership trip to Hawaii. If that doesn't exactly sound like a carbon-zero move, there was a catch. During the event, Anderson had his team weigh all the food waste from their buffets and calculate how many people in underserved communities they could have fed. Then, he had them measure how many gallons of water the team had used and calculate what that number meant in terms of impact. Finally, he *invited*—not mandated—his team to join him on the company's climate change journey.

They accepted his invitation and reached their goal of carbon zero by 2020. Unfortunately, Anderson passed away a year later from cancer, but not before he invited his organization on a new journey: go beyond zero. Today, Interface continues Anderson's work by exploring how to *absorb* carbon from the atmosphere through "factories as forests." Through these efforts, Anderson's vision has outlived and morphed into a bigger one.[1]

Real learning happens when your team members have a stake in the process and are accountable to the outcome, when they get to set their own curriculum, and when they get to collaborate and empathize with each other. To solve the adaptive challenges facing your organization, think in terms of experiences, not training—and while you're at it, take stock of all the knowledge and beliefs that no longer serve you, too.

Remember: Honesty over Harmony

Honesty unlocks efficiency, and empathy unlocks effectiveness.

Workplaces that don't value honesty hide behind the illusion of efficiency instead. Why create experiences and connections when everything can be an email? Why have a series of honest conversations about a tough decision when you can just make a decision in minutes without anyone else's input? Why have a hard conversation when you can build a new,

(continued)

> long process instead? These "solutions" might seem easier in the moment, but typically they only create more problems.
>
> Where there is true honesty, efficiency follows. By embracing the discomfort and naming the thing, not only can you bring issues to the table more quickly but also you can find real solutions more effectively.

Unlearning over Learning

"When are we going to get some training on AI?"

This was far and away the most common question we heard during our hackathon—you know, where the whole purpose of the event was to empower our teams to see what they could discover on their own. We don't blame anyone for asking this question. The idea of training is so ingrained, so institutionalized in our collective organizational psyche, that we're bound to expect that the next round of training is right around the corner.

Leading change is about helping others learn how to tackle complex adaptive challenges. To do that, teams must feel empowered to identify and dismantle the unhelpful knowledge and beliefs that no longer serve them—which is why we're proud to call ourselves an *unlearning and relearning organization.*

Unlearning stems from a growth mindset. In fact, you could say it's the *highest* form of learning. Sure, good, old-fashioned learning is important, too, but that's table stakes. Unlearning requires us to go further. By clearing our mental cache, we become less tempted to integrate new knowledge into old, unhelpful ways of thinking. Instead, we get to take that knowledge and build an entirely new way of thinking around it.

This is why we spent the entire first day of our AI hackathon in dialogue with each other. We recognized that for this effort to succeed, first we needed to identify and discard the knowledge and beliefs that might hold us back. After all, we'd all spent our careers up to that point working in a world where AI wasn't a significant factor. We knew how to do our work without it, we *liked* how we did our work without it, and we resisted the idea that all of this hard-earned knowledge might no longer be useful.

We leaned into that discomfort. We acknowledged that whether we resisted it or not, the AI genie was out of the bottle and work as we knew it would never look the same. Then, we began the process of examining our old knowledge and skill sets. What elements of our work might look completely different in the next six months? What might remain the same? What were we willing to give up, what were we willing to learn, and what are we willing to change?

These were challenging questions, and our conversations reflected that. Still, as the day progressed, a consensus emerged: none of us wanted to wake up one day in a world where everything we knew was obsolete. Even if the unlearning process was difficult, we'd rather change along with the world than get left behind.

That's scary and uncomfortable—even when approached intentionally by running right into the storm. Learning and unlearning are fundamentally vulnerable acts, requiring us to admit what we don't know and to seek help from others. But it's far better to embrace that discomfort and vulnerability than to sit in fear and inaction as you count down the days until AI comes for your job. There's no escape from an adaptive challenge when approached with a fixed mindset—only dead ends.

Of course, the process of unlearning is ongoing. As soon as we accepted that we would have to discard certain of our skills and knowledge sets, a new question arose: how did we approach the actual process of adoption? For instance, did we start with our current systems and workflows and see how AI could augment them? Or, did we blow apart those workflows entirely and start from scratch?

Long term, the latter approach is more beneficial. We understand that AI is not merely an accelerator of our current workflow but also a chance to reimagine it. But that's a bigger change, one that, like most organizations, we will take one step at a time. In the short term, we chose an approach somewhere in the middle.

The Effectiveness Audit

The Effectiveness Audit: A Team Reflection & Action Workbook helps teams explore their relationship with effectiveness, efficiency, and change readiness in a practical, actionable way. To download your free resource, visit LoveAsAStrategy.com.

Be Effective

- ◆ Think about a time you prioritized efficiency over effectiveness. What was the result, and what might you do differently if you could revisit that moment?
- ◆ Have you ever been on the receiving end of a tool or process that was mandated rather than explained or invited? How did that approach affect your behavior and your willingness to change?
- ◆ What does effectiveness mean to you in your current role—and how is it different from just being efficient?
- ◆ What experiences—rather than trainings—have shaped your behaviors or mindsets the most at work? Why do you think those experiences were so impactful?
- ◆ In what ways does your organization mistake speed for success?
- ◆ How do you typically respond when new tools or workflows are introduced? Are you skeptical, excited, resistant, or adaptable? Why?
- ◆ When was the last time you truly had to unlearn something? What beliefs or behaviors did you have to let go of, and how did that feel?
- ◆ What's something your team has learned or experienced together that still shapes how you work today? How did that shared moment change your collective mindset?

- Have you ever participated in a training that looked efficient but failed to create lasting change? What would have made the experience more effective?
- What were some of your biggest takeaways or ah-ha moments from this chapter?

CHAPTER 9¾

A Secret, Bonus Experience

Throughout Part II, we've focused on the six principles of change that bring about a culture of change readiness. These principles aren't a checklist to wave your wand at before diving into the "real" work. This *is* the real work. Put in the effort here, and you're far more likely to see your change effort through. Skip this step, and, well, you saw the statistics we shared in Chapter 1.

But what next? What do you do after you've run directly at a brick wall between platforms 9 and 10 at King's Cross Station? You realize there's more—much more—hiding in plain sight.

There are plenty of methodologies out there. You can even get certified in them if that tickles your fancy. But we believe that anyone and everyone in an organization can adapt and adopt this simple change framework. And remember, even though we have to list this framework in stages, this framework ain't linear (change never is). When it comes to messy human change, you'll stop, start, reboot, swizzle, and reswizzle like a game of *Chutes and Ladders*. So, if experimenting (stage 4) leads you to a new uh-oh (stage 1), that's not a bug of the process, but a feature.

With that out of the way, here in this secret, totally unlisted portion of our book, we present to you our humble approach to change.

Stage 1: Uh-Oh (The Change Trigger)

We've been having the same meeting for six months with no progress. Uh-oh. The technology we built our business on is being phased out and replaced by artificial intelligence (AI) next year. Uh-oh.

Our biggest client hasn't returned our calls in three weeks. Uh-oh.

A social media post about our company just went viral for all the wrong reasons. Uh-oh.

The materials we depend on just doubled in price overnight. Uh-oh.

Big or small, exciting or urgent, change often starts with an *uh-oh* moment. These could be internally motivated (we've gotta reorg to grow) or externally motivated (a new administration comes to power). That's the calling card of an adaptive challenge—and usually you're starting to spot other symptoms of a bigger problem too. Maybe you can't figure out a particular strategy, or maybe certain initiatives are stalling. No matter what the symptoms are, you and the rest of the team are flummoxed.

Congratulations, you've just experienced a change trigger that you can no longer deny or delay. You may not know the extent of the adaptive challenge you're getting yourself into yet, but you do know it's not as straightforward as a technical challenge, so it's time to lean in and see what you can uncover.

Stage 2: Diagnose (Change Interrogation)

In the diagnosis stage, your job is to interrogate your adaptive challenge to make sure you understand it and surface any ideas on how to address it.

To conduct a successful interrogation, you need people, systems, and tools to interrogate—with love, of course. Talk to everybody you can. Stop them in the hallways. Get on their calendars. Ask as many questions as possible to establish and uncover the institutional knowledge and belief systems at play. In other words, think of yourself as an investigative journalist, with empathetic curiosity as your primary tool. To appreciate the common causes of the challenge, you must suspend your judgments and biases, as any assumptions you make could hinder your solution or bring you back to the drawing board.

Most leaders become victims of their experience at this step and take things at face value, quickly resolving that this current challenge is identical to one solved in their past. Their solution is then just a rinse and repeat. It rarely works like that (ask us how we know). Spend most of your time on the human condition of the situation: the feelings, beliefs, experiences, behaviors, and communal lore. We have always been surprised at how much these elements intersect with the structures, policies, processes, and tools that need adjusting.

Stage 3: Plan and Get Ready (Change Community Formation/Change Planning)

Now that you've diagnosed the adaptive challenge, it's time to lay out your vision for solving it. Keep it clear and concise so it's relatable, memorable, and repeatable. Your change vision is one of promise, but the journey to get there will require loss—and that loss may not be equal among all of those affected. The better you understand and can account for those losses, the better you will be able to contextualize and present the change vision. This work will also inform your decisions regarding who should help you plan and lead this change effort, which might be different than your traditional change management team.

Once you have identified your change leaders, enlist them in your efforts to create a culture of change readiness, and do whatever else you can to flood the zone with honesty and trust within this core team. They are not here to receive orders or simply disseminate your asks and preferences. They are here to contribute to the how of your what and why. To get these contributions, create an environment of psychological safety so your team members feel empowered to engage in healthy conflict and dialogue while sharing their unique perspective on the planned change. Together, this team's collective intelligence, as well as any evidence from past effective change initiatives, expedites transformation.

Here, lean on the six principles of change as much as you can. Embrace discomfort. Prioritize relationships. Wield your influence. Do whatever it takes to get people bought in and on board.

Stage 4: Experiment (Change Pilot)

Few change initiatives are rolled out all at once without stress testing the plan first. Our AI hackathon, for instance, was rolled out in stages—first with leadership and then with different segments of the organization. We failed smart, learned from it, and optimized our experiment for a scaled rollout. Remember what we said in Chapter 7: as long as you're learning and adapting, you're doing it right. Even the worst ideas can eventually lead to big breakthroughs.

We've learned that long, exhaustive change plans that are baked in a series of closed-door meetings are either ineffective or abandoned once they encounter real life. We've also seen that the one-note checklists that treat every change the same either fall flat or do more harm than good. You know the checklist: a long email or two, a virtual town hall with a poorly designed PowerPoint presentation, a boring computer-based training module, and a rushed one-on-one with an ill-informed and underprepared supervisor.

Let's stop that. We have seen more success internally and with clients by turning our change plans into a series of experiments and experiences that are gated by feedback and observation. Our goal became effectiveness, not a completed delivery. Yes, these experiments sometimes failed, but those failures also gave way to new ideas that eventually led to success. The lessons gained from these experiments blessed us twofold: (1) we had a valid approach for broader rollout, and (2) those who participated in the experiment were either evangelists in the rollout or coconspirators in a replacement experiment.

Stage 5: Communicate, Collaborate, Commiserate

Your pilot will yield a lot of new learning and feedback. Time for another round of interrogations (again, with love). Get in front of as many people as you can through team meetings, one-on-ones, and other internal channels. Listen, learn, and understand—and document everything.

Remember, when leading change, you are asking someone to change their beliefs and behaviors. We learned that we had to meet people where they are, to make their pain our pain. Whenever we judged or dismissed that pain, we encountered resistance.

This is why communication, collaboration, and commiseration are so important. Communication goes beyond email and chat threads.

We reimagine our communications as experiences, knowing that experiences shape our beliefs as humans. We don't shy away from email and chat, of course, but we instead ask where it fits in the experience we are creating for this change.

To be clear: experiences do not have to be expensive productions or weeklong retreats (although, as you're about to see in Part III, we are somewhat partial to both). The experiences we support are those that capture the attention of the audience, inspire a shift in thinking, and engage our team members as they work through their doubts, concerns, and fears.

Similarly, collaboration is an experience. A conversation can be an experience. A meeting can be an experience. Whatever the context, the goal is to put more thought into those everyday tactics to transform them into experiences.

Finally, while commiserating may sound negative or counterproductive, in reality, it builds trust with the most affected parties. Besides, when it comes down to it, commiserating is just listening with empathetic curiosity and journalistic integrity. It's not that different from how we believe we should behave anyway to make people feel seen, heard, and validated. Through commiseration, you gain a deeper understanding and new perspective on the impact, and unlock your ability to collaborate and communicate effectively.

Stage 6: Measure, Remind, Reward

Any successful change project requires accountability—not punitive accountability, of course. More like "How can we help people operationalize these changes?" accountability. As a change leader, your job is to measure, support, and reward, whether through kudos, fun perks, or unique benefits.

As you examine the results, don't just look for the hits but the misses as well. No change project goes off without a hitch. Always be looking for what could be fixed, what could be better, and what could be abandoned entirely. Measurement is not simply completion when it comes to change. Performance is the ultimate measure, but before that materializes, your change measures should include both qualitative and quantitative indicators. Leading change isn't just about creating change readiness, but about keeping your teams engaged with the big picture. If no one is sure whether their effort is paying off, then that effort will likely taper off.

And socialize what you've learned. Your path to implementing change may unlock ideas for congruent or upcoming change initiatives. Sharing learnings can stop the vicious cycle of failed change. We document our change experiments into playbooks that are living documents that help expedite future plans and build efficiency within our effectiveness.

Stage 7: Rest

Build rest into your change process. Even in a culture of love, even when you've prioritized change readiness and everyone is rowing in the same direction, the work of change is taxing. Either make a plan to rest, or your body will make those plans for you.

But rest isn't just important for our bodies. It's important for our relationships as team members. Resting and connecting creates empathy, a cornerstone of love. With opportunities for rest and reflection, we also get opportunities to reconnect and celebrate our wins together. With these deeper relationships comes more resilience, and with that resilience comes more wins. So few teams take the time to celebrate and count even the small victories the team has gained through their change journey. Rest and celebration are intentional acts, not accidental.

This is why we developed the alternating four-day workweek—and why we offer three weeks of vacation for everyone regardless of tenure, an additional two weeks of mandatory paid time off at the end of year, cultural retreats, and a number of other initiatives designed to help our people maintain their mental and emotional health and readiness. Rest is beneficial in whatever form our team members take it. Maybe they use that time to run errands, help a spouse with childcare, catch up on movies or shows, care for aging parents, go on a date, or literally anything else that isn't work related.

The idea is that having time for personal pursuits recharges our batteries for the professional ones. This isn't just good for us humans, but good for business. In a shocking twist, it turns out that a rested workforce is a happy workforce. The more we prioritize rest as a core aspect of our culture, the more our retention rates improve.

A RISING TIDE LIFTS ALL BOATS

You know those cutouts on every sidewalk that allow wheelchairs, strollers, and people lugging suitcases to navigate from the street to the sidewalk with relative ease? Those have only been around since the 1970s. In the years after the Civil Rights Movement, Americans with disabilities began lobbying federal and state governments to create cutouts in the sidewalk so they could get on and off the sidewalk safely. The campaign quickly gained traction, as other groups began to throw their weight behind the cause.

Sounds like a slam-dunk cause, right? To a degree, it was. The effort was successful, and today, sidewalk cutouts are considered the norm. However, at the time, many resisted the idea, claiming the change would cause construction delays and make cities unlivable.

Fortunately, once the change took root and everyone saw these cutaways' clear benefits, those objections quickly died down. While these cutaways were originally thought to benefit only those in wheelchairs, in the end, everyone benefited—from parents with strollers to delivery people with large dollies. And in a surprise twist that no one saw coming, the death rate for pedestrians plummeted, too, improving outcomes in wonderful and unexpected ways.

There is a common belief that if we do something to help others, only they will win, while we stand to lose. In application, that's rarely true. Intentionally addressing the adaptive challenges of a small group often creates benefits for the larger group as well. In those situations, everybody wins.

Think about this as we move ahead to Part III. When you approach change with love and intention, the result is often not what you expected—it's better.

You've come to the end of our secret, bonus experience. How do we wrap this up?

Oh yeah—mischief managed.

Ready for More?

To learn more about our change methodology, visit LoveAsAStrategy.com.

PART III

The Impact of Change

Change is often felt before it can be measured. When powered by love, the results don't happen in a moment, but build over time. Why? Because change requires courage, and courage can only come when there is love—love of hitting the goal, love of each other, love of doing the right thing *because* it's the right thing.

Love gives us the courage to face discomfort, to prioritize relationships, to practice empathetic curiosity, to experiment, to wield our influence, to be effective. If love is the leading indicator, change is the lagging indicator—the result of days, weeks, months, even *years* of intentional, courageous work.

Here in the final part of the book, we're going to draw a straight line from love to results, starting from the experience of a single family and radiating out in the world.

Get your tissues ready, y'all. It's about to get all kinds of inspiring.

CHAPTER 10

Personal Change

"**Mr. and Mrs. Anwar**, I'm sorry to say this, but Mohsin has a suspected intellectual disability."

It was December 8, 2018, and Mohammad and his wife, Yulia, had just had their world turned upside down.

"What do you mean by disability?" Yulia said. "Can you help us understand what you mean?"

"I'm afraid we don't know enough yet to tell," the doctor replied. "We'll need to do more testing before we can say with any certainty, but no single diagnosis I'm aware of would completely account for what we've observed. Most likely, you're looking at multiple diagnoses."

Mohammad swallowed hard as the shock washed over him. All the hopes and dreams he'd held for his son were reset in an instant.

The diagnosis explained a lot—why his son, Mohsin, had been almost entirely nonverbal, why he was prone to sudden outbursts, why he appeared unwilling or incapable of following even basic instructions. As the doctor explained, these traits would likely persist. Mohsin might never learn to talk, use the bathroom, or fulfill his basic needs. He would probably need constant care and attention his entire life.

Mohammad and Yulia thanked the doctor for his time and drove home in silence. There was so much to say, so many questions to ask, but where to begin? It was an impossible conversation—one made all the more challenging by the fact that Mohammad didn't have time to have it. He was set to fly to India for a work trip that evening.

On the flight, Mohammad was restless, his mind struggling to process the conversation and all the uncertainty that came with it. What happened next? What would Mohsin's life be like? Mohammad's life? His family's life? The doctor's diagnosis had only brought more questions—and, with them, fear.

The day-long flight from Houston to Bengaluru is taxing even on a routine trip with clear skies and no complications. But Mohammad had just received the shock of his life. All he wanted was to be home with his wife to share and grieve together as they turned their attention toward a scary and confusing future. Instead, he was forced to process in a cabin full of strangers as the plane took Mohammad further and further from the one place he wanted to be: home.

What Now?

Over the next several years, Mohammad, Mohsin, and the rest of the family became intertwined in a complex and confounding system in which they were forced to navigate social, educational, and health care processes that didn't always know how to accommodate a person with Mohsin's unique qualities.

However, while specialists agreed on the diagnosis, they provided no consensus on caring for or supporting Mohsin. Each physician and specialist they spoke with provided a different, often contradicting, set of recommendations from the previous doctor—from medicine to protocols to education:

"He'll never be able to do x."

"He'll only be able to do y if he takes medicine."

"He'll only be able to z if he doesn't *take this medicine."*

Each physician was convinced their approach was best and did their best to convince Mohammad and Yulia to follow their recommendations above all others. But with so much contradictory information to process and decide on, whom could they trust? It was like being caught relaying messages between feuding parents, who seemed intent on never speaking to each other under any circumstances. At one point, Mohammad remembers the pediatrician asking him to confront the neurologist about their supposedly wrong recommendations. *Great*, Mohammad remembers thinking, *how am I supposed to tell a neurologist they're wrong?*

In addition to playing messenger for these warring specialists, Mohammad and Yulia were tasked with integrating all the various information and managing an entire care program for their son. It was like they had taken on another full-time job. Every week brought new specialized diets, treatment plans, and appointments with educators and tutors. Some of these programs worked. Most of it just felt like added noise in all the confusion. All they wanted was to help their son and get him the care he needed.

Perhaps nothing stands out more in Mohammad's memory of this time than the day they took Mohsin to the geneticist. With a cadre of student residents in tow, the doctor entered the room, encouraged his student to take pictures, and then jumped into an impromptu lecture. "You see how the eyes are far apart and how there's a big gap in the face? That's a sign of intellectual disability," the geneticist said. "Other genetic features point to the same problem. Do you see how his ears are a little drooped?"

"Excuse me, what's wrong with my son's face?" Yulia asked. Mohammad was relieved to hear his wife speak up. He was about to say much worse.

"Nothing, ma'am," the geneticist said with a puzzled look on his face—as if he couldn't possibly comprehend why this stranger would object to anything he just said. "We're just talking about his genetics."

This isn't a doctor's office, Mohammad thought. *It's a zoo.* Finally, once the residents had left the geneticist's side, Mohammad and Yulia got some one-on-one time to speak with the doctor in hopes of better understanding their son's condition. "It's hard to say for sure," the geneticist said, "but he'll probably never be able to speak like you and me, nor will he ever be able to read."

Great. All that humiliation to learn something we already knew, Mohammad thought.

And so it went—dehumanizing visit after dehumanizing visit. Mohammad and Yulia wanted so badly to protect, care for, and help their youngest grow. But after three years, the only certainty they could get was a diagnosis. Finally, definitively, the doctors were able to determine that Mohsin had a combination of intellectual disability, autism, and ADHD.

With this diagnosis came yet another list of all the things doctors and specialists believed Mohsin would never be able to do. Each list item was a new source of grief and discomfort. As any parent would, Mohammad crumbled inside at the realization his son would face so many different challenges. He tried to tell himself to stay strong and rational, but how could he?

During these challenging times, however, came a glimmer of hope. On his mother's recommendation, Chris introduced Mohammad and his family to an intervention specialist named Ms. Bass. Ms. Bass worked as an early tutor for Mohsin, establishing a series of foundational practices with Mohsin—sitting still, solving basic problems, and recognizing certain words and phrases—that would prove invaluable in Mohsin's development.

Mohammad remembers Ms. Bass's first day quite clearly. "Mohsin's going to be just fine," she assured him.

"How can you say that?" Mohammad asked. It was the first time anyone had said anything *encouraging* about his son.

"He knows how to get out of work," Ms. Bass said. "I work with many special needs kids. None of them know how to 'play the game' like Mohsin does. That's usually a sign of intelligence."

This was just the kind of reassurance Mohammad and his family needed. Still, they had a few lessons to learn and many challenges to endure before Ms. Bass's prediction would prove true.

Practicing in Public

On top of care and treatment, Mohammad and his family also had to navigate the many social challenges associated with a special needs child. For better or worse, any society tilts toward conformity, and American culture is no different. Parents are expected to show up in certain ways. Children are expected to do the same. Anything that deviates too far from these norms is frowned on. If a child doesn't conform to the behavior typically expected in society or public areas, then their parents are made to feel guilty in a number of small but meaningful ways.

For example, nights out at a restaurant were always a gamble. Mohammad and Yulia were intent on living a normal life and sharing as many typical family experiences as possible. That meant practicing with their son in public—often to the dismay of other diners. Even a small outburst in a restaurant is usually met with eye daggers and mumbles of displeasure. But while sometimes Mohsin would be well-behaved and happy to enjoy his meal, other times he was inconsolable. Mohammad was a successful business owner who could command a room with his personality and strategic foresight. Yulia was an Olympic Champion, five-time Olympic medalist, and Hall of Fame diver who had seen the world and risen to the very pinnacle of human capability. But neither of them had ever felt smaller and more judged than in those moments.

To some degree, Mohammad and his family knew they would endure challenges like this with Mohsin. But even when you're prepared for these challenges, even where you're determined to meet them with love, it's still hard. You don't know what the experience will be like until you're in it.

Mohammad didn't know what it would feel like for six schools in under four years to reject Mohsin and recommend him for other programs. He didn't know what it would feel like for martial arts, gymnastics organizations, and summer camps to turn Mohsin away. Each organization claimed to be able to accommodate a child with special needs like Mohsin, but each chose to make Mohsin someone else's problem—typically after only a day or two in the program.

Each experience felt like a new barb, a new rejection of Mohammad and his family. Everyone treated Mohsin like a technical problem—*someone else's* technical problem—rather than embracing him for the adaptive challenge he presented. Seeing this pattern play out again and again, Mohammad became frustrated—not with Mohsin, but with all the cold, uncaring systems society had erected to try and "manage" a child like Mohsin.

More than that, Mohammad was exhausted. Caring for a high-energy kid with special needs is a full-time job. Mohammad and Yulia were fortunate to have enough financial stability that Yulia could stay home and care for Mohsin during the week. On the weekends, Mohammad would take over and give his wife a much-needed break. Mohammad was more than happy to do his part and support his family, but it came at a cost: he never truly had a day off.

In this always-on reality, Mohammad came to dread workplace small talk on Monday mornings. When someone asked how his weekend was, he'd shut down. He didn't want to lie and describe his many imaginary adventures, but he didn't want to tell the truth either. He didn't want to burden anyone with stories of his miserable weekends, of feeling unwelcome in his community, of feeling mentally and physically exhausted and unsure how much longer he could go on like this.

This is the real reason we experimented with the four-day work-week: so Mohammad could get a single day of rest while Mohsin was at school. Not wanting to be the kind of leader who took the day off while everyone else worked, we began a set of experiments to solve this adaptive challenge until we found one that worked (see Chapter 7). But even with these workweek experiments, the combined effort of leading a business during the week and caring for a special needs child was pushing Mohammad to his breaking point. Finally, by Christmas 2022, during a family trip to the Virgin Islands, Mohammad had had enough.

It was a beautiful day in the Caribbean. Mohammad and his family were lounging by the beach, enjoying a stay at the nearby Ritz-Carlton. Mohsin was having the time of his life in the shallows, diving into the water and collecting seashells into a bucket. With each plunge of his hands, he came up with a new treasure—including a sea cucumber. And with each new treasure, his excitement grew. This beach was Mohsin's favorite place to be, a place where he could truly be free to play, splash, and create in the sand.

"What are you doing with those seashells?" a voice from down the beach bellowed. Mohammad and his family looked up in unison to find one of the Ritz-Carlton's outdoor staff briskly speed walking toward their area on the beach. "You there, young man, I'll ask you again: what are you doing?"

Mohammad stood and greeted the man. "Hello, this is my son, Mohsin. Is he doing something wrong?"

"Is this your first time to the Caribbean?" the Ritz employee asked, his cop-like tone offering a stark contrast to the khaki shorts he was wearing and the white towels folded under his arm.

"No, but this is our first time to the US Virgin Islands," Mohammad replied.

"Well, it's illegal to remove seashells from the beach," the employee said. "You could get arrested for that."

"I'm sorry, we didn't know that. Thank you for—"

"Hey, *don't touch that!*" the employee shouted.

Mohammad looked down. As he and the guard spoke, Mohsin became interested in the walkie-talkie on the person's belt and began reaching for it.

The staff person lost what little composure he had left. "He can't be touching me! He can't be touching me!" he repeated. Then, pointing a frantic, scolding finger at Mohammad, he said, "This is out of control. You need to get your child in line."

"Please be gentle with him. My son has special needs," Mohammad tried to interject over the Ritz staff shouts. But it was like speaking into a vacuum.

The exchange reinforced Mohammad's growing sense that he and his family were unwelcome. No matter where they went, the world existed only to dehumanize his son and shame him and his wife as parents.

Mohsin and his family were unwelcome at the park, where parents regularly demanded that Mohammad apologize for Mohsin pushing someone or cutting in line to use the slide. And yet, no children or parents ever apologized to Mohsin or Mohammad when their neurotypical kids would call Mohsin a loser and tell him to get lost.

Mohsin and his family were unwelcome at Mohsin's school, where the then-seven-year-old was accused of sexual assault, questioned by the police without a parent present, and subjected to a battery of intrusive actions that violated his rights, even though the child had no concept of sex, sexuality, or sexual behavior. The investigation was eventually dropped when it became clear there was no mal-intent—all Mohsin had done was hug another kid while the two were playing together—but not before Mohammad was made to feel completely powerless to protect his son and somehow made to feel responsible for his son's supposedly "deviant" behavior.

Mohsin and his family were unwelcome at Universal Studios, where the family in front of them on the (now defunct) Fast and Furious ride kept yelling at Mohsin to shut up after he began crying halfway through. They'd spent thousands of dollars to come to the park, and now Mohammad was afraid to take his son on any other rides and enjoy them as a family for fear of public shaming.

Mohsin and his family were unwelcome on the flight to St. Thomas to the Ritz-Carlton at the US Virgin Islands, when a passenger became upset with Mohsin for repeatedly opening and closing the tray table. Instead of speaking to Mohammad and Yulia about the issue—who were right there in the seats next to their son—he demanded to the still nonverbal Mohsin that he leave him alone and let him sleep. What a way to kick off the vacation.

Mohsin and his family were unwelcome a day later at the Ritz-Carlton swimming pool, when a parent reprimanded Mohammad because his son had splashed water on their daughter. Because heaven forbid, someone gets wet in a swimming pool.

All these thoughts washed over Mohammad as he and his family trudged sadly back to their hotel room. Exhausted, Mohammad started to check his emails. A survey popped up: The Ritz-Carlton wanted to know how their experience was going. "Let me tell *you*," Mohammad started typing, feeling years of pent-up anger begging for release.

Now, if there's one thing you should know about Mohammad, it's that he knows how to weaponize an angry email. Back in the Moh 1.0 days, when he presided over Softway's toxic culture of misbehavior, his digital rants were legendary. Perhaps none of Mohammad's nasty grams better represents this period than the infamous "refrigerator email," where, in an epic onslaught of all-caps emphasis and an army of exclamation points, he torched whatever goodwill he had left in the company and demanded that the staff drop what they were doing and empty the refrigerator of all its contents. (See our first book for the whole ALL CAPS rant.)

Now, nearly ten years later, Mohammad could feel that old 1.0 version of himself bubbling under the surface. The urge to absolutely torch the Ritz-Carlton staff, their outdoor staff person, and any other collateral employees grew strong. But then he caught himself. He had come so far since then. Did he really want to undo all that work just so he could make the Ritz staff feel as small as they had made him and his family feel?

No. He didn't.

But still, the Ritz team *had* asked how their trip was going, and Mohammad *did* still believe in honesty over harmony. So, in as direct and measured a tone as he could muster, he proceeded to explain why their stay had been less than perfect.

Send.

Within an hour, Mohammad received a call from the hotel manager. The next thing they knew, there was a knock at the door, and hotel workers poured in with gifts—including a stuffed iguana and turtle for Mohsin. For the next twenty minutes, the manager and Mohsin played a game with the iguana and a few other gifts, the manager clearly understanding the need to make amends.

As the manager and her team prepared to depart, she apologized again to Mohammad, Mohsin, and the rest of the family. Then, she explained that, in addition to their apologies and gifts, the Ritz-Carlton team would also be reviewing their policies to make sure no families were made to feel unwelcome and would provide additional training as necessary. Finally, they offered to host Mohsin at the hotel's kids club and personally entertain him and his sister so Mohammad and Yulia could have a few hours to themselves.

In this instance, the Ritz-Carlton chose their hard. They could have dismissed Mohammad's feedback or justified the staff's unnecessarily threatening behavior. They could have chosen not to read the feedback at all. Had they done so and continued down this path, they would have set themselves up for a bigger reckoning—and, therefore, a bigger challenge—somewhere down the road.

Instead, they listened to Mohammad's concerns and worked quickly to rectify them. Apologizing isn't easy. Showing up at an angry family's doorstep to make it right isn't easy. Playing with a child with special needs who you've never met isn't easy. The Ritz team chose the challenge of rising to the moment rather than the challenge of fixing a bigger problem later.

And through this choice, the Ritz-Carlton made Mohammad's family feel loved again.

Retreat

The Ritz-Carlton's effort to make things right with Mohammad and his family was genuine. That's who the Ritz is, and that's what they do. But while Mohammad came out of that trip feeling elated, there was still the real world to contend with—a world that Mohammad had begun to lose faith in.

Since 2016, Mohammad had been on a mission of love, determined to bring humanity back to the workplace. Now, he was no longer sure that vision was worth pursuing. Why bother bringing humanity back to the workplace when his fellow humans had shown him and his family anything *but* humanity in public spaces? The very humanity Mohammad had so enthusiastically committed himself to was the same humanity that had excluded, disowned, and mistreated his son. Rather than feel love for his fellow humans, all Mohammad felt was resentment.

It would be so easy to sell Softway and give up this fight, Mohammad told himself. And he almost went through with it. But should he? Would that be the right thing to do? Could he look at himself in the mirror afterward, knowing what he had given up?

Lost, angry, and desperately looking for answers, Mohammad attended a wilderness retreat as part of his fellowship program with the American Leadership Forum (ALF) in Colorado. (Full disclosure: Mohammad isn't supposed to talk to anybody about what he experienced on this retreat, so don't tell anyone from ALF about this part of the book, okay?)

On the retreat, Mohammad had one objective: to practice deep, unstructured introspection about the challenges plaguing him. During the retreat, after trekking nearly nine miles into the wilderness with his cohort, Mohammad sat in his sleeping bag, gazing at the stars. It was only thirty-nine degrees outside, but the day's activities and Mohammad's anxieties were more than enough to take his attention off the cold. Watching the steam from his breath dissipate into the night air, Mohammad could only ask himself a single question, *What am I supposed to do?*

The next morning, Mohammad set out on an eight-hour solo trek. With no cell phone, watch, or any other digital device, Mohammad had no sense of time and little sense of direction. His only instruction from the ALF team was to listen for the sound of drums toward the end of the day. That would signal to him and the others that it was time to make their way back.

Out on his own, Mohammad found a secluded place on a hill and under some trees. Then, he slowly unpacked his lunch, laid out his yoga mat, and grabbed his ALF-provided notebook and pen. He would use his time to meditate and journal. Nothing else. Mohammad examined the prewritten questions in the journal. They encouraged him to consider his career, his purpose—things like that. He ignored them all and focused instead on exploring his relationship with his son.

At first, the writing was disjointed, fueled by confusion, resentment, and a lot of questions:

Why is this happening to Mohsin? Why has the world disowned him?

Why is this happening to me? *Why is Mohsin in my life? Why did God give him to me?*

Am I being punished? What did I do to deserve this?

Mohammad wiped his eyes, the tears already running down his cheeks and dripping onto his journal with a quiet *pat, pat, pat.* Already, he felt ashamed of where his thoughts had taken him, but he continued on: *WHY? WHY MOHSIN? WHY ME?!?*

Not expecting the emotions to rise up so quickly, Mohammad took a deep breath and steadied himself. Then, to help him process this onslaught of thoughts and feelings, Mohammad decided to write a letter to his son. Time stopped. Mohammad's head and hand became synchronized, almost as if someone else was doing the writing for him. Yes, he was the one putting the words down on the page, but each new word was a surprise—a revelation—an answer to the questions that had been burning inside him for years.

He finished the letter. Then, he looked back at one of the questions he had scrawled in his journal: *Why is Mohsin in my life?*

Then, he heard an answer: *Mohsin is here to teach you unconditional love. He is here to teach you patience.*

Mohammad gasped. He heard the voice—*his voice*—as clearly as if someone was sitting right next to him. But it was just him. Alone. In the woods. Overwhelmed by the voice speaking through him, Mohammad sat back, closed his eyes, and listened.

Who are you to not love humanity? Mohsin loves the very same humans who disown and mistreat him.

Who are you to give up on humanity? Mohsin teaches you every day how to become a better human, a better father, a better coworker, a better citizen. Mohsin is your teacher—your blessing—and his message is unconditional, unquestioning love.

Mohammad blinked. It was true. Mohsin was an affectionate, loving child, always ready to greet others with a smile and a hug. He didn't care that the systems he was a part of functioned to exclude him. He didn't care how other kids treated him. He still hugged the same teachers who complained about him daily. He still hugged the same kids who made fun of him and tried to get in trouble. In every day, every moment, every opportunity, Mohsin was the literal personification of love and joy. To Mohsin, no room was scary, and no person was a stranger. When Mohsin walked into a room, he made it his job to greet everyone with warmth and love.

Mohsin was a *gift*. He had always been a gift. And Mohammad had so much to learn from him. Here he was, a grown-ass man whose main message in life was focused on love, and yet, when he entered a room, Mohammad didn't feel love. He felt deferential, shy, apologetic. Worse, he carried these feelings with him whenever he would take Mohsin out in public—whether out shopping, to the airport, to the gym, anywhere. Ever since the diagnosis, Mohammad had been terrified about how people might react to his son—a projection of his own self-consciousness about how people might respond to *him*.

But whenever he let go of those fears and allowed his son to be truly and authentically who he is, the most wonderful thing happens: people lit up. They would be genuinely surprised by Mohsin's warmth and engagement, and most would happily engage right back.

If only more adults could interact with each other like my son, we'd have peace, Mohammad thought to himself.

Seeing this clearly for the first time, Mohammad understood that his role as Mohsin's father wasn't to push back against a system that had failed to recognize his son's humanity but to create space for that humanity to thrive, to meet that system with patience, empathy, and compassion and show the world why Mohsin was such an incredible blessing. If he could embrace and amplify the love that his son gave so willingly, then he could help others recognize the gift his son was as well.

Mohammad finished writing, looked around at the forest around him, and tilted his head down the hill to see if he could hear any distant drum beats. Nothing. *Great*, he thought, *I'll use the rest of this time to write everyone else in my cohort a letter*. And that's exactly what he did. Each letter was filled with words of encouragement, love, connection, and empathy, describing everything he had learned about them in the short time he had known them. When the drum beat came, he happily trudged down from his position on the hill, rejoined the group, and distributed his letters to the returning travelers.

To this day, members of his cohort still reach out to Mohammad about the letters he wrote and their impact on them. It's not that there was anything particularly profound in those letters. It's just that he bothered to write them and share a small piece of the love he felt at that moment.

Through that experience, Mohammad remembered something essential about change: it started with him. He couldn't spend his days waiting for the world to change for his son. He couldn't spend his days waiting for his son to change for him. If he wanted to *see* change, he needed to *be* change.

Because of this realization, Mohammad returned from the retreat a changed man—a renewed father, husband, and friend. This new perspective manifested in every action—in how he treated his wife, in how he treated his daughter, and, most of all, in how he treated his son. He began to see the world through Mohsin's eyes—through the eyes of unconditional love. This new mindset radiated out in his behaviors, creating a cascade of changes in every aspect of his life.

In one telling example, Mohammad met with a neurologist on Mohsin's behalf. Yulia had long ago given up on this doctor—who had been nothing short of insufferable with every visit. This time, Mohammad brought a secret weapon: a copy of our first book, *Love as a Business Strategy*.

After Mohammad presented the book to the neurologist, the doctor's attitude completely changed. For the next forty-five minutes, he sat with Mohammad, learned about him, and treated him like the living, breathing person he was rather than a problem parent to be managed. During this conversation, the doctor even shared something about himself that Mohammad hadn't known: he, too, had a child with special needs.

As they were wrapping up their meeting, the doctor gave Mohammad one last bit of advice. "Set up a trust fund for Mohsin," he said. "He's not going to be able to live on his own, and you'll need to set up special needs service later in life." It was good advice—great advice. And Mohammad never would have received it unless he had decided to become the change he wanted to see.

Because Mohammad now treated doctors, educators, and administrators as Mohsin's allies, Mohsin's outcomes began to improve. Mohsin began learning more, making headway in speech and mathematics.

Because Mohammad and his family felt more comfortable taking Mohsin out in public, Mohsin became more acclimated to social settings. He developed more personal tools for adjusting, behaving, and working with his peers. The more tools he developed, the more Mohammad and Yulia could help him grow further.

Because Mohammad joined a martial arts class with his son and committed to love and play together, Mohsin was accepted as part of the group and celebrated. This outcome was far from guaranteed. Mohsin's Muay Thai instructor, Coach Paul, originally invited Mohammad to join the adult class so he could join his son on the floor and help manage him. Because Mohammad showed up for his son, Mohsin was embraced rather than shunned. The experience has been so rewarding that Mohammad now assists in instructing the kids' class. To this day, Coach Paul says Mohsin is the strongest kid in the class, pound for pound.

Because Mohammad removed the barriers for others to see and love his son, Mohsin made a best friend. A real, honest-to-goodness best friend—who lights up whenever Mohsin is around and was the first to RSVP for Mohsin's first-ever birthday party when he turned nine.

All the things the doctors had said Mohsin might never do, he was doing. Never in his life did Mohammad expect to see so much progress in his son in such a short amount of time. He never thought he'd get to send a video of Mohsin reading on his own to us in our running text thread. He never thought he'd see Mohsin develop the physical and cognitive abilities to build Legos, complete jigsaw puzzles, or take showers and use the bathroom on his own. He never thought he'd ever hear his son say, "Can you help me, Baba?" so he could reply with a smile, "Yes, son. Always. I love you."

Mohammad never expected to see so many people show up to love, care for, and support his family. Once he opened his heart to them, Mohammad saw little glimpses of humanity everywhere.

Mohammad appreciated his friend and ALF classmate, Doctor Andrea, in an entirely new way. After hearing Mohammad's story and understanding his and Yulia's need for small breaks when they could enjoy each other's company without having to be parents, Doctor Andrea offered to babysit Mohsin on occasion—which she continues to do to this day. This kind of care and community were always available to Mohammad and his family. However, Mohammad never realized it until he changed his perspective.

More than anything, Mohammad appreciated Chris, seeing the special bond his friend and his son had shared for years. Chris first met Mohsin one night after dropping Mohammad off at home from the airport. As they arrived at the house, Mohammad invited Chris in. "There's someone I want you to meet," he said.

Chris walked into the dining room to find Yulia, Mohammad's dad, and a little stranger just out of sight behind a column.

"Mohsin," Yulia said, "There's a special visitor here to see you."

Chris poked his head around the column, locking eyes with the little stranger, who had been craning his neck to see around the pillar and get a glimpse of this so-called special visitor. Mohsin smiled. Chris smiled back, and the two have been thick as thieves ever since.

Whenever Chris is around, Mohsin makes Chris feel especially welcome. He hugs him, laughs with him, sits in his lap, and sings along with Chris as his favorite Beyoncé songs bump over the speakers. To this day, if Mohsin sees his dad on a video call with Chris, he gleefully shuts down the conversation to chat with his special friend.

From the first diagnosis of Mohsin's learning disability, Chris was steadfast in his belief in Mohsin. "Our bodies are fearfully and wonderfully made," he told Mohammad. "Write down everything the doctors have told you Mohsin will never do, and let's cross them off together as he proves the doctors wrong." One of the greatest pleasures of his life has been to sit with Mohammad, smile as Mohsin ticks off box after box, and beam with pride as this special child defies all expectations.

But it's not just Chris who is such a believer in Mohsin. Chris has his entire family and extended community in Mohsin's corner. His mom advocated for Mohsin at his school when different challenges arose and introduced them to Ms. Bass, one of Mohsin's earliest champions. The last question Chris's dad asked him before passing away in early 2025 was, "How is Mohsin doing?" Chris's brother and sister-in-law, who once met Mohsin and watched in awe as he went from person to person, giving hugs and making smiles, are convinced they have never felt a love more authentic and gentle than Mohsin's. Even Chris's church prays for Mohsin every Sunday, surrounding and supporting him with the same unconditional love that Mohsin has radiated into the world.

Of course, there are still challenges. There will always be challenges.

Some challenges are endearing, like when Mohsin uses a hair dryer to dry his wet shirt instead of taking it off and throwing it in with the laundry. Other challenges are frustrating but to be expected, like when Mohsin encounters cruelty and indifference from kids and adults—which he doesn't understand and doesn't deserve. Still, some challenges are harder. Some days, Mohsin's impulses will get the better of him, and he'll descend upon Mohammad and Yulia in a flurry of punches, kicks, and scratches.

The old Mohammad would turn into a scold in these moments. "Mohsin, *stop!*" he'd shout, grabbing his son by the wrists. "That is not acceptable behavior. I *need* you to understand that!"

Such a response would never work because it *could* never work. Now, Mohammad knows that he can't control what his son does, but he *can* control how he responds.

So, he takes a breath, embraces discomfort, and asks, "What do you need? How can I help you?" By greeting Mohsin with the same unconditional love that he greets the rest of the world, Mohammad is able to create the space for Mohsin to move past the moment and have his emotional needs met.

Change Starts with You (Redux)

This book almost didn't happen. Our entire reorganization almost didn't happen. Somewhere in the multiverse, there is a reality where Mohammad never went on that ALF retreat, sold Softway, and abandoned Love as a Strategy altogether. Overcome by the sense of hypocrisy he felt promoting love when all he felt was contempt, that alternate-universe Mohammad cut his losses, retreated into the same cynicism that almost bankrupted Softway in 2016, and lived the rest of his life wondering what could have been.

Thankfully, that's not the universe we live in. Instead, we live in a universe where Mohammad could look at his son, see the boundless love within him, and be changed by the experience.

For years, Mohammad had waited for change. For the doctors, teachers, and administrators who worked with Mohsin to change. For his circumstances to change. For his son to change.

Never once did he think to change himself.

That process didn't begin with positive thinking, overwhelming joy, or even love. It began with a feeling most of us try to avoid: grief. In order to move forward in love with the son he had, Mohammad first had to grieve the son he *thought* he would have, to grieve the future he'd imagined for that son, and to accept that this person and that future may never come to be. Only by laying this imagined son with his imagined future to rest could Mohammad truly embrace the son he had, to accept him as he was, and to love him with *all* his heart, no matter what the future held or who he became.

It's a difficult feeling to describe, but one that many parents of children with special needs understand all too well. After Mohsin's diagnosis, Mohammad struggled to separate out the profound sense of grief he felt from the very real love he felt for his son. Eventually, he realized it was an impossible task. For Mohammad, grief and love are intertwined, complex, interdependent. To understand the full scope and range of his feelings, Mohammad needed to experience them together—not just once, but in an ongoing, renewing cycle.

Regardless of when you read this book, Mohammad will still be oscillating between his grief and his love for Mohsin. That push and pull will always be present will every setback, with every milestone, with every birthday. However, while Mohammad understands that his grief will always be a part of the experience, it's his love for Mohsin that keeps him moving forward.

Once Mohammad accepted this as natural—that it was okay to grieve and love his son at the same time—the world changed around him. Suddenly, he saw support instead of resistance, progression instead of regression. As we were writing this chapter, the leader of a school district we had been working with reached out to Mohammad and Yulia for their input in creating an integrated school system where students like Mohsin would interact freely with the more neurotypical student population. As part of the training for teachers as they prepare for the rollout, Mohammad was asked to deliver a sort-of keynote and experience for the roughly 120 teacher leaders at the district. While the initiative and invite were in response to a government mandate, the school's superintendent remembered Mohammad's story of his experience with Mohsin, and he believed that story was just what the gathered teacher leaders needed to buy into the program. From rejection to acceptance, it's a full-circle moment for Mohsin's story.

Big changes begin with small changes. Small changes begin with small shifts in mindset, beliefs, and attitudes. They're felt before they're measured—and soon grow too powerful to be stopped.

But they all begin with a single person, choice, and act. To change the world, your organization, and your team, you must first be willing to change yourself.

When Mohammad allowed himself to see his son differently, the experience forever changed him. It made him a better father, a better family member, a better neighbor, a better friend, and a better leader.

As humans, we thrive in environments where we feel respected and valued, where our ideas won't be ridiculed, where feedback can be given and received without fear of retaliation, and where we know our efforts are meaningful and affect others. When you feel safe and included, you enjoy your job more and infuse your work with a sense of purpose, belonging, and resilience.

But to receive that feeling, we must also create it.

After recommitting to his relationship with Mohsin, Mohammad saw the value of this lesson more clearly than ever. Finally, reinvigorated and recommitted to bringing humanity back to the workplace, he was ready to embody the change he had felt and lead Softway in a bold new direction.

What's Your Change Story?

For help understanding how your own story can be a powerful catalyst for change, see our self-reflection guide (along with other resources related to this chapter) on LoveAsAStrategy.com.

Personal Change

- How do you typically respond when life disrupts your expectations or dreams? What happens to your perspective when things don't go the way you hoped?

- Can you think of a moment when you realized you were carrying unconscious judgment—toward yourself, others, or the world? What helped you notice and shift that mindset?

- What role does vulnerability play in your personal growth? How comfortable are you with allowing others to witness your discomfort or transformation?

- When have you experienced institutional or systemic dehumanization, even in subtle ways? How did that shape your beliefs about others—or yourself?

- In your own life, who or what has served as your greatest teacher—especially someone or something you didn't expect to learn from?

- How do you handle emotional or relational exhaustion, especially when the world seems indifferent to your struggle? What helps you recharge authentically?

- Have you ever felt like giving up on something you once believed in deeply? What helped you hold on—or let go—in a meaningful way?

- How do you balance the desire to advocate for change with the need to maintain hope and love for those who resist it?

- What small shift in your mindset, belief, or behavior has made the biggest impact on your life or leadership?

- When was the last time you greeted a challenge with unconditional love instead of control, frustration, or retreat? What changed as a result?

- If you wrote a letter to someone who has changed your life (for better or worse), what would you want them to know about the impact they've had?

- How does seeing the world through someone else's eyes—especially someone who is often excluded—transform how you show up as a leader, parent, or peer?

CHAPTER 11

Team Change

It was Jeff's birthday. After enjoying a peaceful morning, he looked down to see his phone buzzing. It was Mohammad.

"Happy birthday!" Mohammad said giddily. "What are you doing for lunch?" Then, with no pause to inhale or let Jeff answer the question, "Let me take you out." Lucky for Mohammad, Jeff said he had no plans, and they agreed to meet up for sushi.

"So, how was the retreat?" Jeff asked once the pair was seated. It was a rhetorical question. Mohammad was practically vibrating with excitement, ready to spin off into the stratosphere if he wasn't immediately invited to talk. *Ah, so* that's *why Mohammad wanted to take me out to lunch so bad*, Jeff thought. *Whatever. Free sushi. I'm in.*

"I'm really not supposed to tell you about anything that happened at the retreat," Mohammad said, looking downbeat for just a moment. Then he looked back up at Jeff, a look of playful mischief crossing his face. "But how can I not? It's the best thing that ever happened to me!"

Having given himself permission to ignore all the rules, Mohammad then proceeded to divulge the entire experience to his longtime friend. How he had been struggling as a father to Mohsin, how his experience traveling to the Caribbean had almost broken him, and finally, how the ALF fellowship retreat completely shifted his perspective in two important ways. First, Mohammad realized that if Mohsin could love everyone unconditionally—even if they didn't love him back—he could, too. Second, he realized that for a person to be changed, they must *experience* change. "We're not doing that enough at Softway," said, reflecting on this final insight.

"That sounds like quite the trip," Jeff said.

"You have no idea," Mohammad said. "I'm not sure there is any way I can explain it adequately. You'd have to experience it yourself to truly understand."

Then, hearing his own words as if someone else had said them, Mohammad's eyes lit up. He had an idea. Once again, his body began to vibrate, as if he were on the verge of achieving a higher plane of existence. Niagara Falls started flowing in reverse. All of Jupiter's moons aligned. The entire universe bent to Mohammad's will. Then, Mohammad glitched out of the building and flew off toward some unknown destination, just like Neo in *The Matrix*. From somewhere deep within Jeff's mind, he heard Mohammad say, "I'm sorry, Jeff, I have to go. I'll Venmo you money for the bill later."

Jeff looked around to see if this was a prank or if Mohammad really had become some kind of cosmic being. Then, seeing nothing else out of the ordinary, he shrugged and looked down at the plate of sashimi in front of him. *This is entirely too much food for one person*, he thought. Then he remembered it was his birthday and ate every last bite.

As Jeff took that plate of sashimi down, he reflected on what Mohammad had just shared. For well over a year, Mohammad had felt stuck, like the world was out for him, his family, and his company. And, since he was the head of the company, when Mohammad felt stuck, Jeff and everyone else felt stuck. As goes the leader, so goes the rest of the organization.

If Jeff and Moh's lunch was any indicator, Softway was about to go to the moon and beyond. After all, experiences aren't just moments in time but connected like a chain. Jeff didn't know how just yet, but he knew that Mohammad's transformation at the ALF fellowship retreat was about to change everything—how we showed up to our families, how we showed up to work, how we showed up to our clients, how we showed up everywhere.

Most leaders don't change with their business. They expect their organization to change around them and their desires. That's not leading with love.

Mohammad understood this when he first pivoted Softway toward a culture of love beginning in 2016. He moved out of his office and sat with his teammates on the front lines. He traveled to India and asked his employees' forgiveness for years of misbehavior. He wrote open, vulnerable emails that always ended with "I love you all!" He embodied the change he wanted to create.

But change isn't linear. Sometimes we leap forward, sometimes we stumble backward, and sometimes we just slip into old habits without realizing it. That's exactly what happened to Mohammad as Softway prepared to transform again in 2023 and 2024. Caught up in his own adaptive challenges with Mohsin, Mohammad forgot to consider how he was showing up to Softway—and he forgot to consider how he would change alongside his company as it undertook a massive reorganization. The ALF fellowship retreat reminded Mohammad of the kind of leader he wanted to be, and now, once again, he was all-in.

Now that he had experienced a profound personal change, Mohammad needed to turn that change outward. By creating an environment where everyone at the company could commune with each other, unburdened from the demands of their day-to-day work, Mohammad hoped to lead each team member through their own personal change journey. To do that, Mohammad decided that Softway would host a company-wide retreat in India.

Just like when we implemented the four-day workweek, we thought the idea would be a slam dunk. It wasn't. Some people were worried about the financial cost. Others worried about the idea of Softway effectively shutting down for a whole week. Still others worried that we wouldn't be able to pull it off. Did we realize how hard it was to coordinate a trip for almost a hundred people from half a world away?

We understood these concerns well enough—and we even shared some of them. The logistics *would* be tough. Even in a country as large as India, finding a venue in the wilderness that can house almost a hundred people is difficult.

But that was just a technical problem, one that we were able to sort out in due time. Lying underneath this technical problem, however, was the *real* question—the adaptive challenge everyone felt, but that no one could get their heads around: *why?* Why had we decided that a company-wide retreat was necessary to kick off our transformation effort?

Because meaningful experiences trigger meaningful change. Without creating an *unforgettable* experience for our team, our grand reorganization plan might never take hold.

Time to Worry?

It takes a lot of work to plan an international trip for nearly a hundred people. For the next several weeks, we were in near-constant contact with our counterparts in India to make sure everything would go off without a hitch.

But in all that planning, there's one thing we forgot—or, at least, one thing we hadn't been able to get to: the presentations and exercises we would use to introduce our teams to the planned change journey ahead.

And we weren't worried about it at all.

Well, *Mohammad* wasn't worried about it, anyway. The rest of us were terrified.

If Mohammad had a nickel for every "We haven't planned!" or "We don't have any content" he heard in the weeks leading up to our retreat, he'd probably have enough for about a quarter-tank of gas for the company van. But as we stressed over everything we didn't have, Mohammad focused on what we *did* have: trust.

Mohammad saw the strength of our relationships, our ability to lean into our discomfort, ask questions, and let the most qualified person lead in the moment. To him, that was the perfect environment for a high-performing team to work its magic. So what if we didn't have a plan? So what if we didn't have the content? We had a team who could figure it out.

Did it feel a little uncomfortable to throw caution to the wind of Hurricane Moh? Absolutely, but as the eye of this logistical hurricane, he was as tranquil as can be.

Mohammad wasn't being cruel. He just wanted to re-create the conditions that made the ALF fellowship retreat so successful. During that experience, Mohammad also wasn't given any information to plan with. All he knew was that he'd be in the wilderness by himself, and everything he needed would be provided. Mohammad believed we would increase our chances of success if we followed the same formula.

Don't tell him we said this (we can only hear "I told you so!" from him so many times), but almost immediately as we approached the date of the retreat, we saw time and again that he was right. In fact, had we given in to our silly little impulse to "plan" and "make content," we would have had to throw most of it away anyway.

Here's how it went down. Chris and Jeff arrived in India several days early to help coordinate the effort, while Mohammad was set to fly in the night before the retreat. (Frank skipped out on the retreat because he had a Disneyland vacation already planned with his family.) A day before the event, right as Mohammad was boarding his flight in Houston, we were hit with some surprising news: a statewide strike, or *bundh*, was set to start, and the strikers planned to block all lanes on major roads, making it near impossible for large buses to maneuver, let alone cars. By 6 a.m. the day our event was set to start, all roads would be shut down, leaving us with no means to get our very large group to the retreat site. We had to pivot.

We texted Moh on the plane as soon as we heard the news. "I told you so," he said. "Something unexpected was always going to happen."

"Yes, you did tell us so," Jeff sighed, rubbing his eyes. "So, what do you have in mind?"

Jeff waited for an answer. Then he looked back down at his phone. Mohammad had not responded to the text.

Now, we wouldn't put it past Hurricane Moh to not respond to us in a moment like this to get us to lean into our discomfort. But it was nothing so nefarious: Mohammad just had spotty in-flight Wi-Fi, as international flights often do. Miles away, somewhere over the vast ocean, Mohammad was now just as worried as the rest of us.

So, just as any calm, rational person would do when their Wi-Fi was spotty, Mohammad decided to text everyone and anyone he could think of: the resort, the bus company, his old economics professor at the University of Houston, anyone who could give him some information and insight about what was going on. "Why is nobody responding?" he groaned. Then, he paused, took a deep breath, and considered his situation. Here he was in a flying metal tube thousands of feet in the air, traveling over the ocean at five hundred miles an hour. This moment was a scientific miracle, and he was upset because he couldn't communicate through the clouds to his teammates?

We'll figure this out, Mohammad told himself. *We have good people on the ground. They don't need me.*

Maybe *need* is too strong a word, but Chris and Jeff certainly would have enjoyed his input. They were supposed to be using this time to finally set the agenda and produce the content. Instead, they were stuck with a four-alarm travel problem that threatened to end the trip before it even began. After all, how do you get a bunch of jet-lagged people to their hotel in the Indian wilderness when all the roads are closed?

Finally, about an hour later, Mohammad's Wi-Fi finally stabilized enough to chat over text with Chris and Jeff, who were crammed into a small situation room with the rest of the Indian leadership team. Once Mohammad was caught up on the situation, he issued his decision: "Okay, let's bus everyone to the site overnight."

Hurricane Moh struck again. And then he went off the grid again.

Right about the time Frank was whipping through the fake mines of Big Thunder Mountain Railroad, a still-warm churro in his hand, the rest of us went into full-on scramble mode. We called the resort to tell them we'd be arriving early. We called the bus company to get them to the office immediately, where a throng of weary travelers sat waiting for instructions. They thought they'd be staying in a hotel in Bengaluru for the night before disembarking, but then we called them all to the office at midnight without an explanation.

Then Hurricane Moh's texts started pouring in.

"Are we confirmed for the buses?"

"Will the hotel be charging extra?"

"Why isn't anybody answering me?"

Oops, did Jeff and Chris accidentally switch their phones to silent mode? Hard to say. They were too busy getting things done to notice.

When Mohammad landed in Bengaluru, everything was ready to go. So, we piled into our buses and set out for our destination:

a beautiful hotel in the jungles of India. We arrived at the hotel just before 6 a.m., beating the impending bundh by mere minutes. Or, we should say, we arrived *near* the hotel. The buses were too big for the narrow roads and sharp turns, so we had to go the final mile on foot, luggage in tow.

Everyone was on low rest, no one knew exactly what was happening, and nothing seemed to be running smoothly. And yet, as we looked around at the group, we were shocked at what we saw: nothing but laughter and smiles. And a few yawns—but they were happy yawns.

After another forty-five minutes or so, we reached the site, and everyone found their rooms and collapsed in their beds. Everyone, that is, except us. Time to plan activities, set the daily agendas, produce our teaching content, and sweat a thousand other small details. We learned as we went, constantly pivoting as the need arose. When an activity proved too difficult to implement, we scrapped it. When the weather looked like it might turn, we moved the planned activity indoors. When a giant centipede scurried across the room and sent Jeff squealing and leaping Michael Jordan–style across the room, we allowed ourselves a good ten-minute giggle break and then got back to work.

I Love It When a Plan Comes Together

How can a company of nearly a hundred people transform the stress of sudden change into excitement? Mohammad was certain he had the answer. The rest of us were about to find out if his theory of the game was sound. As we set about designing the retreat experience, we started with a few ground rules:

- ◆ No laptops or electronics. We needed to disconnect from the day-to-day of our work.
- ◆ Put experiential communication front and center through every exercise, session, and presentation, and tie those experiences to our change story through unique, focused experiences.
- ◆ Tie every session to one or more of our six principles of change: embrace discomfort, prioritize relationships, practice empathetic curiosity, experiment, wield your influence, and be effective.

Just as Mohammad predicted, it all came together. Over the course of the retreat, we led our teams through a variety of fun-but-uncomfortable experiences.

Of all the experiences we designed, one of the most uncomfortable was right there in our baseline rules: no phones, no laptops, no work, no agenda, no *busyness*. The way we see it, busyness is the new comfort—and we wanted to pluck them completely out of their comfort zone. For many, it was the first time they had been away from all the normal trappings of their lives—their calendars, their devices, their homes, their families—for *years* (if not ever). Only two laptops came with us on the entire trip, and Mohammad ruled over them with lock and key.

Out in nature, away from the hustle and bustle of our lives, we used nature to ground ourselves. This played a significant role in getting everyone to open their hearts and minds and to consider themselves and each other in new ways. We meditated both in the morning and in the evening, listening to the sounds of nature, feeling the breeze on our faces, hearing the birds calling to each other in the canopy above. Each was a sacred experience, and each was totally lost on us in the course of our daily lives. Eventually, what at first seemed uncomfortable became rejuvenating and refreshing. As our bodies matched the rhythms of the world around us, we became okay with not knowing what was happening at work, what was happening at home, or what would happen next on the agenda. We became comfortable with uncertainty.

And then, just as everyone was starting to feel really good, we decided to climb a nearby mountain. A decently large one, too—about 7,500 feet above sea level. And absolutely no metaphors were derived from the experience.

We had no idea how to climb a mountain. We had no idea what the terrain would be like. We had no idea how long it would take us to summit and come back down. And we had no idea why the weather refused to cooperate with us. Didn't it know we were trying to create a transformational experience?

As we trudged up the muddy terrain, the skies opened up, the wind howled in our ears, and the clouds threatened to swallow us entirely. The rain didn't fall so much as surround us, making it difficult to see more than five feet ahead. At any minute, we felt like we might fall. And yet we soldiered on—in the most uncomfortable experience we could have planned.

The clouds parted just as we summited, the weather finally wising up to the symbolism of our transformational journey. As we stood atop the mountain, a group of eighty-plus drenched and dazed non-hikers, we heard a mix of gasps and sobs.

"I never expected this."

"I never knew I could climb a mountain."

"I was sure this was impossible."

But it wasn't. We had done it. We had conquered the mountain—both metaphorically and in reality. And that victory unlocked something in us. Suddenly, we understood. We understood what it meant to embrace discomfort. We understood what it meant to prioritize relationships—to trust, support, and encourage each other. We understood what it meant to be interwoven and unbroken. (Hey, that has a nice ring to it . . .)

This was worth it.

Too much happened on this trip to include in this book. We blindfolded people and marched them through the woods. We trekked for hours in silence to an abandoned temple overtaken by monkeys—just crazy monkeys everywhere. We heard and saw animals we'd only ever glimpsed in nature shows. Everywhere was beauty. Everything was a lesson.

Through each unscripted experience, we changed—as people, as teammates, as an organization. We now had an unbroken bond, a common language. From that day forward, we knew without question what we were capable of, not just as individuals, but as a team. If we could endure this together, we could endure *anything*.

As the saying goes, sometimes you have to slow down to speed up. Had we focused merely on transmitting knowledge, we could have gone through the entire change conversation during a one-hour all-hands call. It certainly would have been the cheaper way to communicate change. But this experience wasn't about knowledge. It was about *understanding*. It was about creating a culture of change readiness by leading with love. It was about taking the time to do things right so we wouldn't have to go through all this again several months later.

But here's the thing: the retreat was only the *beginning* of our organizational change journey. We didn't immediately leap into new roles and a new structure when we got back to work the next week. Instead, we spent the next few months having the important conversations necessary to ensure everyone was bought into our change program and ready to do their part—which often meant working in a new role and context. These were honest, vulnerable conversations intended to create dialogue and understanding—and as you saw from the stories of Saif, Greg, and Saquib, we didn't always get them right. However, by giving ourselves the time and space to have these conversations, we never felt rushed either. From September 2023 to May/June 2024, this was the work—and it was the most important work we could do.

This is what Love as a Change Strategy looks like in action—not a sprint, but a marathon. Ultimately, it isn't about reaching the finish line in record time. It's about the experience and accomplishment itself. It's about being effective.

So, What Did We Learn Here?

You could interpret this story in different ways. One interpretation would be that we procrastinated all our planning until the very last minute and got lucky. For everyone not named Mohammad, it sure felt that way. But Mohammad knew we were up for the challenge, he knew we had the knowledge and the talent, and he knew we were ready to pivot—like all change-ready teams need to be. Here are a few things we learned from the experience.

SUCCESS DOESN'T COME FROM PLANNING

Change-ready teams don't need to preplan everything. They don't throw everything to the wind, either. The sweet spot is somewhere in the middle. Sweat the important details, set what you have to set, and let the six principles of change guide the rest. Even if we didn't know exactly what all our exercises would look like, we knew their feel and shape, because we knew our vision for our reorg and how these principles factored in.

As we reviewed employee feedback on the retreat, we saw note after note praising how well planned the event was. They were shocked to find out we had never even aligned, practiced, or known how everything would flow together. Even during events, we often pivoted, added, created, and cut entire elements.

In that way, we were learning as we went—just as we would again once our reorg was officially underway. We embraced the power that change can bring, and we let that power guide our next moves. By experimenting live and showing our willingness to embrace discomfort and uncertainty, we helped move our teams further toward change readiness.

PRIORITIZE EXPERIENCES

Experiences inform learning and belief, not preparation. As thought leader Steven R. Covey famously said, "Begin with the end in mind." Even if we didn't know all the details, we did know what kind of experience we wanted to create.

We built everything with this experience in mind. It was like having a preset framework that enabled us to quickly plan, iterate, and revise in the moment. Sometimes it might have been nice to have more certainty and lead time, but we could work confidently knowing that as long as we worked toward the target experience, we'd never stray too far.

Plus, we also had a secret weapon: we knew how each other worked and how we complemented each other, and we trusted everyone to play their part. We're kind of like a heist team, except instead of robbing the Bellagio, we lead change with love. Mohammad is the visionary, laying out the broad strokes of the scheme and turning the rest of us loose to figure out the details. Chris is the mouthpiece, the public front. He can see a slide deck for the first time and immediately speak smoothly and intelligently about whatever's on the screen as if he's rehearsed the presentation a dozen times. Jeff is the right-hand, rule-creating man, focused on logistics and execution—all with a healthy dose of empathy. Frank is the wildcard—a left-handed, throw-out-the-rules, and punch-through-the-box kind of guy, bringing levity and humor to get to the most creative, emotional outcomes.

THE INVESTMENT IS WORTH IT

No phones or laptops. No business as usual for an entire week. A big expense we hadn't budgeted for (which was spent wisely and was worth every penny). The more details we unveiled about our plans, the more resistance we encountered—from project managers to the sales and accounting teams.

Better to flush out that resistance early than have it poison your change operation. Better to spend on your people early and often so you can put your money where your mouth is.

Most organizations don't give up revenue or actively invest in their workforce, much less take them on a week-long retreat for change readiness. Any "logical" business leader would say, "We don't have the time or resources for this."

We're not just any business. And we dare you to embrace the discomfort and join us. Embrace the discomfort of running a retreat without planning all the details. Embrace the discomfort of foregoing revenue for a week. Embrace the discomfort of being led blindfolded by a coworker through the jungle. Every time you do, that's one more investment in yourself, in your team, in your organization. That's how you create change readiness at a large scale.

And remember: it all starts with a vision—and a commitment to create meaningful experiences. That vision doesn't mean you have to travel to the Indian wilderness. But that vision shouldn't be delivered in email form. Get out there. Get outside the box. Create the experiences that will bring the six principles of change to life. The outcome could literally save your organization, transforming it from an organization with a leader to an organization with a culture of leadership.

If you can achieve that, we can tell you right now that the cost in time, revenue, or expenses will be more than worth it. Invest in your people up front, and the rewards will more than follow.

The Team Transformation Planner

If you don't have much experience creating experiences, we've got your back: the Team Transformation Planner. This interactive toolkit will help guide you through the process of designing meaningful experiences—including how to build them, and, most importantly, how to set your *why*.

For more information, visit LoveAsAStrategy.com.

Change Yourself, Change Your Organization, Change the World

Any hardship—whether it's personal or professional—is an opportunity to change for the better. With a growth-focused mindset and an embrace of love and humanity, you will come out the other side stronger.

This is the lesson Mohammad learned with his son, Mohsin, teaching him what it truly means to allow yourself to be transformed and inspiring him to facilitate that experience for others so they can undergo their own transformation. In that way, an individual transformation became the trigger for a much larger organizational transformation.

As we've changed, so has our relationship with our clients. We've always been invested in our clients' success, but now we understand more clearly than ever that we are not just selling a product or service to increase revenue. We are helping others to thrive and overcome any hardship they may face. When we lead with empathy, we share empathy. When we share empathy, others receive it and retransmit it.

By embracing our humanity and putting ourselves at the center of any change we want to see, we rehumanize ourselves, we rehumanize our work, we rehumanize those who benefit from our work, and, as we'll see in Chapter 12, we rehumanize the world.

Team Change

- ◆ Think back to a moment of personal transformation in your life. What sparked that change, and how did it ripple outward into your relationships or work?
- ◆ Mohammad realized that meaningful change requires meaningful experiences. How often do you or your team rely on experience rather than instruction to spark transformation?
- ◆ Have you ever tried to lead change while staying the same yourself? What was the result—and what would you do differently in hindsight?

(continued)

- ◆ What does being all-in look like for you when it comes to supporting organizational change?
- ◆ How does your team respond when things don't go as planned? What behaviors emerge in moments of chaos— and what do they reveal about your culture?
- ◆ What kind of experiences would you design for your team if time and budget weren't constraints? What's holding you back from doing a version of that now?
- ◆ What adaptive challenges are you or your team currently facing? How might intentionally embracing discomfort help you navigate these challenges?
- ◆ What were some of your biggest takeaways or ah-ha moments from this chapter?
- ◆ Share a moment of self-awareness about your leadership after reading this chapter.
- ◆ What, if anything, will you change or adjust about how you lead or behave based on what you've read?

CHAPTER 12

Organizational Change, Global Impact

"I don't understand. This is a joke, right? There's no way this is the real presentation."

Frank and Chris looked at each other. Then they looked back at Mohammad.

"Um . . . no joke. This *is* the real presentation," Frank said meekly. Chris nodded in approval.

Remember in Chapter 7 how we said you never want to disappoint an Anwar? Well, Frank and Chris had just done it—and at the worst possible moment.

Mohammad let out a sigh, rubbed his eyes, and looked at his watch. 1 a.m. In just seven hours, they were set to deliver a keynote to the entire company during a big off-site event designed to cap off Softway's week-long reorg rollout in India. And the presentation was hot garbage wrapped in gym socks.

That was not the reaction Frank and Chris expected. In their minds, this keynote was proof that they'd attained full enlightenment, ascending from the mortal plane to commune with the gods. Such achievement deserved a slow clap at minimum, if not an immediate raise.

Instead, all they got were the tired, crestfallen expressions on Mohammad and Jeff's faces.

Caught flat-footed, Frank began to rattle off all the reasons why their keynote was pitch-perfect.

"It's got humor, amazing success stories, and even some plot twists! *So* many plot twists."

"You won't really get it until you hear it for the first time."

"Come on, that dance number in the middle is going to change lives! Chris and I have been practicing for weeks."

With each new statement, Frank sounded less like he believed what he was saying and more like he was trying to spin a disaster into a heroic feat. But Moh and Jeff weren't buying it.

"I'm sorry, guys, but there's no way we can use this as it's currently written," Mohammad said. "The past few days have been incredible and need to be celebrated. This isn't incredible and it should not be celebrated."

Oh, well. Honesty over harmony, right?

Now, to be fair to Frank and Chris, it wasn't that they had slacked off or otherwise put off the work. In fact, they'd spent the past month crafting a presentation they had sincerely been proud of.

But they weren't sharing any of their work. Every time Mohammad or Jeff had asked to see the presentation, Frank and Chris were evasive. Frank kept mumbling something about "synergy." Chris said it was going to be a big surprise.

Finally, about 1 a.m.—the morning Frank and Chris were set to deliver the presentation—Mohammad managed to wrestle Chris's laptop away and get a look. What he saw was both garish and confusing. Whole slides were dedicated to famous billionaires—Steve Jobs, Colonel Sanders, the guy who invented Bose speakers, and, of course, Beyoncé. Flanking these ultra-stylized slides were lofty expressions like "overcoming adversity" and "failing without fear."

It all looked pretty slick, but it all felt pretty soulless. Where was *Softway* in all this? What about all of the work we'd done over the past few days? What about our goals? What about the future of the company? What about love?

Must've slipped their minds.

Chris and Frank thought they had a good idea, but they didn't ask anyone to gut check them. As a result, they'd taken the keynote in the wrong direction. If this week had taught us anything, we weren't on the verge of the biggest change in the company's history because of the Colonel's secret recipe. We were on the verge of change because of *our* secret recipe.

That was the story we needed to tell. And there was still time to do it—about six hours, to be exact.

So, how did the new keynote go? Were we able to pull off a miracle in those six short hours? We'll get there. But to understand the ultimate impact of that moment, let's back up a bit so we can tell you the full story in context.

As shared in Chapter 11, in October 2023, Softway led a company-wide retreat for our Indian team, where we embraced discomfort, prioritized relationships, and focused on building a culture of change readiness within the organization. For the next few months, we engaged in important conversations with individual team members to ensure Softway was ready to make the next leap and hit the start button on our planned reorganization (see Part II). This work culminated in another trip to India in February 2024, this one focused on finally kicking off the reorg with a bang.

In true Softway fashion, we wanted to create an experience out of the rollout—to inspire, to connect this plan with our larger organizational vision, and to align each individual with their potential to impact the world through their work. As we saw it, the only way to accomplish that was through something big—something so big, in fact, that it would take an entire week to get through.

Here's a day-by-day recap of the experience, showcasing how we brought all our hard-learned lessons and six principles of change together to create an unforgettable rollout.

Sunday: T-Minus Four Days to Off-Site

We approached each day of this weeklong experience as a different stage of the emotional journey we wanted to guide our team members through. Day 0 was our "soft landing" day, where the only goal was to get the good vibes flowing.

Many in the organization were still en route to Bengaluru. In fact, the travel itself was part of the experience. All flights, all bus or cab fare, were all carefully planned and paid for to make sure (1) everyone was able to attend, and (b) no one had to stress out over the logistics of their trip. Everyone arrived in Bengaluru on time, comfortable, and well-fed.

And when we say well-fed, we mean well-fed. Sunday morning, for everyone who had already arrived, all the Indian and visiting US leaders cooked and served everybody an East-meets-West breakfast, replete with uppam, pancakes, and other tasty dishes. For many new folks, this was the first time they'd seen senior leadership—in this or any company—actually roll up their sleeves and make their teams a meal. For those more tenured folks, it was a comforting reminder and a sign that we were getting back to the heart of what mattered most: taking care of our people.

For the rest of the day, the objective was simple: rest, relax, connect, and set the foundation for the rest of the week. An all-company dinner capped off the night, and then it was off to bed so we could all greet the next day with fresh eyes.

Well, off to bed for everybody except the leadership team. That night, we got together for the first of our nightly alignment and recap conversations. This was our chance to debrief and pivot, if need be. What were we hearing? What were we feeling? What issues were coming up? Nothing much came out of this conversation on Sunday, since we hadn't launched anything yet, but this nightly routine became an essential check-in tool throughout the week.

At the end of our debrief, Mohammad looked at Frank and Chris. "How's Thursday's keynote coming along? Are you ready for feedback?"

Frank and Chris smiled at each other. "You'll see," Frank said.

But behind the knowing grins, Chris was feeling . . . not contentious, but let's say unresolved. In the weeks leading up to the event, he had felt unaligned in terms of what the event would look like and how everything would unfold. Without knowing the full arc of the week, Chris had felt like he and Frank were aiming at a moving target when designing their keynote.

To combat that worry, and because they still weren't entirely sure how things were going to play out, he and Frank decided to play it safe and stick to the broad strokes of the emotional journey: And the best way to do that, they decided, was to put on one great big spectacle.

It's easy to see why this idea wouldn't have worked in hindsight. But at the time, given the context and their own progression on the change journey, it made total sense.

Monday: T-Minus Three Days to Off-Site

With the mood good and our bellies full after Day 0, we then proceeded to the next stage of the emotional journey: establishing the problems facing our company and building alignment on our case for change.

For the first several hours, we recapped everything we had discussed during the culture retreat, which nearly the entire organization had attended (but not Frank, who, lest we forget, was at Disneyland). Not only did this remind everyone of the good vibes from a few months ago, but it also served as a primer for what we'd be asking of everyone this week. We wanted to emerge from this rollout united and excited, and to do that, we would need to draw on everything we had learned about transformational growth, conflict, and discomfort.

In the afternoon, we hosted breakout sessions with existing managers, outgoing managers, incoming managers, and individual contributors who had been with the organization for ten years or more. Especially for those who would no longer be in leadership roles, we wanted to start this group on their change journey early so they could be strong advocates later in the week, when the rest of the organization learned their new roles.

During these sessions, we had an initial conversation about what our reorg would look like, and what the roles and responsibilities would entail for them as managers. More important, we stressed our appreciation for them and made every effort to honor them for their work. The reorg wasn't about people performing poorly and needing to be replaced. It was about acknowledging that we needed to change in order to grow, and for most of us, that meant sitting in a different seat than the one we had been accustomed to. Throughout these meetings and the dinner that followed, we were careful to make sure that our communication and messaging didn't all come from the same leader, but rather from the leader who had the strongest relationships to a particular group. Mohammad led one discussion, Greg led another, Chris led another, and so on.

That night, during the debrief, Mohammad asked again, "Can I see that keynote presentation? I'd hate to have us pull another all-nighter on Wednesday."

"Almost ready," Chris said, with just a hint of uncertainty in his voice.

Tuesday: T-Minus Two Days to Off-Site

Next up on our emotional journey: embracing change. If our teams could understand the core problem we set out to solve, they would appreciate the thought process that went into our decisions so that, by the time we revealed our new org chart, everyone had context for and clarity about those decisions.

In the morning session, we began with the problem statement and worked backward. In truth, we faced many challenges:

- An extremely flat org structure
- Scarce opportunities for individual growth, development, and career progression
- Gaps and ambiguities in leadership, authority, and accountability
- Transactional collaborations, rather than relational or strategic ones

Our core problem, however, centered on the ineffective division of labor between our American and Indian teams, which had led to friction, siloing, and organization-wide inefficiencies. We explained how these ineffective systems had all arisen from Mohammad's unexamined beliefs about the Indian team, even though they made little sense on paper, and we apologized for creating and perpetuating what had essentially become a two-tiered system within the company. Our reorganization would break those silos, destroy old power dynamics, and create stronger, more integrated teams.

Next, we presented a clear case for our planned change and explained why a full reorganization was the best way to meet our goals. We started by considering the cost of *not* changing. What beliefs about our team, clients, geography, and other factors were we holding on to, and how were those beliefs holding us back? What opportunities became available if we embraced this organizational change? Through questions like these, we encouraged everybody to think about their own mindsets, attitudes, and beliefs and how they might affect their response to the change journey ahead.

Then, we highlighted the ten goals we believed our reorg would help us achieve. (What can we say? We're ambitious.) As we demonstrated, each goal was tied to a specific set of metrics that integrated into our new de-siloed organizational structure.

Eventually, the conversation led to the obvious question: how did this change affect everyone's jobs? We led with the good news: nobody was losing their job or seeing a pay reduction. This reorganization was about helping Softway realize its growth and revenue potential, not about cleaning house or getting greedy.

To underscore that point, we rolled out the reorganization in three stages. First, we unveiled the new org chart itself, without any names attached to the new positions. Then, after lunch, we went a layer deeper, breaking down the org structure department by department. Through these conversations, teams began to understand what we were trying to accomplish in terms of our three-year, five-year, and ten-year goals, and they began to sense what role they might play within the new structure.

Through these efforts, we hoped to bring everyone along the same change journey that Jeff had brought us on nearly a year before, when he levitated above the conference room table. That day, we accepted as truth that if we wanted to grow as an organization, we couldn't make the reorg about what positions we wanted for ourselves or believed we were entitled to, but what positions benefited the company the most. For this reorg, we explained, we wanted to design an org structure without specific people in mind, figure out what we needed in terms of skill sets and capabilities, and then come back and map names to those roles.

Finally, with our case for change and approach to the reorg clearly established, we revealed who would occupy each newly created role. Then we held our breath and waited for the response.

And then we heard it. Applause. Cheers. Laughter. Congratulations. With each new name we announced, the room celebrated and embraced the person and their new role, thrilled for them and the opportunities they would have in the company.

A sensitive discussion like this could have been a disaster. But we'd learned from our past mistakes, and, for our company-wide rollout, we put in a lot of work to empathize with the experience of learning of a role change—even if that change appeared relatively small. How would it feel to see your name in a different spot in front of your peers? What context and assurances would you want to have? How could we communicate these changes so they were seen as a way to accelerate a person's career goals? Everything we didn't do well for Saquib, we vowed to do well for the rest of the team to guide them through the experience and help make it, dare we say it, *fun*.

Once we had thoroughly discussed the details of our reorganization, we hosted an all-company dinner and town hall, opening up the floor to anyone who wanted to ask questions. We wanted the organization's full commitment to our reorg, no matter how uncomfortable it was to get here. So, we promised we wouldn't leave until everyone in the room had a chance to speak their mind, ask questions, challenge a decision, and so on. Some difficult topics came up, and we lived up to our word to walk through them one by one.

For any team members hesitant to ask questions in an open forum, we also offered an anonymous survey, with a promise to share the results and answer questions the following night at our follow-up next town hall/dinner. We promised that anybody who left their name would have the opportunity for a face-to-face conversation the following day to ensure they felt seen and heard.

That night, during our alignment debrief, we began to review the submissions and requests for one-on-ones from our team members, which, to our relief, were far fewer than we had anticipated. But, by getting a sense of this feedback as a whole, we were able to align as a team to pivot, adjust, and refine our approach for the next day.

Mohammad gave Frank and Chris a pass on the keynote that night after we'd reviewed all the questions and requests for one-on-one time.

"We'll talk about that presentation tomorrow," he said. "Be ready."

"Oh, we will," Frank said (un)knowingly.

Wednesday: T-Minus One Day to Off-Site

Whew. Step 3 of the emotional journey was a big one. For Step 4, we wanted to take the pressure off and allow our newly assigned teams time to meet, engage, and build relationships.

We kept Wednesday extremely flexible, expecting a deluge of one-on-ones and private question-and-answer sessions with team members who were either struggling or needed some specific context. The deluge didn't come (yay!), so we had plenty of time to meet with everyone who wanted to meet, connect with them, and purposefully spend time to answer questions and address anything they were struggling with. Some genuine concerns were raised, but many of our conversations focused on answering small questions and discussing team members' potential for growth in the company.

That evening, we had our second of two town hall dinners. Once again, we opened the floor to everyone who wanted to share their thoughts. We also shared the results from the anonymous submissions we received so we could address them publicly. This wasn't to embarrass or shame anyone, but to embrace discomfort and talk about these concerns openly. As we saw it, if one person had the question, then others likely did as well.

During this discussion, we stressed the idea that change wasn't linear. Even though we'd given a great deal of consideration to the reorg and the rollout, not everything was set in stone. Things would continue to change as we learned more. (And in the months that followed, that's exactly what happened.)

Finally, to wrap up the evening, we conducted a poll with a single question: are you committed to this change? While we wanted the organization's full commitment, we wanted to *earn* that commitment, so we encouraged everyone to respond honestly. We tallied up the votes, and then revealed the results.

Eighty-seven responded yes. Only two said no.

We couldn't believe it. We were expecting, at best, to get about a 60 percent positive response. We got 98 percent. We'd always been confident in our plan, but we hadn't expected such near-unanimous buy-in.

Throughout this book, we've described the impact of Mohammad's belief that the Indian members of Softway couldn't serve in customer-facing roles or have the same access to leadership opportunities. This belief was shared and retransmitted by many within the organization—American and Indian team members alike. In the weeks leading up to our rollout event, many of Softway's Indian team members learned of some of our planned changes and had expressed a range of concerns. Some believed the effort was too little, too late. Others shared in the belief that they shouldn't hold certain roles and resisted the idea of change. We were prepared for this resistance to continue and to continue working through our team members' discomfort. But, as the results showed, that work would be unnecessary. Our rollout had been a success.

Unfortunately, the high of that success was short-lived. Later that night, Frank and Chris were finally forced to share their big keynote, the one kicking off the off-site, with Mohammad and Jeff. As you know, it was a disaster. We had to capitalize on all this goodwill and wrap up this experience with a bang. The question was, how?

We weren't sure, but over the next few hours, we worked to make it happen. Then, after a brief nap, we were ready to unveil keynote 2.0 to the world.

Thursday: The Off-Site

Finally, the big day. Despite not having our keynote presentation dialed in until just a few hours before, this off-site at a fancy five-star hotel was otherwise locked and loaded. For several weeks, Chris had worked with different teams to produce swag kits with fabric swatches, candy, t-shirts, and even a short book describing our vision.

Once everyone had filed into the beautifully ordained conference hall, it was finally time for the moment everyone had been waiting for: our keynote.

Chris and Frank walked out onto the stage, sans any fancy light-show or pyrotechnics. They looked at each other, smiled, and dove in.

"Usually at big keynotes like this, speakers try to wow you with quotes and stories from Steve Jobs, or Colonel Sanders, or Beyoncé," Frank said. He looked out across the hall to see Mohammad and Jeff bury their faces in their hands. He winked. *You were right, guys,* he wanted say. *We get it now.*

Chris continued Frank's thought. "But what do these billionaires have to do with *our* change, *our* opportunity? Nothing at all. Today, we thought we'd do something a little different. We thought we'd talk about *our* stories and experiences."

Oh, if only everybody knew how much work it had taken to arrive at such an obvious conclusion. This was how the presentation always should have been—the only way it ever *could* have been.

Frank and Chris began by sharing the big challenge of capturing the reorg in a simple, memorable internal transformation brand. We knew our reason for change: de-siloing the American and Indian areas of our business so we could move forward as one. But that phrasing didn't exactly roll off the tongue.

As a company of both American and Indian origin, Softway was a melting pot of backgrounds, skill sets, and cultures. This diversity made us strong, resilient, and capable of handling any change that came our way. And yet, we hadn't behaved that way for most of our existence. Moving forward, we wanted to create a Softway that reflected our commitment to people-first change at an organizational level—a Softway that was aligned and unified, like a tapestry.

After a little more work, Frank and Chris explained, we arrived at a perfect transformation brand that summed up our reorganization effort: interwoven and unbroken.

Or, as Chris said to the crowd: "interbroken and unwoven."

Perfect.

We were so excited by our new transformation brand and what it meant for our future. We'd discussed it for hours. We'd made a cool paisley/plaid design that blended both Indian and American cultures. We had loads of internal swag with that design ready to go.

But, when the big moment came to announce it, Chris flubbed the delivery.

Standing across the stage, Frank could feel a laugh forming in his throat and bit down hard on his lower lip. Somewhere in the back, Moh and Jeff fell over themselves, gasping for air. Finally—*finally!*—we had something we could use to make fun of Chris forever.

Of course, Chris, being the consummate professional that he is, rolled with the flub as if it never happened. Just as he had messed up our transformation brand, we as a company had missed opportunity after opportunity to come together. It wasn't that we were a *bad* company, he explained, but some aspects of our organization were broken. How could we take those broken elements and remake them as unbroken? How could we take what was unwoven and make it interwoven?

As he explained, an interwoven company meant a globally integrated structure for growth from both organizational and personal perspectives. It also included operational visibility, empowerment across disciplines and roles, and the deployment of power sharing to stop silos.

An unbroken organization practiced real, interpersonal connection and trust. Within the workplace, we would exhibit honesty, a willingness to work through conflict, an openness to knowledge sharing, an inclination toward strategic collaboration, and an alignment of goals. Communication should happen within and outside the hierarchy, eliminating the limitations of hierarchy.

Through this transformation, we would lead change with love and usher in a new era for Softway—an era where we expanded our mission to bring humanity back to the workplace and focused on *impact.*

If you're like us, you and your organization likely don't stop to consider its impact on others' lives. It's hard to. No one can be involved in every single project, every single decision, every single outcome. As a result, most of us only have an inkling of the true impact we've helped create.

"The impact you have is *everything,*" Frank said. "So, now that we are moving forward as one company—interwoven and unbroken—we wanted to share with you all the ways that you're creating impact through your work that you probably never stopped to consider."

And so, we shared a few of our favorite stories showing the impact our team at Softway was having on the world.

- ◆ We shared the story of BioBridge, a company that supplies blood and tissue to hospitals. Despite hating the title of *Love as a Business Strategy*, they used the principles within that book to transform their culture—and in so doing, optimize its services, significantly reduce attrition, improve cash flow, and scale its operation to save countless more lives across the world.
- ◆ We shared the story of Houston Methodist, a leading hospital that houses the DeBakey Heart and Vascular Center—one of the premier heart facilities in the world. Working alongside Siemens, a large technology conglomerate, we helped develop an artificial intelligence–driven process to scan human hearts and determine which corrective device a patient would need *before* surgery. Through this work, the doctors at Houston Methodist have been able to reduce the time on the table for their patients—improving success rates, accelerating recovery, and enabling hospitals to increase the number of surgeries they could perform per day.

◆ We shared the story of Guyana Enterprise. After the South American country discovered vast oil and gas deposits within its borders, a consortium of businesses, including the Guyanese government, partnered with us to (1) rewrite operational rules for how government and private enterprises worked together, (2) develop a messaging and behavioral framework to guide all decision-making and team building related to their oil and gas resources, and (3) take meaningful steps to improve the nation's economy while also protecting its biodiversity. This effort has helped bring an extra dimension of security and confidence among Guyana's small population as they work to usher their nation into a new era of economic prosperity. As a result of our work, and at the time of this writing, Mohammad sits on the steering committee for Guyana Enterprise.

◆ We shared the story of a major HVAC manufacturer on a mission to promote more energy-efficient solutions to reduce environmental impact and promote sustainability. Through our partnership, we have helped this manufacturer reduce its carbon output by 246,000 tons and reduce energy use in homes and businesses by 30–40 percent—resulting in a 30 percent net drop in carbon emissions for the entire continent of North America.

As we moved through these examples, the members of our organization sat in wonder at everything they had helped accomplish. For many, it was the first time they really understood that, with just a few keystrokes in Houston or Bengaluru, they had the power to contribute to something far beyond their lives, their needs, and their dreams.

"*This* is what you're a part of," Chris said as the presentation wound down. "*This* is how you're changing the world. Thank you all for what you do every single day."

Cheers erupted from the audience. Smiles, tears, pride, and delight. Not clapping for Chris or Frank on stage, but for *us*. One team. Interbroken and unwoven.

And then, we launched into a big song-and-dance number, complete with top hats, canes, and a chorus line of dancers. Mohammad tried to rush the stage to stop it, but Jeff put a hand on his shoulder. "Let them have this one, Moh. Let them have this one."

Man, wouldn't that ending have been something? Like something out of a movie.

For the rest of the trip, we let the good times roll. Later that afternoon, we held a surprisingly emotional panel, where we got very real and addressed some long-standing hurt in the company. There were many hugs and many tears, but we'll save that story for another time.

Then, that evening, we had the alumni meetup, where veterans of Softway from as far back as twenty years showed up to rub elbows and share old stories. This event brought together many alumni who had departed during the reign of Moh 1.0 before he had discovered Love as a Strategy. Their presence stood as a testament to the effort Softway—and specifically Mohammad—had put in to make amends in the years that followed. The next two days were reserved for more team building, where our only agenda was to hang out, enjoy each other's company, and celebrate.

Throughout these final two days, we kept hearing how shocked everyone was at the level of care that had gone into the week. As one team member shared with Frank, "How could I *not* get on board with this when all my concerns were heard before I even shared them?"

And then, it was over. We had pulled it off. Not only had we set the path, but our people actually wanted to follow us down it. Where, a year earlier, even we as a leadership team were unsure of what we were about to embark on, now we were walking that path *together*.

Do Something That Matters

Here's the last part of the failed keynote story we've been holding back. Even after Frank and Chris realized they hadn't understood the assignment, even after we realized we only had about six hours to make things right, even after we realized we had no presentation at all, we knew we still had each other. And we'd been in way stickier situations. Before diving into the hard work of pulling a miracle presentation out of thin air, Mohammad asked if we could clear the air first.

"Guys, I need to talk about how this experience made me feel," Mohammad said. "I feel like you intentionally hid this from me."

"We did," Chris acknowledged.

"I'm sorry, Moh," Frank said. "We thought we had something good and we wanted to dazzle and surprise you with it."

"Thank you. That's all I needed to hear," Mohammad said.

"Are we all good?" Jeff asked, ready to get to work.

Everyone nodded, and we dove in. Together this time.

All the hustle and bustle fell away, and it was just us—bouncing ideas, hitting that stride, enjoying the heck out of the moment. All that mattered was our ability to do it together, to rely on each other, interwoven and unbroken, and united by love.

What a feeling.

You can have that feeling, too.

You might not realize it, but small things have large impacts. Mohammad had a revelation about his relationship with his son, which led him to reevaluate his relationship with his people, which led him to reevaluate his relationship with his company and his contribution to the world—his own personal Love as a Change Strategy.

Little moments save lives. By changing our behaviors and committing ourselves to being the change we want to see, we can change how the world works. Elections matter. Social movements matter. But in our experience, what matters most is how we show up to the world and what we put into it. By bringing humanity back to the workplace, we can change the hearts and minds of those around us, who will in turn change the hearts and minds of their leaders, of their clients, of their families.

Yes, you can still make a profit—a very nice profit. You can even increase that profit—all while doing right by your people and the planet.

And if none of these lofty goals come to fruition? If Love as a Change Strategy never delivers the returns you were looking for? It's still worth it. At the very least, you'll have created a better place for yourself and your coworkers, a place where people are given opportunities, feel rejuvenated, work with purpose, and feel a sense of trust.

It may not sound like much on the face of it. But to us, it's *everything*.

But if this is the change you want to create, you have to do it. You can't just sit on the sidelines, read a book about love, and wish for things to be different. Change starts with you—and getting there won't be easy.

Love as a Change Strategy Works

Impact matters. We can think of no greater honor in this world than helping others help others. Our Impact Storytelling Guide offers a framework for collecting and sharing organizational impact stories internally and externally.

For more information, visit LoveAsAStrategy.com.

Organizational Change, Global Impact

- ◆ How easy can your team identify the impact their work has on society?
- ◆ How might your organization better articulate its impact on society, both locally and globally? What stories of impact might you be overlooking?
- ◆ Tell a story of impact to the group—what are those moments of impact from your team or organization that you don't often share with others?
- ◆ When planning organizational change, how can leaders balance the need for decisive action with making space for everyone's voice to be heard?
- ◆ How can organizations better trace the line from individual contributions to broader impacts, making those connections visible to everyone?
- ◆ What were some of your biggest takeaways or ah-ha moments from this chapter?
- ◆ Share a moment of self-awareness about your leadership after reading this chapter.
- ◆ What, if anything, will you change or adjust about how you lead or behave based on what you've read?

CHAPTER 13

Choose Your Hard

Some say when faced with a choice, there's an easy way and a hard way. But that's not true. There's no shortcut to success. No silver bullet. No "easy" button.

There's only the hard way.

Saving money is hard, but so is being broke.

Working on your marriage is hard, but so is being in a bad marriage.

Learning a new language is hard, but so is mastering your first language.

Love is hard, but so is hate.

Making decisions is hard, but so is indecision.

Change is hard, but not changing is harder.

You get the idea. No matter what your situation, the path before you is hard. But here's the good news: you get to choose your hard. You can choose to be like the herd of cattle and run away from the hard, or you can choose to be like the herd of buffalo and run headfirst into it.

There are two paths you can take: the path of comfort and the path of the hard.

But here's the thing about choosing comfort: you're only setting yourself up for a bigger challenge down the road. Choosing comfort in the moment has consequences, stretching out into our futures until eventually we're called to pay a price—with interest.

The problem is, we rarely notice that the futures we create are the consequences of the choices we *didn't* make. We don't stop to think about the role we played in keeping that bad employee around and the loss in relationships and effectiveness our organization suffered as a result. We don't stop to think about how we need three meetings to make one decision because no one is addressing the elephant in the room. We don't recall when someone closer to the problem sounded the alarm, and we dismissed the issue for lack of data, composure, or status, which is a stall tactic in the face of elephants. But just because we don't notice them, these connections are here all the same.

Whether you embrace discomfort or flee toward comfort, you're going to face challenges either way. Things are still going to be hard.

So we say choose your hard. We say run right into the storm. Get messy. Get muddy. Get through it.

To understand why, let's travel through space and time to a world of alternate universes where Jeff, Frank, Chris, and Mohammad chose comfort instead of choosing their hard so we can see the consequences that followed.

Jeff Ignores the Elephant in the Room

Jeff had a choice. He could have chosen his hard, levitated above the table, and called the elephant out in the room, or he could have chosen not to let his discomfort guide any of his decisions and kept it all to himself.

We asked Jeff what might have happened if he had chosen the latter. First, he said, "Well, I'd probably still be in a leadership position, which might be nice." Then, he stopped making jokes, chose his hard, and answered the question.

First, the leadership team continued on with their patterns of avoidance. Everyone knew the hard conversations they needed to be having, but no one felt comfortable having them. The longer the team delayed, the more urgent its work became. Eventually, the reorg devolved from a well-considered change program into a series of drastic actions and escalations with no guiding vision or set of principles to ground them. It happened—kinda—but because we forgot to take a people-first approach and prioritize relationships, the effort never really took off, and it basically became a very expensive flavor-of-the-month.

Take the new org chart, for example. In the prime timeline—*this* timeline—we carefully considered the roles and responsibilities we needed first and then considered the best person within the organization to fill that role. We made the boxes, and then we attached names to them.

Instead, in the alternative timeline where Jeff ignored the elephant in the room and never achieved full transcendence, we skipped straight to reassigning people—we stuck names to boxes without considering whether we needed those boxes in the first place.

Because we didn't practice empathetic curiosity when thinking through our reorg, we struggled to justify our decisions and rationale for why certain people had their shiny new role or title. After all, how can you explain a choice when you haven't properly thought through the impacts? So, instead of leading with love, we led through fear and mandate—accept the new role, or else.

Does this outcome represent the darkest possible timeline? Not really. Softway would have continued on, but our vision of bringing humanity back to the workplace would have taken a serious, possibly fatal, hit. Seeing their opportunity for more influence, leaders would have created their own little fiefdoms. Some groups would have given the new reorg a try and then reverted to the way things were. No one would've given each other any feedback as long as work was getting done. We would have become unwoven and ever-broken.

Because Jeff chose the comfort of keeping his mouth shut, even though every fiber of his being was telling him he had to say something, we would've kept the status quo, prioritized tenure rather than need-based roles, and focused on fixing everyone but ourselves. Frank, for instance, would have stayed comfortably in his lane doing his creative projects and avoiding all growth and challenges. He would have never stepped up to lead the creative team in India because he never would have considered it an option.

Instead of playing to win, we would have played not to lose—not to lose comfort, not to lose convenience, not to lose familiarity, and so on. It would have been a whole lot of work for very little meaningful change. And none of it would have served what we needed.

Frank Chooses Self-Destruction

Frank had a choice. He could have chosen his hard, listened to Dr. Anwar's advice, and gotten serious about his health journey, or he could have chosen to pick up a five-pound bag of Kirkland Signature pretzels on the way home and devour the whole thing in one sitting.

We asked Frank what might have happened if he had chosen the latter. This alternate universe isn't hard to see: it's the one without Frank in it.

This isn't a glib answer. We don't like thinking of that universe and are grateful we're not in it. To make sure that universe never comes to pass—at least, not until he's old, happy, and fulfilled—Frank wakes up every morning, chooses his hard, and builds discipline so he can stay focused and healthy.

The comfort Frank was choosing was literally killing him. It may sound like a strained metaphor, but here's the truth: every time you choose comfort, you're limiting the ability to become a better version of yourself. You're curbing your ability to experience the triumph of overcoming. You're preventing the world from seeing the whole, fully realized person you could have become.

Chris Chooses to Be a Beautiful Liar

Chris had a choice. He could have chosen his hard and taken responsibility for his part in his toxic relationship with Greg, or he could have chosen comfort and continued to sabotage Greg behind the scenes.

We asked Chris what might have happened if he had chosen the latter. Here's what he had to say.

Mohammad put Chris and Greg on the integrators team, but—shocker!—they never integrated. Chris didn't want to, and Greg shrugged about the whole thing. Instead, the two leaders became increasingly siloed, drawing others into their orbit. It was like Softway had two operating structures: the official one that they used for onboarding and reporting, and the real one in which Chris and Greg had carved out different parts of the business for themselves. Just to run his company, Mohammad was forced to have two sets of conversations about every update and decision because Chris and Greg didn't want to be in the same room together. It became so exhausting that Mohammad considered implementing a four-day *weekend* instead of a four-day workweek.

This was not an effective or efficient system. Anyone on the sales team, for instance, had to have two meetings just to make a decision on anything—a meeting with Chris and a meeting with Greg. In those meetings, Chris would present the team member with his approach to selling, Greg would present the team member with his way of selling, and the team member would be forced to choose which approach to follow.

Eventually, the ripple effects of this siloed process spilled over into Softway's client work; Chris worked with his clients, and Greg worked with his clients. If you were Greg's client, you never knew Chris existed—and vice versa. There wasn't any point in doing things otherwise. Because Chris and Greg didn't share and collaborate, bringing them into each other's projects didn't yield any additional value.

And if someone had a problem that required both leaders' input? It was like pulling teeth. First, they'd go to one with the issue, then they'd go to the other, and then they'd go back to the former in order to relay important information and make a final decision. That's a whole lot of bone carrying for very little movement.

This future isn't very hard to imagine. We've worked with organizations where this precise scenario has played out. One company was downright pathological about it. Any time they needed to have a hard conversation, they just split the reporting structure. Ultimately, these splits merely hamstrung the business, creating teams with half the resources, half the people, and half the information they would have had if they'd just been willing to choose their hard.

Mohammad Chooses Hate

You know what? You already saw what Mohammad looked like in an alternative timeline in Chapter 6, when we contrasted the way Moh 2.0 practiced empathetic curiosity while Moh 1.0 very much did not. If we projected that timeline out a little further, we'd see that Moh 1.0 torched his relationship with Saquib, who eventually left the company, which eventually left us without one of our star players to manage a critical account. Revenue lost, goals not met, difference not made. You get the picture.

We yield the rest of this space so Mohammad can lay a little tough love on you. He's been chomping at the bit to do it all book, and we promised we'd let him tell you how he *really* feels about choosing your hard and leading change with love. Deep breath, dear reader. Time to embrace some discomfort. See you on the other side.

STOP KICKING THE CAN DOWN THE ROAD

When you choose to avoid the immediate challenge, the uncomfortable task, the difficult conversation, you're only kicking the can down the road. You're trading today's discomfort for tomorrow's disaster. You're earning a penny in comfort today only to lose ten dollars tomorrow. Easy was never promised, yet so many leaders and business minds have convinced themselves that there is an easy option.

Don't look for easy. Look for the cheapest hard. Chances are, it will come with extreme discomfort and a narrow path. But that's better than the price far too many organizations have become used to: bureaucracy, silos, turnover, wasteful spending, safe havens of mediocrity, and, ultimately, obsolescence. Someone once told Chris that the signature of mediocrity is inconsistency. When an organization's performance is inconsistent, you can't help but to wonder which hard their leaders are choosing.

Avoiding that crucial training session is today's easy. But tomorrow you'll be unprepared, underperforming, and procrastinating when you should be executing.

You're not fooling anyone. You're not getting ahead. You're just delaying the inevitable—and making it exponentially worse.

Choose your hard.

INVEST IN YOURSELF

When you choose your hard, that's money in the bank. You're making an investment in your skills, your resilience, and your future. You're building a foundation of strength and confidence that will serve you well in the long run. When you choose comfort, however, that debt will eventually come due with interest.

Ask yourself, how does it feel to be in debt to yourself? Not great. That's a quick way to erode your confidence and fail to live up to your full potential.

Choose the path that challenges you to grow, the path that leads to a *better* future, not the same one. Prove to yourself and others that you have what it takes to succeed through adaptive challenges, discomfort, and pain.

Choose your hard.

THE RESULTS ARE WAITING FOR YOU

So stop looking for shortcuts. Stop making excuses. Start taking ownership.

Just because you love your team doesn't mean you have to love all their choices. If you see your sales team kicking the can down the road, for instance, choose honesty over harmony. Tell them what you see. Be the example that empowers them to choose their hard more often.

Show your team how to book that meeting. Show them how to stop waiting for the client and write that proposal. Show them how to stop being tactical about which networking meeting to attend and how to dive right in. Get your reps in.

When you try to take the easy way out, you're just making things harder for yourself. No leads are going to come down your pipeline if you don't put in the work. Sometimes, that's all it takes. The results are there for the taking.

Choose your hard.

DETERMINATION, DISCIPLINE, AND CONSISTENCY

As humans, we seek comfort because we lack the determination, discipline, and consistency necessary to keep choosing our hard and stay on track.

The bad news is that there are no shortcuts to choosing your hard. There are no time-logging tools that will make this easier—not even Sortd will save you if you're not committed to it. The hard thing will always be the hard thing. But as stoicist Ryan Holiday famously said, the obstacle is the way.

You know everything you need to get started. Determination is your *why*, your reason for getting up in the morning and committing to change. Discipline is doing the hard thing even if you hate it in the moment because you know it will pay off in the future. Consistency is the willingness to do it all again tomorrow.

Every day, practice determination, discipline, and consistency. Wash, rinse, repeat. Just remember: simple doesn't mean easy. You still have to choose your hard.

Choose Love

Okay, that wasn't so bad now, was it? Now that you've graduated with your No BS from Moh University, here are a few final thoughts from all of us.

When you choose comfort over your hard, nothing ever gets done—at least, not all the way. Whatever change you had initially intended becomes bogged down by endless process making and second-guessing. Time is wasted, nothing gets done, the scope and ambition of your initiative shrinks, and a year later, you're left scrambling to make up for lost ground.

But you know all of this already. You know what it feels like when you choose comfort in the moment. You know what it feels like to tamp down your feelings and let your unforgiveness fester. You know what it feels like to feel checked out from a project that you should have been invested in. You know what it feels like to show up to work with a mask on because you don't trust that you can show up as your full self.

Choosing comfort doesn't create psychological safety. Choosing your hard does.

Choosing comfort doesn't allow you to be yourself at work. Choosing your hard does.

Choosing comfort doesn't further change. Choosing your hard does.

That's it. That's how Love as a Change Strategy works—one choice at a time, one commitment to our shared humanity, one step in the direction of love.

So, here's what we want you to do next.

Right now, there's something in your life or in your work that's been nagging at you. "I should probably do something about that," you say to yourself—and we agree. You *should* probably do something about it.

Maybe you realize that certain team members are poisoning your culture and you need to be honest instead of harmonious.

Maybe you realize the core, unaddressed problem that's sending leadership into a Möbius loop of meetings and you need to raise your hand and suggest a new path forward.

Maybe you just need to do your chores and not let them pile up for future you to take care of.

Maybe you need to stop letting YouTube influencers raise your children and spend some time with them face-to-face.

Whatever the case, it's time to choose your hard.

The world will change no matter what. *You* get to choose whether to change with it. That change won't happen overnight, but it won't happen at all unless you commit to it.

So commit.

Commit to this change every day. Show up for others the way you want them to show up for you. Take that first step into the future you want, not the future you have.

If you can do that, who knows? Maybe one day the rest of the world will join you.

Keep the Conversation Going

Thank you so much for reading our book!

If you enjoyed what you read, here are a few ways to keep the conversation going.

First, our newsletter. Our LAAS (Love As A Strategy) Newsletter is where fresh thoughts, ideas, and stories come together. Join a massive community of leaders who are rethinking culture, change, and what it means to lead . . . with love. Sent straight to your inbox.

Sign up for free at LoveAsAStrategy.com/newsletter. Second, for bonus materials, guides, assessments, planners, toolkits, podcasts, and more, visit LoveAsAStrategy.com. There's tons of stuff for you there, and some of it's bound to be useful.

Third, we'd love to hear from you—and possibly even host an ask me anything with you and your team. Just send an email to laabsbook@softway.com and we'll schedule some time to meet. You can also reach out to us on social media—we'd love to connect.

Thank you for helping us bring humanity back to the workplace!

Choose Your Hard

- What can are you currently kicking down the road in your personal or professional life? What's the true cost of continuing to delay this challenge?

- What's one comfort debt you might still be paying off today—and what would it look like to stop the cycle?

- Think of a time when you chose comfort over discomfort. What were the long-term consequences of that decision? How might the outcome have differed if you had chosen your hard instead?

- What relationships in your work life have you let stay broken to avoid discomfort? What would it look like to choose your hard in that dynamic?

- What is nagging at you right now that you know you should address? What specific hard do you need to choose today? What's stopping you?

- What's the relationship between choosing your hard and the concept of Love as a Change Strategy? How does one support the other?

- What were some of your biggest takeaways or ah-ha moments from this chapter?

- What, if anything, will you change or adjust about how you lead or behave based on what you've read?

Notes

Chapter 1

1. Behnam Tabrizi, Ed Lam, Kirk Girard, and Vernon Irvin. "Digital Transformation Is Not About Technology." *Harvard Business Review*. March 13, 2019. https://hbr.org/2019/03/digital-transformation-is-not-about-technology

2. Walkme Team. "Change Management Statistics You Need to Know." *WalkMe Blog*. June 12, 2024. https://www.walkme.com/blog/change-management-statistics/

3. Tabrizi, Lam, Girard, and Irvin. "Digital Transformation Is Not About Technology."

4. Jayne Ruff. "40+ Organisational Change Management Statistics for 2024." ChangingPoint. April 4, 2024. https://changing-point.com/organisational-change-management-statistics/

5. Ibid.

6. Oak Engage. Oak Engage's Change Report. Accessed October 28, 2024. https://www.oak.com/media/c5llwb4v/oak-change-report-digital.pdf

7. Ibid.

8. WalkMe Team. "Change Management Statistics You Need to Know."

9. Oak Engage. Oak Engage's Change Report.

10. Ibid.; Mark Murphy. "Why the CEO Gets Fired (Change Management and More)." Leadership IQ. Accessed October 28, 2024. https://www.leadershipiq.com/blogs/leadershipiq/35353153-why-the-ceo-gets-fired-change-management-and-more

11. WalkMe. "Change Management Statistics You Need to Know."

12. Newsroom. "Wastage from Digital Transformation Projects Could Reach $2 Trillion by 2026." *Marketing Communication News*. November 1, 2023. https://marcommnews.com/wastage-from-digital-transformation-projects-could-reach-2-trillion-by-2026/

13. Saïd Business School at the University of Oxford. *The Future of Transformation Is Human.* 2022, p. 12. https://www.sbs.ox.ac.uk/sites/default/files/2024-04/ey-the-future-of-transformation-is-human-report.pdf

14. Resilience Alliance. "Change Management Classics: Burning Platform." Accessed October 30, 2024. https://resiliencealliance.com/change-management-classics-burning-platform/

15. Tobi Agbede. "Remote Work Statistics: 50+ Key Facts to Know in 2025." Notta. October 10, 2024. https://www.notta.ai/en/blog/remote-work-statistics

Chapter 2

1. Teju Ravilochan. "The Blackfoot Wisdom That Inspired Maslow's Hierarchy." Resilience. June 18, 2021. https://www.resilience.org/stories/2021-06-18/the-blackfoot-wisdom-that-inspired-maslows-hierarchy/

Chapter 9

1. For more on Anderson's story, see the documentary *Beyond Zero* (2020).

Acknowledgments

To those who helped make this book possible, we are deeply grateful. To Greg, Saquib, Saif, Lacee, Jaya, and Ashley—thank you for lending your experiences and stories to this book. And to Chas Hoppe—our trusted collaborator once again—thank you for your steady hand, sharp insight, and unmatched expertise. This second book, like the first, simply wouldn't exist without you.

From Mohammad F. Anwar

First and foremost, I would like to thank Softway employees past and present. To every person that has been a part of our company, every client, partner, and friend—thank you for being part of Softway's journey and your dedication and support. I also want to express my deepest gratitude to Lacee Maxedon, without whom this book would not have been possible. Thank you for keeping us on track, holding us accountable, and ensuring we had everything we needed to bring this vision to life.

MY COAUTHORS

Writing this book has been a deeply personal journey, and I am profoundly grateful for the support and inspiration I've received. I want to thank my incredible partners in crime: Chris Pitre, Frank Danna, and Jeff Ma. Your collaboration and shared passion have been invaluable.

SOFTWAY TEAM—A DECADE OF DEDICATION

To Ashley Ward, Kristen Gerner-Khan, Greg Duggin, Saquib Hakim, Taban Rashid, Parthibhan Manoharan, Jayasimha Subbu, Farooq Kuntoji, Priyanka George, Senthil Kumar, Saif Khan, Nathan Smith, Sahir Tariq, Abhay Srivastava, Honey Jain, Prabakar Thiruchitrambalam, Neethi Gnanakan, Siddhartha Chowdhury, Roy Gonzalez, Nishi Gulnaz, Shabeer Ahmed, Tajjamul Pasha, Hurmath Unnisa, Suresh J., and all the other employees who have been with

Softway for over a decade: your unwavering trust and loyalty have been the bedrock of our journey. You had every opportunity to seek other paths, yet you chose to stay, build, and believe. This book is a testament to your dedication, and I am eternally grateful.

SHAKILA BEGUM AND ABDUL ANWAR (MOM AND DAD)
To my parents, I am forever indebted to you for your sacrifices and hard work. You instilled in me the values that guide my life and set an example of how to lead with love. Thank you, Mom and Dad, for everything.

FAIZUN ANWAR (SISTER)
To my only sister, Faizun, thank you for being my big sister and for all that you do for me and my family. You and Suhail took me into your home and ensured I received an education, providing much-needed support when I needed it most. I am extremely grateful for that.

KHALEEL ANWAR (BROTHER)
To my brother, Khaleel, thank you for your trust and for empowering me to start Softway. Softway would not exist had it not been for your push and encouragement. I am extremely grateful for your power of empowerment, which shaped me and Softway into what it is today.

TAJ ANWAR (BROTHER)
To my brother, Taj Anwar, managing director of Softway in India. Despite being my elder brother, you have supported me in my dreams and have always been there to support me through thick and thin, going where I choose to go with the direction of the company. Your continued support, belief, and faith in me and Softway are strong like a bedrock, and I am grateful for all that you do for Softway and our team.

SIRAJ ANWAR (BROTHER)
To my brother, Siraj, thank you for always being there to support me whenever I need it, whether it is helping with Mohsin or anything else. I am always grateful for all that you do to encourage me and support me through my journey and career. Thank you!

YULIA PAKHALINA (SPOUSE)

To my beautiful wife, Yulia, your sacrifices and unwavering support make everything possible. Your relentless efforts to ensure both our kids Mohsin and Sufia get everything they need to be successful in life is something special. Your relentless efforts to help Mohsin improve and develop have only empowered me to do more for him, which in turn has actually helped me do more for our organization and create impact in the world. Behind every successful endeavor is your strength and love. I love you to the moon and back.

MOHSIN ANWAR (SON)

Mohsin, this book exists because of you. You teach me every day what it means to love unconditionally and to practice patience. Your resilience, confidence, and warmth are your superpowers. I hope that one day, you will read this book and know that you are making a profound difference in the world, defying all expectations. I love you more than words can say.

SUFIA ANWAR (DAUGHTER)

Sufia, I am deeply inspired by your empathy and unconditional love for Mohsin and everyone around you. Your ability to understand and support others is a gift that will serve you well throughout your life. I am incredibly proud of the person you are becoming. Stay humble and keep spreading your love.

WAQAR FAIZ (MENTOR)

Thank you to my spiritual mentor, Waqar Faiz, for your invaluable life lessons and guidance. Your wisdom and support have been instrumental in my personal and professional growth.

SOFTWAY—PAST EMPLOYEES

To all the past employees of Softway, thank you for your contributions. I apologize for any hurt or mistreatment, intentional or unintentional. Your experiences have shaped my leadership and my understanding of humanity.

SOFTWAY—CURRENT EMPLOYEES

To my current Softway team, thank you for believing in our vision and purpose. Your faith, accountability, and honesty drive me forward. Without you, none of this would be possible. I am forever grateful for your commitment.

CUSTOMERS—PAST AND PRESENT

To our past and present clients, thank you for your trust and partnership. You have been mentors and inspirations, and I am honored to serve you.

COACH TOM HERMAN

Coach Herman, though we have never met, your words have deeply affected my leadership. Your message of a culture of love and resilience, as the former head coach of the University of Houston Football team, inspired me to transform Softway. Thank you for your profound influence.

COACH KELVIN SAMPSON

Coach Sampson, your wisdom and insights on culture and resilience, shared through your press conferences as the head coach of the University of Houston Basketball team, have been a constant source of inspiration. Your ability to lead through adversity and build a winning team has profoundly influenced my leadership. Thank you for showing us how to cultivate a culture of success.

DONNA COLE

Thank you, Donna Cole, for nominating me to the American Leadership Forum (ALF) Fellowship program. Without your nomination, this book would not have existed.

NORY ANGEL

To Nory Angel, thank you for your trust, partnership, and encouragement in my continued journey of self-discovery and growth.

ALF CLASS OF 59

To my ALF Class (American Leadership Forum) of 59: Rakesh Agrawal, Adolfo Melara, Andrea Link, Bobby Hilliard, Catherine Horne,

Chasiti Horne, Diane Maben, Diana Zarzuelo, Frances Villagran-Glover, Ge'Juan Cole, George Farah, Jeff Mechlem, Kelly Waterman, Kerry McCracken, Lorie Westrick, Maria Reeve, Mariela Poleo, Michael Moore, Robert Gondo, Ruth Turley, Sue Smith, and Teneshia Hudspeth. Thank you for being there for me throughout our fellowship. This journey, which taught me so much about leading change, would not have been possible without each of you. You have all contributed, directly and indirectly, to the creation of this book.

ALF FACILITATORS
To the facilitators of the ALF fellowship: Judy Le, Sean Fitzpatrick, Shaina Holm, and Nory Angel. Your guidance and leadership through this program started my journey in understanding what it means to lead change with love. Thank you.

UNIVERSITY OF HOUSTON
To the University of Houston, thank you for providing the foundation for so much of my life. It is where I met the first love of my life, my wife Yulia Pakhalina, received my education in computer science, and began my journey as an entrepreneur by starting Softway at the age of 20. The university also introduced me to the transformative power of a culture of love through the University of Houston football team and Coach Herman, and the importance of a culture of winning and resilience through the University of Houston basketball team and Coach Sampson. Thank you for your continued support and inspiration in my mission to lead change in the world. I will be a forever Coog and proud alumni.

From Frank E. Danna
When I was a kid, I didn't really dream about a career—I just wanted to own a cool car with decent AC and a sweet sound system. I had no concept of adulthood or success or how life might unfold. The only thing I was sure of, especially as a teenager, was that hitting your mid-thirties meant you were "old as heck"—with one foot in the grave.

Yet here I am, far from that grave.

Looking back on life's winding path—its surprises, its depth, and the people who've walked it with me—I'm filled with gratitude. Every day brings something new, awe-inspiring, and wonderful.

Our first book, *Love as a Business Strategy*, sparked something deep within us. For me, it wasn't just a bucket list moment—it gave me clarity. It was in writing that book, in my early thirties, that I finally understood what I wanted to be when I "grew up."

I wanted to be someone who changed the world.

Cliché? Maybe. I can literally feel you rolling your eyes. But through that first book, this one, and everything ahead, I hope you'll see that changing the world starts with changing ourselves. When you change one life—starting with your own—the ripple effect is immeasurable—and the world is a lot smaller than you think.

MY WIFE, MEGAN

You are the anchor that keeps me stable and buoyant. You help me become a better man, father, and human being. Our relationship and love grow in beautiful new ways, each year together better than the last. Your passion for life, compassion for others, and leadership are changing the world, too.

MY CHILDREN

Emma and Levi—you are my light. You are both brilliant, bold, and beautiful. Through your eyes, I glimpse the future—your future—and the significant mark you'll leave on this world. You each possess unique gifts to accomplish extraordinary things: my little world changers—though, when I look at you now, I see you're not so little anymore.

MY PARENTS

Writing this book challenged me, particularly when sharing experiences in Chapter 3. Reconciliation remains complex but ongoing. Forgiveness is real, and it is powerful.

KIM AND KURT, MY MOTHER- AND FATHER-IN-LAW

Your stability, dedication, and example have shown me what true love embodies. Thank you for that priceless gift.

MOHAMMAD

You are a powerful force for good—a generous soul who pushes people beyond comfort zones with love, holds them accountable, and creates space for those who won't create it for themselves. You continue to exemplify what it means to love and care for the world.

JEFF, CHRIS, AND MOHAMMAD, MY COAUTHORS

We've circumnavigated the globe together many times, solved wild and complex challenges, built businesses, and grown through life's experiences side by side. I couldn't imagine better companions for this journey. Thank you for showing me we accomplish more together than alone. I love y'all.

EVERYONE AT SOFTWAY

Our work is so much bigger than you and me. And I'm thankful that your dedication, desire, and commitment are steadfast. We've built a really special place at Softway, a place that must be protected (and one that must be shared). I love you all. Together, we are bringing humanity back to the workplace.

DWELLING PLACE CHURCH

Thank you for being a house of restoration and global impact. We've found our family (and our destiny). Tear the loaf.

OUR CLIENTS (AND ANYONE WHO'S HEARD OUR STORY)

Thank you for allowing us to share our experiences, struggles, and failures with you. Thank you for entrusting us to guide, direct, and shape your organization's future through our services and products. We're grateful that our story and our team have been part of your journey and impact. And to future clients . . . can't wait to meet you!

TO THE READERS OF THIS BOOK

I'm both honored and amazed that you've invested your precious time to read or listen to these words. I hope you've discovered genuine value and opportunities for growth through our stories.

SPECIAL THANKS

To Ben Stiller, Dan Erickson, and the entire *Severance** cast and crew. Okay, this may seem like a weird one, but go with me here. Your show has actually become an invaluable connection point in our work, helping people recognize they are whole individuals both inside and outside the workplace. Severance has enhanced our ability to communicate the importance of bringing humanity to work rather than "severing" oneself into different personas to try to hide what was never meant to be hidden.

NORY ANGEL AND MY ALF (AMERICAN LEADERSHIP FORUM) CLASS 65

Journeying with this extraordinary group—some rightfully claim it's the best class ever—has been profoundly inspiring. Your collective drive to elevate yourselves and others exemplifies true leadership. Thank you for welcoming me into something beautiful.

From Jeffrey F. Ma

Writing this book has been a journey—not just of words on a page but of growth, change, and an unshakable commitment to helping people rediscover humanity in the workplace. After the success of *Love as a Business Strategy*, I realized that a shift in perspective can truly transform lives. This book is a continuation of that mission, born from the lessons I've learned since the first, the experiences that have shaped me, and the personal evolution I've undergone.

MY COAUTHORS

Mohammad, Chris, and Frank—you are my brothers in this work. We've been in the trenches together, making sacrifices, pushing through late nights, and staying committed to the belief that love belongs in leadership. This book, like our journey, exists because of our shared resolve.

MY WIFE, MAGGIE

Your unwavering support and willingness to walk this path alongside me mean more than I can put into words. You challenge me, inspire

---

*If you haven't watched this masterpiece yet, please do so immediately. It'll go down as one of television's most outstanding achievements. You can borrow my Apple TV+ login if you'd like.

me, and remind me every day what love in action truly looks like. To my kids, Cody and Penelope—you are my greatest teachers. Your innocence, curiosity, and boundless love give me purpose. When the road felt long, you kept me going. I want you to know that your dad is always working to be better, not just for the world but for you.

TO EVERY LEADER AND TEAM I'VE HAD THE PRIVILEGE TO WORK WITH

Thank you for your honesty, your trust, and your vulnerability. Your willingness to share your struggles and allow me to walk with you through them has poured life into this book.

There have been moments along the way—conversations with readers, stories shared, lives changed—that have served as reminders of why this mission matters. Those moments fueled this work, reminding me that love is not just a lofty idea but a tangible force that can reshape how we lead, how we work, and how we live.

As I grow older, my focus sharpens. What matters most is ensuring that my children inherit a world where love is the foundation, where they can be fully themselves without fear, where their work has meaning, and where they are embraced as they are. That starts with me. If this book helps even one person see the power of love in change, then it is a success.

BEAR-BEAR AND FROGICO

And finally, a special shoutout to Bear-bear and Frogico—two stuffed animals who have been constants in my children's lives, offering them the same comfort and love that I hope to instill in the world. They deserve a place in these pages, because love, in all its forms, should be celebrated. I know they'd be thrilled to see their names printed in a book.

The birth of my son Cody lit a spark in me—a spark that has turned into a flame guiding my every step. And my daughter, Penelope Love Ma, carries a name that reminds me of my purpose every day. My hope is that this book, and the work I continue to do, make them proud.

SPECIAL THANKS

A special shoutout to the humans in my ALF class 64, who have taught me so much and continue to inspire me to do this work. Thank you for your friendship and love.

From Christopher J. Pitre

While writing this book, I experienced a lot of change in my personal life, the largest being the death of my father. He won't get the opportunity to read what's in this book, but I know how proud he was of me, as those were the last words he shared (after asking about Mohsin). This book will be a reminder for me of the loss of a parent and the gaining of self-care, respite, and confidence in my point of view.

MY FAMILY

Thanks for the love and support. Losing Daddy was difficult, but we're not without hope. We have each other and the memories. We also have gumbo and sweet potato pie, his favorites, to comfort us.

MOHSIN

My bright light in a dimming world. I wish I said it first, but Beyoncé beat me to it. There are so many roses but none to be picked without thorns, so be fond of your flaws, dear Mohsin. While the world may not see your light at times, it will have no choice but to grow from it. Here's to you being what God promised, your parents dream, and you dare. I'll always be your best friend and biggest fan, even if you choose to befriend someone else.

MY COAUTHORS

What a road we trod! Though filled with highs and lows, laughter and tension, shade and support, we are thick as thieves. A brotherhood of the highest order. Thanks for showing up even when I thought it wasn't necessary and for pushing me to learn from my overdone strengths. (You'd probably want me to say mistakes there, but the journey we're on would be over too soon if I relented here and now.) Kidding. Thanks for pushing me to share and learn from my mistakes.

MY SOFTWAY TEAM

We continue to change and reinvent ourselves without losing our humanity or sanity. We are not always the most prim and proper or overly structured, but we have grit and heart. We do well by each other and our clients, which is only possible because of how amazing and resilient we are. Thank you each for the support, kindness, gulab jamun, and jokes you've gifted me over the years. Whether you've graduated to other organizations or have stayed on the journey, your contributions to Softway are undeniable.

MY ALF CLASSMATES

I have to pay tribute to my American Leadership Forum (ALF) Class 62 family. Each of you have given me tools, perspective, and encouragement during this challenging year. While our official time together has commenced, I find myself retreating to our learnings, conversations, and jokes in times of stress and change. I hope you see bits and pieces of all of us in the contents of this book. Amy Wright, Amy Hinojosa, Angel Harris, Armando Orduña, Blake Ellis, Bob Newhouse, Chad Burke, Chris Brown, Edward Shipper, Jamal Razzack, Kavon Young, Kim Williams, LaToshia Norwood, Laura Vargas, Lauren Caldarera (my buddy), Liliana Rambo, Linda Lorelle, MaryJane Mudd, Max Moll, Peter Stout, Richard Baker, Shampa Mukerji, Shariq Ghani, and Rev. Stanley Phill—you're my circle. (Special shout out to Judy Le and Sean Fitzpatrick as our facilitators!)

MY GW COLONIAL INAUGURATION CABINET OF 2004

It's been over 20 years since we graced the halls and streets of GW (The George Washington University), welcoming the class of 2008 into life at Foggy Bottom and Mount Vernon. I wouldn't be a freshman orientation leader if I didn't annoy at least one person by calling you all out in this section. The reunion we held in the Poconos as we were planning this book rejuvenated me and reminded me of the first time I felt love in the workplace. You each have gone on to build lives, careers, and families that I admire and enjoy following. Thank you for planting a seed that still has roots in my pursuits.

About the Authors

Following the cultural transformation of Softway (Softway.com), Mohammad, Chris, Frank, and Jeff cofounded Culture+ (culture-plus.com) and created the Culture Rise training experience, along with other culture-based products, services, and experiences. Since the release of their first book, *Love as a Business Strategy*, the team has continued to expand their impact as renowned keynote speakers, sharing their story on stages around the world.

Their work has evolved into a global movement, Love As A Strategy (LoveAsAStrategy.com), a growing ecosystem of content, resources, and experiences designed to help organizations bring humanity back to the workplace.

Love as a Change Strategy is each author's second book.

Mohammad F. Anwar

Mohammad is the youngest of five children and was born and raised in Saudi Arabia by Indian parents from Bengaluru. He graduated from the University of Houston (go Coogs) with a BS in computer science and started Softway at age 20, where he still serves as president and CEO.

Mohammad lives in Sugar Land, Texas, with his amazing wife, Yulia, a Russian diver and five-time Olympic medalist, and his beautiful children, Sufia and Mohsin. In his spare time, he enjoys fitness, watching college sports, and butchering American idioms.

Frank E. Danna

Frank, the oldest of six children, can often be found perfecting the art of brewing, drinking, and sharing coffee with friends and family. Frank is an entrepreneur at heart, having successfully sold his first startup at age 25.

Frank is a pop culture connoisseur, world traveler, and citizen of Disneyland. In his spare time, he bakes award-winning cookies, makes silly videos, and enjoys fitness (to offset the cookies). Frank lives in Houston, Texas, with his gorgeous wife, Megan, and awesome children, Emma and Levi.

Jeffrey F. Ma

Jeff spent the first decade of his career working in the video game industry, from game testing to project management. He continues to bring his love for games into everything he does, from playing with his kids to training and coaching leaders.

Jeff has a burning passion for board games, magic tricks, Agile, and growth mindsets. He was born and raised in Texas, where he and his beautiful wife, Maggie, dote on their wonderful children, Cody and Penelope.

Christopher J. Pitre

Chris is a student of the world and enjoys anthropology, history, travel, and culinary experiences. His interests in global cultures naturally led him to travel around the world, co-facilitating Culture Rise, a leadership development training program, and managing client relationships globally. Chris is a native Houstonian who loves everything Beyoncé. He has a BA in business administration from The George Washington University in Washington, DC.

About Softway

Softway (softway.com) is a people-first consulting firm that helps evolving businesses transform in the areas of technology, communication, and culture. In 2015, after a toxic workplace culture nearly bankrupted the company, Softway's leadership team—including authors Mohammad F. Anwar, Frank E. Danna, Jeffrey F. Ma, and Christopher Jordan Pitre—made a bold decision: to rebuild the business on its greatest asset—people.

The team chronicled that journey in their first book, *Love as a Business Strategy*, a raw and inspiring blueprint for leading with love in the workplace.

Love as a Change Strategy continues that mission. It shares the next chapter of Softway's story—one of reorganization, reinvention, and growth—and offers practical human-centric principles for driving sustainable transformation and lasting impact within anyone and any organization.

Culture+

In 2021, Softway launched Culture+ (culture-plus.com) to scale the impact of transformation. Co-founded by the same leadership team, Culture+ delivers leadership training, products, and immersive experiences designed to help organizations activate meaningful change.

From the Culture Rise experience to tailored Culture Practice Workshops and products like the Culture Counter Measurement tool, Culture+ equips leaders with the training, tools, and techniques to transform any workplace.

Love as a Strategy

Love As A Strategy (LoveAsAStrategy.com)—or LAAS for short—is a movement built to bring humanity back to the workplace.

More than just an idea, LAAS is a hub for tools, resources, and experiences that help individuals and organizations put love into action. Everything referenced throughout this book lives here—from discussion guides and workbooks to podcast episodes, videos, articles, and our weekly newsletter. It's all designed around one core belief: business gets better when people come first—and *love is the strategy* that makes it possible.

Index